About Island Press

Since 1984, the nonprofit organization Island Press has been stimulating, shaping, and communicating ideas that are essential for solving environmental problems worldwide. With more than 800 titles in print and some 40 new releases each year, we are the nation's leading publisher on environmental issues. We identify innovative thinkers and emerging trends in the environmental field. We work with world-renowned experts and authors to develop cross-disciplinary solutions to environmental challenges.

Island Press designs and executes educational campaigns in conjunction with our authors to communicate their critical messages in print, in person, and online using the latest technologies, innovative programs, and the media. Our goal is to reach targeted audiences—scientists, policymakers, environmental advocates, urban planners, the media, and concerned citizens— with information that can be used to create the framework for long-term ecological health and human well-being.

Island Press gratefully acknowledges major support of our work by The Agua Fund, The Andrew W. Mellon Foundation, Betsy & Jesse Fink Foundation, The Bobolink Foundation, The Curtis and Edith Munson Foundation, Forrest C. and Frances H. Lattner Foundation, G.O. Forward Fund of the Saint Paul Foundation, Gordon and Betty Moore Foundation, The Kresge Foundation, The Margaret A. Cargill Foundation, New Mexico Water Initiative, a project of Hanuman Foundation, The Overbrook Foundation, The S.D. Bechtel, Jr. Foundation, The Summit Charitable Foundation, Inc., V. Kann Rasmussen Foundation, The Wallace Alexander Gerbode Foundation, and other generous supporters.

An Indomitable Beast

An Indomitable Beast
The Remarkable Journey
of the Jaguar

Alan Rabinowitz

◐ **ISLAND**PRESS   Washington | Covelo | London

Island Press is a trademark of The Center for Resource Economics.

Library of Congress Control Number: 2014933248

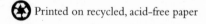 Printed on recycled, acid-free paper

Manufactured in the United States of America
10 9 8 7 6 5 4 3 2 1

Keywords: Island Press, jaguar, corridor, connectivity, apex predator, big cat,
Wildlife Conservation Society, Panthera, trophic cascade, were-jaguar, indigenous
Mesoamerican cultures, indigenous South American cultures

This book is dedicated to my wife, Salisa, and my children, Alexander and Alana, who put up with all my years of work and travel so that I could help be the voice for the big cats.

Contents

Illustrations

Plate 1

Geologic time scale of the Cenozoic Era, sometimes called the Age of Mammals. *(Adapted from Geological Society of America, www.geosociety.org/science/timescale/.)*

Plate 2

The "Dancing Jaguar" at Copán, Honduras, part of the architectural and sculptural complex characteristic of the Classic Era of Maya civilization, which lasted from the fifth to the ninth centuries. *(Photo by Steve Winter, Panthera.)*

Plate 3

Map of approximate time periods, locations, and distribution of major pre-Columbian civilizations. *(Map by Lisanne Petracca, Panthera.)*

Plate 4A

Map depicting the state of our knowledge of jaguar abundance and distribution in 1987 in the United States, Mexico, and Central America. *(Adapted from Swank and Teer, 1989, fig. 1.)*

Plate 4B

Map depicting the state of our knowledge of jaguar abundance and distribution in 1987 in South America. *(Adapted from Swank and Teer, 1989, fig. 2.)*

Plate 5

Maps illustrating the extent of knowledge regarding jaguar distribution, breeding populations, and point observations by experts attending the 1999 meeting in Mexico City. *(Adapted from Sanderson et al., 2002, fig. 1.)*

Plate 6

Known breeding populations of jaguars, called Jaguar Conservation Units (JCUs), compiled from expert data in 1999 and a second survey of experts in 2006. Background colors represent different jaguar geographic regions (JGRs). *(Map created and modified by Kathy Zeller and Lisanne Petracca, Panthera.)*

Plate 7

Early map of the potential travel pathways or corridors connecting known Jaguar Conservation Units throughout the jaguar's range. *(Map by Kathy Zeller, Panthera.)*

Plate 8

Landscape permeability for jaguar movement throughout the jaguar's existing range. Dark green represents optimal travel routes, while lighter shades indicate barriers to jaguar movement. These data indicate that nearly 80 percent of the jaguar's historic range still allows for potential jaguar movement. *(Map by Kathy Zeller, Panthera.)*

Plate 9

Jaguar traveling in daytime during the dry season at the edge of a cattle ranch along part of the jaguar corridor in the Pantanal, Brazil. *(Photo by Paul Goldstein.)*

Plate 10

Prioritization of Jaguar Conservation Units and the jaguar corridors to help direct limited manpower and financial resources to critical areas of the jaguar corridor. *(Map by Kathy Zeller, Panthera.)*

Plate 11

A jaguar crawling under a cattle fence during the night in order to move through a cattle ranch in the corridor. *(Photo by Steve Winter, Panthera.)*

Plate 12

Country map of Colombia (2010) showing the highly threatened remaining jaguar corridors (in purple) linking the jaguar populations of Mexico and Central America to the rest of South America. *(Map by Kathy Zeller, Panthera.)*

Plate 13

Female jaguar (staring into camera) with subadult male offspring moving through an old oil palm plantation in the jaguar corridor of Colombia. *(Camera-trap photo by Esteban Payan, Panthera.)*

Plate 14

Early map (2007) showing a single, narrow corridor through Honduras, with a possible break north of San Pedro Sula in Honduras. *(Map by Lisanne Petracca, Panthera.)*

Plate 15

Known jaguar corridors through Honduras in 2010, after further ground-truthing, showing continuous connections and two possible corridor pathways between Guatemala and Nicaragua. *(Map by Lisanne Petracca, Panthera.)*

Plate 16

Representation of the grid system employed to ground-truth jaguar corridors between Jaguar Conservation Units. *(Map by Lisanne Petracca, Panthera.)*

Plate 17

Jaguar track found during ground-truthing survey along the northern coast of Honduras. *(Photo by Steve Winter, Panthera.)*

Plate 18

A jaguar chased up into a tree before being sedated, examined, and radio-collared by our research team in Brazil. *(Photo by Steve Winter, Panthera.)*

Plate 19A

Examination and measurements of paws (width: 125 mm, or 5 inches) of sedated jaguar. *(Photo by Steve Winter, Panthera.)*

Plate 19B

Examination and measurements of dentition of sedated jaguar. Note broken upper right canine. *(Photo by Steve Winter, Panthera.)*

Plate 20

Expansive landscape mosaic of the northern Pantanal of Brazil. *(Photo by Steve Winter, Panthera.)*

Plate 21

Free-ranging cattle during the dry season on the vast open landscape of the Pantanal. Such open areas have traditionally been maintained by fire and cattle grazing. *(Photo by Steve Winter, Panthera.)*

Plate 22

Jaguar visiting an old cattle kill on a ranch in Brazil's Pantanal. *(Photo by Steve Winter, Panthera.)*

Plate 23

Jaguar swimming across a river as it moves through its range to hunt caiman and capybara along the riverbank. *(Photo by Steve Winter, Panthera.)*

Plate 24

A Tolupan woman in Honduras, the first person to open up to me about her people's beliefs regarding the Masters of Animals. *(Photo by Steve Winter, Panthera.)*

Plate 25

The author (far left) taking part in the first signing of a Memorandum of Understanding (MOU) in Colombia to officially acknowledge the jaguar corridor with former vice president Francisco Santos Calderón, along with the minister of forestry and the director of national parks. *(Photo by Panthera.)*

Plate 26

Local Maya schoolchildren being brought to the Cockscomb Jaguar Preserve in Belize to be taught about jaguars and other wildlife. *(Photo by Becci Foster, Panthera.)*

Plate 27

A jaguar along the riverbank in Brazil's Pantanal watching tourists in a small motorboat who are there to see jaguars and other wildlife. *(Photo by Paul Goldstein.)*

Plate 28

The indomitable beast leaping for a piece of food hanging from a tree in Brazil. *(Photo by Steve Winter, Panthera.)*

Prologue

I WAS FIVE YEARS OLD, walking hand in hand with my father through the massive doors of the Lion House at the Bronx Zoo, built half a century before my birth. It had been a particularly bad week at school for me and though my father and I never talked much, he knew one of the few places that made me happy. I slipped away from his grip and rushed forward, the clopping of my shoes on the wooden floor drowned out by the cacophony of sounds from the caged, restless cats. The sun beamed through the skylights as I rushed past the lion, the leopard, the tiger, letting the wild, musky smells engulf me. There was only one cage I was interested in right now.

I could see before I reached him that the jaguar had stopped pacing and was waiting, staring out to identify the approaching sound. Reaching the cage I leaned against the safety railing, meant to keep people from going too close to the bars, and faced my cat. It was always the eyes that drew me in, eyes that seemed filled with perpetual pain. Ignoring any people standing nearby, I started whispering in a voice that no one else could hear, stepping inside a private world to speak about thoughts and feelings that no one else in my life was privy to. That no one else in the world deserved to hear.

Twenty-six years later, I was in the jungles of Belize, following the largest jaguar tracks I had ever encountered. There was a new animal in my study area and I wanted to know where it was headed, hoping I might catch a rare glimpse of it. But hours later, after all tracks and sign had long since disappeared and darkness was closing in over the jungle, I turned to go back to camp. As soon as I turned around, I froze. There he was. The jaguar I had been tracking so relentlessly had circled around long ago and had been tracking me. If it had rushed me with my back turned, I would never have known what hit me. I shivered, realizing how exposed I'd been. Though I could detect no malice in the jaguar's stance, I was frightened. Not entirely sure what to do next, other than not run away, I squatted down and wrapped my arms around my knees to make myself small and non-threatening. Having no clue as to what to expect from the jaguar, I was still surprised by what happened next: he sat down also.

I was scared and I was awestruck at the same time. The jaguar never took his eyes off of me. And for a long moment, I remembered the feeling I had staring into the face of the jaguar so many years earlier as a child at the Bronx Zoo. Only this time, the sad, broken child immersed in his private world was now a more confident man, and in the eyes of this jaguar there was only wildness and strength. I leaned forward a little, as I had done so often by the cage at the zoo.

"It's all right now," I whispered. "It's all going to be all right."

Chapter 1

In the Beginning . . .

M Y EARLIEST MEMORIES are filled with pain, embarrassment, and coming to terms with the reality, reinforced by adults, that I was one of life's broken creatures. Born with a debilitating stutter and placed in public school classes for "special" children, I found it easiest to live inside my own head and withdraw from the world of people as much as a child can. My place of greatest comfort in those early years was the closet in my room in my parent's New York City home. In this small, dark world, I felt normal, I wasn't scared to speak, and I could live out my fantasies. My companions, a little menagerie of chameleons, green turtles, garter snakes, and hamsters, were the only living beings around me that seemed to listen but not judge. They had feelings, but they too had no voice to express themselves. They were me.

My parents were World War II–generation Eastern European Jews. They were sympathetic to my disability, willing to try anything that might help me—speech therapists, psychologists, medication, and hypnosis. But when nothing worked, they resigned themselves to the fact that I was simply "different" and nothing would be gained by talking about it. They believed that life's difficulties, of which they had experienced many themselves, were managed without discussion, without emotion, without self-pity. So I talked to my little pets and cried only when I was alone in the darkness of my closet.

My father, a high school physical education teacher in New York City and a former army paratrooper from the 82nd Airborne Division, was a dominant presence in my childhood. Drilling into me the idea that I would have to fight my way through life, physically and mentally, he taught me to how to box and wrestle. Meanwhile, he battled his own demons in a way that created a house filled with tension, one that rarely heard the sound of laughter. The greatest kindness my father showed me were the trips to the Bronx Zoo, when he would take me to the Lion House and leave me alone to wander among the big cats. He had no idea how or why those animals helped me. He just knew they did.

Visiting with the big cats at the Bronx Zoo taught me early in life that you could be big, strong, and clever, yet still locked inside a cage from which there was no escape. Despite this sobering realization as a young child, I also realized that if the cats and other animals at the zoo had a human voice, if they could cry, laugh, or plead their case, they would not be locked up so easily in small cages for display. They would never have that human voice—but I would, I was sure of it. And when I found that voice, I promised the cats at the zoo, every time I visited them, that I would be their voice. I would find a place for us.

Much of my childhood is a blur, with all the painful memories long buried somewhere in my brain. I had few friends and rarely socialized with others. As a sixth grader I once stabbed my hand with the point of a pencil in order to avoid having to speak in front of the class. There were fights and bloody noses, stints in detention, and visits to the principal. I was never the first to lay a hand on someone, even when teased or bullied, but I never backed down from confrontation. My grades were adequate but not stellar, except in science, which I considered to be the language of the real world, apart from the perceived reality of human beings. In 1970, desperately wanting to escape my home and experience more of the world, I applied to and was accepted into McDaniel College, a small liberal arts college in the hills of western Maryland.

I took all the science courses I could handle while I figured out a possible career path. During my second year of college I was taken on a camping trip into the Allegheny Mountains of Appalachia where, for the first time, I felt safe, alone, and at peace in the outside world. After that, at every opportunity I would head off from my college dormitory into the woods to camp or hike, sometimes with the few friends I had made, often alone. In my junior year, I enrolled in a new course that was offered at the college—animal ecology. Two weeks into the course, I realized I had found my profession, the way to use science to save animals. Only one thing was still missing—my voice.

In the summer before my last year of college, my parents told me of an experimental clinic for severe stutterers in upstate New York that they had heard about. I applied immediately. After two months of intensive therapy and continual practice of manipulative mouth exercises, I gained control of my speech for the first time in my life. I was still a stutterer. Part of the therapy, in fact, was the acceptance of the fact that there was no magic pill to cure me and that I would always be a stutterer. But now, with the knowledge and the tools they had given me, I could be a fluent stutterer. I could speak an entire sentence, even an entire thought, without my mouth locking up. And I could fulfill the promise I had made to the cats so many years earlier.

After graduating summa cum laude in both biology and chemistry, I enrolled in a PhD graduate program in ecology and wildlife biology at the University of Tennessee in Knoxville. The years that followed, which I spent living and working in the Smoky Mountains, conducting research on bats, raccoons, and black bears, were the happiest, most fulfilling years of my life so far. I was still uncertain about the future, but for the first time in my life I was happy in the present. Then I unexpectedly found myself in contact with the man who would help set me on my life's path and, in the process, become my lifelong mentor and friend, Dr. George Schaller.

George Schaller, at the time, headed the International Program at the Wildlife Conservation Society (then the New York Zoological Society) based at the Bronx Zoo, and was at the University of Tennessee visiting my professor, Dr. Mike Pelton, one of the world's leading experts on black bears. In 1980, while in the last phase of writing up my PhD dissertation, I was asked to take Schaller for a hike into the Great Smoky Mountains National Park, where he wanted to compare the black bear habitat of this region to what he was seeing while working on the Giant Panda in China's Wolong National Nature Reserve. The result of that excursion into the mountains with George was that, after completing my PhD, I was on a plane to the little, newly independent country of Belize in Central America to survey jaguars. And my employer was none other than the Bronx Zoo.

Belize was my testing ground where, as a field scientist, I would measure my commitment to working and living in remote areas under uniquely challenging situations. Despite the challenges, it wasn't really much of a test for me. Setting up my home in a wild jungle, with lots of animals and among people of a different culture and language who had no preconceived ideas about me, couldn't have felt more right. When I returned to New York after the eight-week survey and presented the results, Schaller asked me to continue the work and to initiate a two-year study on jaguars. Such research in the jungles of Central America had never been done before. I couldn't have been happier.

Whatever I had had to overcome for the jaguar survey was nothing compared to the setbacks and hardships I now faced capturing and placing radio collars on jaguars at the abandoned timber camp I had selected as my study site, an area called the Cockscomb Basin. I persevered, because failure was never an option. Eventually, I broke new ground with my jaguar research and accomplished what no one else had ever done in conservation—setting up the world's first jaguar preserve. But it came with a price. My study was to cost the life of one of my workers, inflict lifelong injuries upon myself, and change the lives of many Mayan families forever. I was also still too young and inexperienced to understand the larger implications of what I was doing, or to put into perspective my new understanding of jaguars and the people with whom they lived. Some clarification came when I wrote my first book, *Jaguar*, reflecting on my feelings about these events in their entirety. Most of my understanding, however, would come much later.

After I left Belize, the new Jaguar Preserve received unexpected international recognition and praise. In 1988, two years after the preserve was formally designated, His Royal Highness Prince Philip, president of the World Wildlife Fund International, visited Cockscomb Basin Wildlife Sanctuary and presented an award to Ignacio Pop, one of my Mayan field assistants and now first warden of the preserve. Meanwhile I had transitioned from research scientist to staff scientist with the Wildlife Conservation Society, and Schaller was encouraging me to go further afield and work with other wild cat species that needed research and recognition. The work in Belize and the research on jaguars was now to be continued by others. Or so he and I believed.

Over the next two decades I worked in Thailand, Borneo, China, Taiwan, Laos, Malaysia, Russia, and Myanmar, tracking, studying, and gathering new data on clouded leopards, leopard cats, Asiatic leopards, and tigers. Whenever and wherever I could, I sought out wild areas, collected data, and tried to convince governments to set up new or larger protected areas that gave wildlife a secure home. I contributed to the designation of a World Heritage Site in Thailand and set up a more than 31,000-square-kilometer (12,000-square-mile) complex of contiguous protected areas in northern Myanmar, including the world's largest tiger reserve in Hukawng Valley. During these expeditions, while searching for some of the last northern strongholds of the Indochinese race of tigers, I discovered a new species to science, the most primitive living deer in the world, and I rediscovered the only race of Mongoloid pygmies, the Taron, in a tiny, remote mountain village in the eastern Himalayas. While writing scientific and technical papers, I documented all my thoughts, feelings, and adventures in more popular books: *Chasing the Dragon's Tail*, *Beyond the Last Village*, and *Life in the Valley of Death*.

In the following years my efforts for a time were focused on one species alone, the tiger. The world's largest and most iconic wild cat was rapidly sliding towards extinction. Though revered as a cultural symbol throughout Asia and the world, the tiger's parts were so highly valued by the Chinese medicinal trade that a dead tiger was much more valuable than a live one. But by the time the world took serious notice of plummeting tiger numbers, there were few left in the wild. We were losing the battle for the species.

What I had seen in my work with the tiger made me worry all the more about the jaguar. Fortunately the jaguar's situation, while deteriorating in many areas through hunting and loss of habitat, was not yet close to that of its larger cousins, the tiger and the lion. But that could change quickly, as the supply of tiger bone was diminishing and the insatiable demand turning to the parts of other big cats—lions, jaguars, and leopards. My other concern was that the research and conservation of jaguars that I had thought would follow my work in Belize and that of other early jaguar researchers had not happened to any great extent. The jaguar preserve in Belize was plodding along, a few more people were working on jaguars in different parts of their range, but 15 years after setting up the preserve, we didn't seem to know much more about the life of this cat or even its distribution than when I had first started working on the species. And no one seemed concerned.

In 1999, I obtained funds from the Wildlife Conservation Society to organize the first-ever meeting of the world's jaguar experts so that we could bring together and assess the information already known about this species and devise a strategy for moving jaguar research and conservation forward. While the jaguar was much better off than the world's other big cats—tigers, lions, leopards—conservation actions had to be taken now while the species still had a chance. I wanted consensus on a set of priorities that would set the stage for saving the most important jaguar populations throughout the species' range. This, in itself, would be a daunting task. What I was not prepared for, however, were the new scientific data on jaguars that would emerge at this meeting, data that would rock the conservation world and move us far beyond any conservation model we had previously imagined for the species.

As will be explained in later chapters of this book, the science that led to the realization of the existence of what I call the Jaguar Corridor was a huge leap forward in understanding how to save this species, and possibly others. It also presented an almost insurmountable task of figuring out how to use very limited resources to carry out the conservation actions that were necessary. The resulting program, the Jaguar Corridor Initiative, would take more than a decade before we could see significant results of all our efforts, and much more time before the entire corridor could became a reality.

But part of the reason behind the writing of this book is that I still wanted more. After three decades of witnessing the continual declines in big cat populations worldwide, I wanted to understand what had brought the jaguar to the unique place it occupied in the carnivore conservation world. What biological, cultural, and political factors of the New World and the people who inhabited it allowed there to be a twenty-first-century range-wide jaguar corridor unlike anything else that existed with any other living big cat species? And as I gained a greater understanding of "jaguarness," how the jaguar was indeed different from the other cats—in structure, in temperament, and in behavior—I also wanted to explain what seemed inexplicable, perhaps even unscientific. I wanted to understand the essence of the animal I had spent countless hours watching and talking to as a child, then following, studying, and fighting for as an adult. An essence that earlier people seemed to have seen and understood.

Why had I been so attracted to this animal more than all the others in the Lion House at the Bronx Zoo? And if there was something special about this cat, something that helped comfort

and motivate a troubled, insecure child, could a better understanding of the true nature of jaguarness help us not only to save
jaguars but to help humans in their own quest for survival? In the
course of my search, I explored unexpected realms—from the
deep paleo-history of the species, to the cutting edge of DNA science and population genetics, into the complex layers of human
cultural, political, and social dynamics—all of which moved me
towards a deeper understanding of the question of jaguarness.

In the end, I believe I found the answers to my questions.

Chapter 2

The Pleistocene Jaguar Corridor

FEELING MUCH OLDER THAN MY 42 YEARS, I sank to my knees in snow as we crossed a gully and climbed towards the top of the plateau. Gasping for breath, I forced myself to speed up just so I could move one step ahead of the man beside me, Russia's premier living tiger expert, Dimitri Pikinov. Dimitri grunted, lengthened his stride, and moved ahead of me again, never taking his eyes off the ground while he scanned intently for the telltale tracks or sign of the animal we were there to find. I smiled to myself, pleased I had at least elicited a grunt, then planned my next attack when we hit a downhill slope. It was a game that both of us played, while pretending we were not. Though I had no expectation of outpacing Dimitri on his home turf and in sub-zero weather, the physical challenge

9

and the competition with a man I respected was exhilarating. I was giving him a run for his money, of that I was sure. The voices drifting downwind from behind us were our fellow cat experts, Drs. Howard Quigley and Dale Miquelle, who were quietly amused at this test of wills between Dimitri and myself that started with our first meeting in Vladivostok and had continued into the wintry cold of the Russian Far East. It was primal. Two middle-aged, type-A personalities, pounding their chests.

I welcomed the respite when we crested a plateau and Dimitri finally called for a break. The scene was spectacular. Sheer rocky cliffs dropped down into a forested valley extending into China. Less than a day's drive out from Vladivostok, a city of more than half a million people and Russia's major port on the Pacific, we were in the territory of the world's largest wild felid, the Siberian tiger. We had crossed the path of at least one male tiger already, the largest cat tracks I'd ever seen. But exciting as that had been, that wasn't the animal we were looking for right now. This remnant of seemingly wild and remote unprotected forest was some of the last habitat for the Amur leopard, the northernmost race of leopards adapted to surviving in this extreme cold. One of the planet's most critically endangered big cats, this subspecies was now cut off from all other Asian leopard populations with little more than two dozen individuals trying to survive. That meant keeping away from humans like myself.

I scanned the vista ahead: the Suifen River meandering through the snow-covered boreal forest. Dimitri suddenly rushed over to a large tree nearby and hunkered down over what looked like another set of tracks, though much smaller than what we'd seen previously and heading to lower ground. When he grinned, started speaking to himself in Russian, and then waved me over, I knew he had found tracks of the rare leopard. I stayed back a few moments longer, closing my eyes to try and picture the last Amur leopards traveling the riverine corridor below in their struggle to hang on to their tenuous existence. But my mind's eye played a trick on me, conjuring up a pattern of rosettes on the large stocky form of a jaguar instead.

Even then, halfway across the globe, approaching the end of the twentieth century, and more than a decade after I started my work in Belize with wild cats, my mind was never far from jaguars. I knew I stood on the continent of their origin, but until that moment I had not thought about what it meant for them to travel and survive the harsh, cold landscape of the Russian Far East, perhaps crossing paths with leopards and tigers. Only now, years later, do I remember standing on that Russian mountaintop, and I wonder if that image in my head was portentous. I am convinced, albeit in retrospect, that I saw the first glimmer of what I would one day call the Pleistocene Jaguar Corridor in those moments when I visualized the jaguar in that landscape.

Buddhist teachings state that one's destiny is not mapped out beforehand, but is shaped according to the conditions already present at the time of one's birth as well as all the other factors that can be changed through one's own efforts. To begin to understand how the jaguar arrived at where it is today, I realized I needed to examine the conditions that shaped the species' existence. I had to go back to the beginning.

Over the approximate 4.6 billion years of our planet's existence, the origins of the big cats in general and of the jaguar in particular are relatively recent events. While the earliest mammals date back to the Triassic period of the Mesozoic era, approximately 220 million years ago, the actual dominance of mammals on our planet occurred only in the last 65 million years, after the extinction of the dinosaurs and when the continents and oceans began to resemble what we see on modern maps today. Fossil evidence of the first felid-like carnivores is sparse, appearing in the mid-Tertiary period, 25 to 30 million years ago.

The earliest fossil evidence of what are considered the first real cats (Felinae) dates back about 9 million years. Then, within a relatively short evolutionary time span, these early forms branched into eight ancestral lineages: Panthera, Ocelot, Puma, Lynx, Bay cat, Domestic cat, Caracal, and Asian leopard cat. Rapid diversification within these lineages might have occurred between 3 and 6 million years ago when sea levels were as much as 100 meters (330 feet) above present levels, thus limiting movements over large areas and forcing ecological partitioning of resources. But such rapid diversification, along with an incomplete fossil record, makes our knowledge of their evolutionary history inexact and based almost exclusively on molecular phylogenies, or genetic differences.

Until recently, the oldest known fossil remains of the genus *Panthera*, the big cats, were from the East African Laetoli Beds in Tanzania, dated at approximately 3.5 to 3.8 million years ago. Phylogenetic research (evolutionary history) of modern *Panthera* showed a taxonomic grouping of the lion, the leopard, and the jaguar, separated from the tiger. The tiger appeared to have branched off before any speciation occurred within the lion/leopard/jaguar group. In fact, the oldest complete skull of a pantherine cat, estimated at 2.2–2.6 million years old and found in China, *Panthera zdanskyi*, was thought to be the most primitive species of the tiger lineage. It was at least half a million years after the tiger when the first jaguar-like *Panthera* cats (*P. onca toscana*), the stem population, came on the scene and started to disperse across Europe.

A recent discovery by Z. Jack Tseng and his associates of a fossil pantherine from the Tibetan Himalayas, named *Panthera blytheae* and dated between 4 and 6 million years old from the late Miocene–early Pliocene, extends the known fossil record for these cats back approximately 2 million years and provides definitive proof for the Asian, not African, origin of the pantherines. Furthermore, Tseng and his associates' analyses, using both the fossil record and molecular phylogenies, shift at least 75 percent of all the divergence events in the pantherine lineage back to the Miocene, up to 7 million years earlier than previously estimated. If these analyses are correct, the implications of such a radical shift in dating results needs more careful examination.

A defining period for the cats was to be the beginning of the Ice Ages, 2–3 million years ago, and the Pleistocene in particular. The Pleistocene is the best-known period of the glaciations, or "Ice Ages," in the earth's history, when ice sheets covered all of Antarctica, large parts of Europe, North America, and South America, as well as small areas in Asia. In North America, sheets of ice stretched over Greenland, Canada, and the northern United States. The glaciations of the Pleistocene were not continuous but consisted of several glacial advances punctuated by interglacial stages, during which ice retreated and a comparatively mild climate ensued.

When the ice sheets spread and sea levels dropped, new land bridges were formed, facilitating migrations that allowed isolated cat populations to redistribute themselves, interbreed, and start creating greater genetic linkages among the cat species of the Western Hemisphere, Eurasia, and Africa. Beringia, a land bridge connecting Asia to North America, emerged as sea level fell at least 55 meters (180 feet) from the present level. Now with both the Beringian and the Panamanian land bridges in place (the latter emerging 2.5–3.5 million years ago), animals had open pathways into new areas. These movements enabled the felids to rapidly evolve into one of the earth's most successful carnivore families, inhabiting all the continents except Antarctica.

The extreme climatic shifts taking place during this period were unforgiving. Species that did not migrate or that got trapped in refugia either adapted or went extinct. During at least 17 glacial-interglacial cycles of the Pleistocene, many of the biggest and strongest of the carnivores, including at least 80 percent of the known large-bodied felids at the time throughout different regions of the world, would go extinct. And those cats and other carnivores that did survive did so through a combination of luck and tenacity. Among them was the jaguar, a species that would be severely tested and shaped by these times. In the end, it would be the jaguar's tenacity that set it apart and helped facilitate its survival.

The jaguar I envisioned that day along the Russia-China border, making its way through cold, sparsely forested regions, might have taken more than a million years to get there. But that jaguar was heavier and longer limbed, better adapted to the rigors of the high-altitude extreme environments than its modern descendant. Still, it would have been struggling to survive as it made its way along river corridors from Central Asia and across southern Siberia, through a harsh, changing landscape. Had it wandered too far to the southeast, where I had been, it likely would not have survived.

Fossil evidence from England, Germany, and Spain indicates the presence of jaguars into at least the middle Pleistocene in Europe. The cause of the eventual extinction of the European jaguar, after surviving numerous glacial-interglacial cycles, remains a mystery. Computer models using modern jaguar life-history data as a proxy for European jaguar populations suggest a scenario where three extensive land masses, in the Balkans, Italy, and Iberia, provided refuge during glacial periods for isolated big cat populations such as the European jaguar. But even such refuges, however large, were isolated and cut off from each other. If jaguar populations survived in these areas for 1,000 years or longer, random environmental events and inbreeding during subsequent glaciations could have led to the expression of lethal recessive genes that would have caused the fragmented populations of the European jaguar to have declined and eventually gone extinct. This was an early manifestation of the importance of the phenomenon of genetic connectivity, a crucial factor in the jaguar's survival elsewhere. Once travel pathways or corridors between seemingly disparate populations were severed, isolated jaguar populations, even in large areas, were prone to extinction.

As many European jaguar populations blinked out, some jaguars survived by finding their way farther north to the then-existing land bridge of Beringia, connecting Eurasia with North America across the Bering Strait. As the jaguar entered North America and headed southward, it left the likelihood of extinction behind. Forging ahead and breaking new ground, this jaguar was now on the verge of creating a new chapter for the species.

There is still uncertainty about when exactly the jaguar arrived in North America; early estimates are based on a single premolar found in Arizona that is nearly 2 million years old. Now it is believed that this tooth was not from a felid at all, and that transcontinental dispersal probably brought the jaguar to North America during a glacial period a million years later. Only much later did jaguars make their way to Central and South America, not before the late-middle to late Pleistocene, 280,000–510,000 years ago.

For many decades, the European and North American jaguars were considered to be three separate pantherine species. But with little evidence indicating a clear separation of European and North American jaguar paleo-populations, it is now believed that they all derive from a single phylogenetic lineage—possibly the same jaguar species—including the modern-day jaguar. Obvious morphological differences between early and late forms, however, point to the likelihood of at least three distinct races of European jaguars between the late Pliocene and the mid-Pleistocene. The North American jaguar that crossed the Beringia land bridge became a separate race, 15–25 percent heavier (up to 210 kilograms, or 463 pounds) and with larger skulls and dentition than current living jaguars. But with fossil evidence showing that the North American jaguar lived at the same time that the European jaguar still survived, this means there was a single circumpolar jaguar population that was eventually broken up by fragmentation and local extinction, leaving the living American jaguar as the only survivor—the hero of this story.

Piecing all this information together, we have a picture of primitive jaguars dispersing out from Asia and across Europe more than 2 million years ago. By about 1.8 million years ago, the jaguar is on the scene in Central Asia. Morphological similarities of Asian jaguar fossils of the late Lower Pleistocene and those from Central and Western Europe suggest an extended period of uninterrupted contact between the jaguar populations of Europe and Western Asia. Assuming a preference for riparian areas in forest and open grasslands like their modern-day counterparts, the area surrounding the Caspian Sea provided ideal conditions for the further development of the Eurasian jaguar until the severe climatic disruptions of the Pleistocene glacial-interglacial periods forced the dispersal of the species. Home to the modern-day countries of Russia, Azerbaijan, Iran, Turkmenistan, and Kazakhstan, the river systems of the Caspian Sea region provided ideal migratory corridors for the jaguar as it moved south of the Caucasus, skirting Siberia and up towards the Beringia land bridge to enter North America, where it arrived approximately one million years ago. The travel pathway negotiated by these jaguars from Europe through Asia and into North America, often with extensive disruptions in time and space, is what I call the *Pleistocene*

Jaguar Corridor, the precursor of the modern-day Jaguar Corridor. The realization that jaguars had not only survived dramatic climatic shifts that caused massive extinctions among many other big cat species, but also had navigated circumpolar travel routes to bring them to their current range, reaffirmed my conviction that the jaguar could provide insights into survival and extinction in an uncertain and rapidly changing world.

With the extinction of the Eurasian jaguar, the future of the species now hinged on the North American jaguar. Starting in the early Pleistocene, perhaps a million years ago, when the jaguar crossed Beringia into the New World, the species kept moving southward, becoming part of what paleontologist S. David Webb called the *Great American Biotic Interchange,* crossing the Panamanian land bridge (created 2.5–3.5 million years ago) into South America. Jaguar fossils from Bolivia have been dated to the middle Pleistocene, and those from Argentina to the late Pleistocene. The jaguar arrived in the New World along with numerous other Eurasian cat species.

But not all movement was in one direction. A 2013 discovery of a 5-million-year-old saber-toothed cat fossil in Florida now puts the origin of these famed cats (tribe Smilodontini), with front canines exposed as much as 17 centimeters, or 7 inches, in the New World, crossing Beringia into Eurasia, not the other way around as previously believed. Research into the American cheetah has been contradictory. Originally believed to have been an early puma, it was reclassified in the 1970s as a relative of the modern cheetah. This suggested that ancestors of the cheetah diverged from the puma lineage in the Americas and migrated back to the Old World. But recent research of mitochondrial DNA has suggested that the American cheetah might, in fact, be more closely related to puma and not to the modern cheetah of Africa and Asia. Fossil evidence of the leopard has never been found in North America, despite this species always having been widely distributed and utilizing a wide variety of habitats and prey. It is possible that because this species flourished during even the coldest periods of the Ice Age, it was not prone to the same pressures of extreme climatic shifts that were driving other species across Beringia and into North America.

Although the lion, once thought to have formerly ranged from Africa through Eurasia and into both North and South America, was believed to be the most wide-ranging wild land mammal of all time, more-recent examination of skull and dental characteristics of the American lion has caused some scientists to speculate that it was not a lion at all. In the 1930s, George Gaylord Simpson speculated that the American lion was actually a giant jaguar, distinct from but related to the North American jaguar. But with morphological similarities of both the jaguar and the tiger, the American lion is not easily assigned to any extant pantherine, and is likely a separate species more recent than either the tiger or jaguar lineages. Whatever it was, there was probably competitive exclusion between the American lion and the jaguar in North America, because fossil remains of both species have rarely been found together.

While the jaguar was entering North America, early man was still spreading across Africa, Asia, and Europe. Those early humans, the terrestrial bipedal hominids of the genus *Homo* who evolved about 2.5 million years ago in Africa, spread into Eurasia about half a million years later and eventually helped ravage the Pleistocene megafauna. Ironically, early man—an outsider to the super-carnivore guilds of Africa and Asia and potential prey rather than predator—did not fare so well himself. Anthropologists speculate that early food procurement by humans involved scavenging carcasses from larger felid kills, an activity that might have shaped the social behavior of early hominids. As many as 22 species of hominids went extinct, at least 11 of which were of the genus *Homo*. Eventually only *Homo sapiens*, our own current species, was truly "the last man standing." And recent evidence indicates that, while the population of humans fluctuated, there were perhaps no more than 10,000 breeding individuals of *Homo sapiens* during nearly the whole of the Pleistocene.

Taxonomically, the felids had a better survival record than the hominids. Today, the cats are divided into two subfamilies, Pantherinae and Felinae, to describe the reconstructed dichotomy between large cats in the pantherine lineage (*Panthera* and *Neofelis*) versus all other cats. Cats of the genus *Panthera* (tiger, lion, jaguar, leopard, snow leopard) have a flexible or incompletely ossified hyoid and a U-shaped bone at the root of the tongue that allows for roaring. The snow leopard, a purring cat, is the exception because it lacks the special morphological features of the larynx that are also needed for roaring.

Only one human species, *Homo sapiens*, would follow the jaguars across Beringia nearly a million years later during the late Pleistocene, when another interglacial period caused warming climates and a retreat of the continental ice sheets. As habitats became drier, forests replaced grasslands and rising sea levels resulted in the inundation of large areas of coastal grazing lands. With such extensive habitat loss, many of the large herbivore species died off, and with their major prey gone, the carnivores soon followed. Only this time, in contrast to the past, this late-Pleistocene extinction event was exceptional in the numbers of large species over 40 kilograms (88 pounds) that disappeared in the Americas. This period claimed at least 33 of 45 genera in North America, and 46 of 58 genera in South America including all mammal species of South American origin over 100 kilograms (220 pounds). Among the cats, this included sabertoothed cats, the American lion, and the American cheetahs.

While extreme climatic and environmental changes were clearly among the causative factors during this late-Pleistocene extinction event, the fact that the disappearance of so many large mammal species coincided with the presence of modern man lends credence to the Blitzkrieg or Overkill Hypothesis, the theory that modern man was a major driver of this particular extinction event. It is speculated that hunters armed with newly developed weapons, such as spears and knives, could easily wipe out large numbers of megafauna not habituated to the human threat. Furthermore, many of the now-extinct animals persisted on islands long after their disappearance on the mainland, despite the dramatic postglacial warming, but then disappeared with the arrival of humans to those islands. This theory proposing humans as the major driving force of this Pleistocene extinction seems most credible in North America, where the appearance of Paleo-Indian cultures around 11,000 years ago coincided closely with some of the continent's greatest-known extinction events ("Indian" being a term for the existing inhabitants that originated with Columbus, who thought he had arrived in the East Indies while seeking Asia).

Early *Homo sapiens* were believed to have colonized Beringia perhaps as early as 20,000 years ago, spreading out into the Great Plains when a corridor opened through what is now the Northwest Territories. There is also evidence that other groups might have arrived, not necessarily by crossing Beringia, but possibly by boat along the coasts of North and South America as far back as 35,000 years ago, prior to the last Ice Age. But it was the appearance of the Clovis people around 12,000 years ago that is closely associated with the extensive megafaunal extinctions in the Americas. This early Paleo-Indian culture, whose name is associated with the town in New Mexico where the characteristic stone spearheads used by these people were first found, supposedly comprised highly proficient big-game hunters. Clovis spear points have been found with the bones of Ice Age animals in many North American sites. The Folsom culture, dating a little later than the Clovis, were also hunters using chipped flint points and a variety of other stone tools to kill large mammals. It is assumed that as humans eradicated game in one area, they moved on to new areas before prey had a chance to learn evasive behavior.

Enjoying a plentiful bounty of a high-protein diet, human hunting groups had high birth and survival rates, while big animals like the mammoths had long gestation periods and thus low birth rates, making them more prone to extinction. While mammalogist Ross MacPhee did not believe that "a few thousand Indian men with pointed sticks could run around a continent and bring to extinction 135 species in maybe 400 years," recent studies suggest that humans likely precipitated extinction in many parts of the globe, but also that the timing, geography, and magnitude of these Pleistocene extinctions would have been different had climatic change not coincided with the human impacts.

While early interactions between jaguars and man might have occurred in Eurasia, the earliest evidence we have of jaguars and Paleo-Indians actually coexisting in the same landscape was found at Schulze Cave in Texas, where skeletal remains of both jaguar and man, dating 4,000–11,000 years ago, were found together. Similar evidence of coexistence with the jaguar's relative, the American lion, is suggested by finds at Ventana Cave in southern Arizona and at Jaguar Cave in Idaho. Remains of Folsom-style projectile points were found at the Arizona site, which was successively occupied for the next 10,000 years by the Cochise, Hohokam, and Piman Native American cultures.

While North American jaguars continued to range into areas that are now the northern states of Washington, Nebraska, Pennsylvania, and Maryland in the United States during the mid-Pleistocene up until the last glacial period 10,000–110,000 years ago, fossils of late-Pleistocene jaguars show them only as far north as Nevada, Kansas, Missouri, and Tennessee. From this time period onward there was a continual restriction of the jaguar's range even farther to the south, probably influenced by additional glacial and interglacial shifts. Eventually the species' range in what is now the United States would be restricted to only a relatively small portion of the Southwest.

And as its cooler, more-open habitats were replaced with warmer forests, the jaguar became smaller in size, with a corresponding shortening of the limbs. This shift in size could be explained by Bergmann's Rule, a correlation between temperature and the surface-area-to-volume ratio of endotherms, particularly birds and mammals. According to this rule, proposed in 1847, larger animals radiate less body heat per unit of mass, and therefore stay warmer in cold climates. Conversely, in warmer climates where heat needs to be dissipated, the higher surface-area-to-volume ratio of smaller animals facilitates heat loss through the skin and helps to cool the body. An 'alternate' theory, proposed by biologist Valerius Geist in 1986, correlates body size with seasonal food availability.

Shifts in geographic distribution with subsequent extinction of local populations of jaguars, from the species' earliest beginnings, through the Pleistocene, and on to recent times, has resulted in severe range contraction from the species' once much more widely distributed Holarctic form. And while the modern-day jaguar species has been described morphologically as a "phenotypic dwarf" and ecologically as a "relict population," I think these descriptions are misleading. The jaguar that emerged onto the stage of modern times was a survivor—smaller and more resilient, a highly mobile and adaptable species that had survived one of the worst extinction events during one of the most turbulent periods of geologic time.

While other megafauna went extinct, the jaguar was re-creating itself. Evolutionary forces that drove the diversification of the numerous sympatric felid species placed the jaguar, morphologically and behaviorally, in an advantageous position. Its 40- to 160-kilogram (88- to 352-pound), short, stocky structure resulted in a solitary, opportunistic, stalk-and-ambush predator that, while mostly terrestrial, was also adept at tree climbing and swimming. Hunting mostly after dark, the jaguar could be active day or night. With a robust skull and powerful jaws as part of a smaller, more compact yet still incredibly powerful structure, the jaguar was capable of taking down prey far larger than itself, or crawling quietly through the underbrush to pounce upon a smaller, unsuspecting meal. With a gestation period of a little more than three months, females could have up to four cubs capable of surviving 12–15 years in the wild or up to almost twice that time in captivity, making it one of the longest-lived cats. What emerged from the Pleistocene and into modern times was an incredibly efficient predator, an animal capable of utilizing all the dimensions of a turbulent, changing world and shifting its behavior between that of a big small-cat or a small big-cat, as circumstances required.

Perhaps if I had been more insightful that day in the Russian Far East as I pictured a jaguar in my mind's eye, I might have had the wisdom to see the existence of the Pleistocene Jaguar Corridor, forged by the resilience of the jaguar and its ability to move through the Palearctic, Nearctic, and Neotropical habitats of Europe, Asia, and North America, respectively. I might have realized the possibility of the modern-day Jaguar Corridor long before it was thrust in my face years later. I didn't yet fully grasp the tenacity and resiliency of the jaguar, nor its ability to move over great distances, unseen and unheralded. This species was undeterred.

But great challenges lay ahead for the species. For on the heels of the modern jaguar was that other group of highly resilient mammals that had followed them through the Pleistocene Corridor and across Beringia, perhaps the greatest mammalian dispersers that ever lived. And what now followed was to prove far more threatening to the jaguar's survival than anything it had yet experienced. Modern man was on the scene.

Chapter 3

The First People of the Jaguar

I WAS ON AN OVERGROWN DIRT TRACK far back in the Cockscomb
Basin of Belize, a former access road cut when the timber company operating there had been on its last legs. One more rainy season and the road would be impassable, I thought as I crept along in
the truck, listening to the static of my radio receiver that monitored
the collars of my jaguars. I was after the radio signal of my newest
jaguar, a young 36-kilogram (79-pound) male I had recently captured in this area and named Xamen Ek, after the Mayan god of the
North Star, a benevolent deity. It was 1984, and at age 30 with my
relatively new PhD credentials I was conducting the first ecological
study of its kind on jaguars in rain forest habitat as a field scientist with the Wildlife Conservation Society. Every day brought new
adventures and challenges. And every day I gained more insight into

the mysteries of how the Western Hemisphere's largest and least-known big cat lived.

Thinking back on the capture of Xamen Ek still made my heart race. I remembered my first sight of him, crouching silently in a far corner of the nearly two-meter-long, one-meter-high (six-foot-long by three-foot-high) cage trap, built of iron rebar and baited with a live pig enclosed at the back. It had taken me several attempts before learning how to build a trap that was strong enough to hold these cats. Then I came up with the idea of building one in pieces that could be hauled far back into the jungle and assembled on-site. The capture of Xamen Ek had been in the most remote trap I had yet placed out in the jungle.

The young jaguar's eyes followed my every move as he flattened his body, as if trying to meld into the ground. Only when I got close enough to the trap to inject a sedative into him did he suddenly lunge at me, roaring, teeth bared, throwing his body against the iron bars of the trap. I fell backward, almost jabbing myself with the drug-filled syringe. He was scared, or perhaps just wary, making him more aggressive rather than more timid as I had seen with the four other jaguars I had trapped before him. He had never seen another human before, of that I was certain. He was too young to have experienced the destructive power of our species yet. I was saddened by the thought that I might now have changed that. He roared and charged me one final time before I jabbed him with the drug. For just an instant, as he pressed against the bars of the trap while lashing out at me, our eyes met. They were the wildest eyes I had ever seen.

Now I was searching for this elusive young cat, a task that was proving increasingly difficult, particularly at this time of year. The rains had wreaked havoc again, washing away sections of what was left of the timber roads. The tires spun, I smelled burning rubber before I got traction again, and the truck struggled out of another rut. Then I heard the grinding. I continued over a short rise before pulling over into a flat, open area, once a holding site for logs from the now-defunct timber operation. As I turned off the engine I knew I had just lost another universal joint—the fifth one in less than two years. I looked over at Cirillo, my Mayan assistant, already gathering his belongings for the walk back to camp. Rather than follow the road, Cirillo got out and started immediately chopping through the dense jungle to make a shortcut. I stayed back a while longer and secured the truck until we could come back with the parts to fix it.

I followed Cirillo's trail, still trying to pick up the radio signal of the young male jaguar, when I literally bumped into Cirillo's back. He stood statue-like, machete in mid chop, staring at the wall of foliage ahead. Only it wasn't a wall of foliage—it was a real wall! Rising up in front of us, along the edge of a creek, was a mound, 50 feet high, that seemed totally out of place. Looking more closely, I could discern square-cut stones protruding from the edge of the mound at different heights. My throat tightened with the realization of what I was looking at. I started to pick out more sculpted stone blocks below the dirt and trees—the base platform of the structure and what appeared to be two terraces above it. We had just walked onto the site of an ancient, undiscovered Mayan ruin, deep in the jungle.

I raced over and climbed the mound, soon standing atop what I assumed to be a small Mayan temple. The timber road where we had just broken down was less than 30 meters (about 100 feet) away. I had driven and walked right by this ancient Mayan site dozens of times, as had others, without knowing it was here. If anyone knew about it, it would have been plundered already.

To the south was a large creek that skirted the ruin and fed into the major waterway of the Cockscomb Basin. The availability of water had likely influenced the location of the temple. I cut another trail back to the timber road to get my bearings, and then I tried to picture the site denuded of forest, as it had been when the Maya were here. The timber road had been cut through the ruin, I realized. The rise over which I had driven my truck before we broke down was part of the larger base platform for the site. I knew that the ancient Maya often elevated their temples and palaces by building extensive platforms or foundations. While this didn't appear to be a large Mayan site by any measure, tons of stone still had had to be quarried and transported here before being cut, shaped, and set into place. And this temple wasn't sitting here alone. How many more ruins were out here in this ocean of green vegetation, I wondered?

Cirillo had not moved an inch from where he'd first been standing. Just as with Xamen Ek in the trap, I wasn't sure if it was fear or uncertainty I saw in his eyes.

"Tell no one where this place is for now," I said to him.

Cirillo remained silent, then turned away and continued cutting our trail back to camp.

It was a few weeks before I could return, both to fix the truck and to bring someone from the Archaeology Department of Belize to the site. Cirillo's uncertainty had by this time turned to intense interest and he now became an active and eager participant in exploring the site. Starting at the temple mound, we cut transects out in four directions. Within the hour we encountered two smaller mounds west of the main plaza. Between the mounds we found a cut circular stone, about a meter and a half (five feet) in diameter but lacking any carvings or inscriptions. On the transect that crossed the timber road, we found another mound alongside an odd-looking pair of oblong stones, about a meter (three feet) apart and each about half a meter high and a meter and a half long (two feet high and five feet long). The others moved on, but I lingered. I rubbed my hand along the length of one of the stones, than sat between them.

Mayan ruins were not entirely new to me. I had visited the extensive excavated temples of Tikal in Guatemala and the much smaller site of Altun Ha in Belize. Since settling in the Cockscomb Basin for my jaguar research, I had tried to understand the obvious disconnect between the present-day Maya, who lived in simple and often squalid conditions, and their incredibly rich ancestral heritage. I'd found no answers at the cleared, heavily visited tourist sites. They were museums with displays—empty mausoleums. And the forest around them, if much remained, was degraded, mostly devoid of wildlife. This was different. I saw it in Cirillo's eyes, the connection between past and present, as he returned with us to explore this site, gently examining the cut stones. This was home to his ancestors, and they were possibly the last ones before us to have touched these stones and walked this ground.

After reporting the information to the Belizean Archaeological Commissioner, at the time a virtual one-man force named Harriot Topsey, I was told I could suggest a name for the site. It was in my head already: Kuchil Balam—"Place of the Jaguar." I was searching for young Xamen Ek when we found this place. The people who had once lived here—built these structures, denuded the forest, and killed the animals—were long gone. This was home to the jaguar now, and Xamen Ek embodied the wildness here.

I looked upon the Maya with whom I lived with new eyes now. They moved around camp almost listlessly, to their huts, to their fields, to their hammocks. Where was the energy of the people who had ruled this land once, who had built great cities, studied the stars, and revered the jaguar? Archaeologists had already determined that the population of this region during the Maya Classic Period was considerably greater than it was now. Why had the jaguar lived while the Maya, the people of the jaguar, died out?

Once *Homo sapiens* crossed Beringia and followed the jaguar into North America, humans were destined to become the dominant factor in the survival or demise of the jaguar. To put recent history into proper context and to understand fully what we will be exploring in this book—the jaguar and the people with whom it lived—we need to do as we did in chapter 2, go to the beginning, with the emphasis now on humans. "Life can only be understood backwards," stated the nineteenth-century Danish philosopher Søren Kierkegaard. To get to the essence of the jaguar and its influence on the people with whom it lived, we must examine not only some of the biological and sociocultural factors of human evolution, but also the interactions between humans and jaguars that shaped cultural beliefs and behavior between these two species unlike anything else seen on the planet, past or present.

The earliest hominids that evolved on what is today the African continent lived on foods that could only be picked or gathered: plants, fruits, invertebrates. Sometime around 2.5 million years ago, or earlier according to some theories, meat obtained through opportunistic scavenging, and later through hunting, became an important component of the diet. This shift towards a more carnivorous diet supposedly led to changes in behavior, use of tools, and larger brain size in evolving man—changes that are said to have "made us human." The eventual transition back to a more omnivorous diet occurred gradually, with shifts in other physiological and behavioral traits, such as the lengthening of the small intestine, more leisure time, and living at low population densities.

For many years, humans were hunter-gatherers, traveling in highly mobile bands of up to 50 members, often an extended family. But as humans evolved from scavengers to predators, their killing apparatus now contained more highly efficient projectile points made into spears and knives, along with specialized tools for butchering and hide processing. *Homo erectus*, appearing about 1.8 million years ago, might have been the first truly predatory human species, and evidence suggests that he scavenged carnivore kills from wild predators. Scavenging may have played as important a role in human foraging as did hunting in early hominids, possibly resulting in some of the first interactions between early man and large carnivores, including jaguars. Studies in modern-day rural Uganda show that even today, humans living among large carnivore communities and armed with simple weapons can successfully chase carnivores from kills. And among the contemporary Hadza people of Tanzania, scavenging still constitutes a significant part of their foraging activity.

The transition from scavenging kills made by other predators to the development of increasingly effective hunting implements and tools forced an increase in the physical and mental dexterity of hominids. Planning hunts involved rational and conceptual thought. Cooperative hunting brought together unrelated individuals, expanding the gene pool for potential mates. Food sharing allowed for increased group sizes and more socialization. Humans learned to use fires to enhance grazing lands and optimize hunting as early as 10,000 years ago, though some believe that the use of fire dates back more than 100,000 years.

But a nomadic existence, whether for plants or animals, did not lend itself to long-term stability and the evolution of civilization. Those changes began when humans shifted from a strictly carnivorous diet to one that utilized the food energy contained in edible plants, but in a methodical, strategic manner—farming. The development of farming, along with the more sedentary lifestyle necessary for such an activity, occurred independently in at least seven different parts of the world at the end of the last Ice Age, about 10,000 years ago.

In the Americas, with climatic fluctuations stabilized by about 8000 BC the South American highlands became a center of early agriculture. The potato, originating in southern Peru, was cultivated as early as 10,000 years ago. Maize or corn was first bred and cultivated in the valleys of southern Mexico about 7,000 years ago. Corn was initially a weed-like secondary food source, but millennia of selective harvesting and replanting increased the size of the corn cob and the number of kernels to produce what eventually became a basic primary food throughout North, Central, and South America. Other food crops soon followed, including beans, squash, sweet potatoes, tomatoes, chili peppers, pineapples, avocados, cacao, vanilla, onions, peanuts, strawberries, raspberries, blueberries, blackberries, and papayas. Over 40 species of economic crops were eventually domesticated in the New World and, today, over two-thirds of all food crops grown worldwide are native to the Americas.

As agricultural practices and tool development became more sophisticated, people learned to manipulate nature to their advantage. Fire was used intentionally to clear large areas of forest understory and thus facilitate the growth of certain plants, resulting in the pre-Columbian savannas of North America. Early irrigation systems were developed by diverting streams, creating canals and water reservoirs. Digging and plowing implements were created. On hilly or sloped terrain, the practice of terracing was eventually used to prevent erosion and water runoff. Even on some of the most seemingly uninhabitable land in places like Amazonia, pre-Columbian farmers of the Guianan coast learned to construct large raised-field complexes to grow crops such as maize, manioc, and squash. Everything that could be done to tame and cultivate the land was done.

It is likely that early man, having spread into the range of the remaining European jaguars only by the mid-Pleistocene, perhaps a million years ago, had little significant interaction with the species. By the Late Pleistocene period, as the last Eurasian jaguars disappeared, the

American jaguar had already spread throughout much of the New World. And at this time, as noted in the last chapter, *Homo sapiens* crossed Beringia over into North America. Many of the largest mammal species would not survive the Late Pleistocene extinctions that took place, at least partly because of the successful dispersal and hunting behavior of early humans in the Americas. But jaguars did survive, only to face their next big threat by a growing and changing human presence.

The transition from nomadic hunter–gatherer to pastoralist lifestyle among early man in the Americas was gradual, and eventually had major implications for land use, population growth, cultural development, and the survival of species like the jaguar. With the tending of crops and the domestication of animals, large numbers of people could be supported in concentrated areas for indefinite periods. The most fertile lands, often the richest wildlife habitats such as grasslands, floodplains, and forest mosaics, were settled first. Then, starting about 2,000 years ago, centralized civilizations developed. As larger numbers of people became more sedentary and more agrarian, extensive areas of prime jaguar habitat were denuded and fragmented. Through use of cooperative hunting techniques, better weapons, and the harnessing of fire, hunters became more proficient. Those who lived among the jaguar were now a force to be reckoned with by the species, already carrying out activities that would henceforth remain the major threats to the jaguar's continued survival—loss of habitat, loss of prey, and the actual killing of the jaguar.

The early human demographics of the New World, discussed in greater detail later in the book, are the key to understanding the seeming paradox of a bountiful paradise alongside intense exploitation of resources in certain parts of the Americas at this time. These demographics played a significant role in jaguar distribution patterns. In the regions of extensive human settlement, land-use practices varied greatly with a continuum from intensive hunting in places like the east Caribbean coast, to intensive monocultures in parts of what is today El Salvador. While some indigenous hunting bands evolved into civilizations with towns and cities, others still lived in small, scattered communities. Despite degradation of extensive areas of prime wild jaguar habitat, human activity was concentrated in defined areas with relatively few people spread over the remaining landscape. Extensive contiguous jaguar populations were safe for the time being. But there was one dramatic change afoot, one that would affect the jaguar significantly—man's newly emerging cognizance of nature.

With reliable sources of food, more leisure time, and increased interaction between large numbers of people, the development of complex cultures was accompanied by a desire to understand, explain, and try to control the surrounding world. Many indigenous people seemed ambivalent towards the natural world: they were both terrified by the uncertainty and power of the environment (drought, floods, earthquakes, hurricanes), yet also pleased and grateful for nature's bounty and the predictable natural rhythms on which they depended for survival. Forests were dark and scary places with dangerous wild animals like jaguars and poisonous plants; forests were also the source of many edible plants, game animals, medicines, and building materials. Nature was neither good nor evil, but there was an increasing realization that the forces upon which people's lives depended needed to be understood and controlled. Gods were created to explain and justify the origin and existence of the natural world in which humans lived, and ritualistic practices were developed to appease and interact with the gods, thus ensuring control and dominance over the future.

Anthropologist Wade Davis believes that shamanism is perhaps the oldest of human spiritual endeavors, born of the hunt and the need on the part of humans to rationalize their killing while also creating a balance between the living and the dead. Some scholars suggest that shamanic relics and rituals might have accompanied the earliest human migrations from Eurasia to the Americas. Davis suggests that perhaps as early as 6000 BC, shamans and medicine men used spirit-derived power from the hunt to benefit their agricultural endeavors and impose control over other aspects of the environment.

But there is little evidence of any complex relationship between indigenous peoples and jaguars until about 1500 BC, when one of the first major pre-Columbian cultures of the New World, the Olmec, came onto the scene. Other civilizations might antedate the

Olmec, such as the Zapotec (1500 BC) from southern Mexico and the Norte Chico civilization (3000–1800 BC) from Peru, but the Olmec created one of the earliest and most sophisticated cultures that helped lay the ideological, religious, and economic foundations for succeeding civilizations in the region. And most importantly, their religious beliefs centered around one particular fierce and impressive deity—the jaguar.

While some ritualistic practices or beliefs connecting humans and jaguars might have been present in the Pleistocene, it was not until the rise of early civilizations and cultures in the Americas that there began a new chapter in the saga of man and jaguar. And it was the Olmec civilization, precursor to the Maya and born in the tropical lowlands of south-central Mexico, that truly set into motion what I term the *Jaguar Cultural Corridor*—the cultural linkage among the people of the jaguar, all those whose lives from the Pleistocene onward were shaped by the apex predator with whom they shared their land, whether they cringed in fear at the animal's proximity, battled for flesh scraps or marrow from its kill, roamed the jungle in a drug-induced state as a shaman "were-jaguar," or used dogs to chase the animal up a tree to be killed.

I first encountered the term *People of the Jaguar* as the title of Nicholas Saunders's 1989 book in which he examines jaguar symbolism among the various cultures that disappeared or were conquered, from the Olmec onward, leaving a vast array of monuments, carvings, and drawings as their legacy. The similarities and continuity of practices and beliefs relating to the jaguar that existed among diverse civilizations, separated in space and time, seemed part of a larger cultural consciousness that was as powerful and evocative as the animal itself. The Jaguar Cultural Corridor encompassed those cultures that existed in a world where the boundary between humans and animals was blurred and where the jaguar was a powerful manifestation of nature's power.

I started to understand some of this that day in the jungle with Cirillo as we tracked the elusive Xamen Ek. When I looked into

Cirillo's face just moments after the realization that we had stumbled upon an almost unrecognizable Mayan temple, hidden by the same jungle in which he had spent his life, I saw the connection. He knew what he was looking upon, and the incongruity between the grand ancestral past of his people and his simple, almost forlorn present was as inexplicable and frightening to him at that moment as it was baffling to me. The connections among Cirillo, the ruins, the jungles, and the jaguar were there plain as day. ·

In chapters that follow, we will explore in greater depth the early civilizations of the region that comprised the Jaguar Cultural Corridor and how they were linked around a core belief that the jaguar's existence was tied to that of humans, both spiritually and in everyday life. While the jaguar was to be feared, it was also to be respected, because the presence of this animal played a role in the health and well-being of the people with whom the jaguar lived. This belief, this human–jaguar linkage, was, I believe, as important to the cultural fabric of the people as it was to the jaguar's struggle for survival.

Chapter 4

When Jaguars Talked to Man

God created man, only after the jaguar had already been put on the earth. Sending the jaguar to the river to fetch water so that he couldn't see what was going on, God fashioned thirteen men from mud, along with twelve guns. By the time the jaguar returned, God was in the process of creating a dog from the mud.

"That animal is for me to eat," the jaguar said.

"No," said God. "The dog is the servant of man and these guns will teach you to respect him."

"I'm not afraid of the gun," said the jaguar. "I'll catch the shots that are fired at me."

So God had the jaguar move away while one of the newly created men shot and wounded the jaguar in the paw.

The jaguar, nonplussed, said, "The dog is for me to eat."

But man told him otherwise and sent the dog after the jaguar, forcing the jaguar up into a tree while the man shot him again in the paw.

"Now you have learned your lesson that you must not eat man or dog. . . . Go away and live in the bush."

THIS CREATION MYTH, told by the Maya in Belize to anthropologist J. Eric Thompson in 1930 and relayed in greater detail in my first book, *Jaguar*, is an elegantly simple depiction of how the Mayan people of this region explained their relationship to both this powerful predator and the evolutionary forces (or God) that put them there. Despite the Maya having no knowledge of the actual events that took place millions of years earlier, this particular Mayan story is surprisingly accurate, placing the jaguar on earth initially dominant to humans until humans learned ways, through weapons and tools, to control the jaguar. While there are numerous versions of the Mayan creation myth, much of the source material came from the *Popol Vuh*, or "Book of Council," dating from the sixteenth century and found in the Guatemalan highlands, which clearly states that plants and animals were on the earth first, and helped the Creator bring humanity into existence.

Creation myths such as these are symbolic accounts of a group's beliefs regarding how the world began and how people first came to inhabit it. There are often multiple versions of such myths, all with plots and characters that convey metaphoric, symbolic, or even historical truths for the society. Such myths also provide answers to deeply meaningful questions and reveal the worldview of the people who share the myth. They help guide one's relationship to both the spiritual and the natural world.

Early myths and stories from major pre-Columbian civilizations reveal the underlying relationship between humans and jaguars, and almost always they share a common theme. The Olmec, Maya, Aztec, and Inca all worshiped the jaguar in some form. Throughout the haunts of the jaguar, different tribes created a varied array of folklore and mystical relationships with this big cat that went far beyond creation myths. Often feared not for it was, but for what it was believed to be, jaguars inspired a universal awe and dread that was predominantly of a mystical nature, the fear of an animal possessed of supernatural powers and only partly of this earth. Such a beast needed to be both respected and controlled.

The jaguar, with its power, ferocity, and valor, was of man's world, yet outside of man's world; it was a strong, secretive animal of the dark, dense forest, linked to the spirit world, godly but not God. God (or gods) empowered man to chase, wound, and even kill this favored species when necessary, despite its otherworldly status. Certain humans, such as shamans, were empowered to use the powerful medicinal plants of the jaguar's world in order to enter that world themselves, become a "were-jaguar"—half-jaguar and half-human similar to the werewolf of European folklore. As explained in the previous chapter, the development of such beliefs and practices, along with the pantheon of gods needed to explain and control the world, were shared by spatially and temporally disparate indigenous cultures of the Americas, creating the underpinnings of the Jaguar Cultural Corridor.

I tried to understand the link between the lives of the Maya and the jaguar while living and working with them in Belize. But while these modern-day Maya lived almost as basic a life as that of their ancestors, they seemed strangely out of touch with their own cultural past. I saw little connecting them to jaguars other than a fear of the animal that led most people to carry guns in the jungle and shoot the jaguar on sight if possible. It was only when I delved into the past, during my first trip to Mexico, that a better understanding of the Jaguar Cultural Corridor started formulating in my mind.

My shirt was already drenched with sweat and sticking to my body long before we reached the hotel in Villahermosa. I was traveling with two friends, Jane Alexander and Ed Sherin, and we had just met up with Victor Perera, another friend of theirs, at the airport. A Guatemalan Jewish novelist, who had spent part of his childhood in Brooklyn, Victor had recently published a book entitled *Last Lords of Palenque* about the lives of the Lacandon, a remote tribe of Maya Indians whom he had lived with and believed to be the descendants of the ancient Maya theocrats. Now Victor was returning to visit their spiritual leader, Chun K'in, whom he had heard was in failing health, possibly dying.

When I was invited to go along on the trip, I jumped at the opportunity. Approaching the end of my jaguar research in Belize and the likelihood that I would soon be walking away from the Cockscomb Basin forever, I still had more questions than answers about the life of the jaguar. But more than that, I was deeply bothered by what felt like a lack of closure, a lack of understanding of the Mayan people and the present-day culture that I had been immersed in for more than two years. Were all the jaguar carvings, paintings, and rituals of the Maya and other past civilizations just cultural artifacts, merely a way to control or sublimate their fear of the bogeyman in the dark closet, a fear that was no longer necessary? Or was something more there, something I still couldn't grasp? I was seeking answers.

Our first destination was the heart of Central America's oldest-known civilization, the Olmec remains at La Venta, in the present-day Mexican state of Tabasco, close to the Gulf of Mexico. I had first heard of the Olmecs while in Belize trying to learn more about the Mayan civilization. Occupying south-central Mexico around 1400 BC and considered the "mother culture" for other major Mesoamerican cultures, the Olmec used the jaguar in their depictions of the world more than did any other civilization. While some of the other early cultures, such as the Chavín of Peru and the San Agustín of Colombia, also had jaguar cults, the Olmec were perhaps the earliest culture to have made the jaguar a central focus of their lives. To the Olmec, the line between man and jaguar was blurred, as depicted in their very distinctive carvings, masks, and pottery decorations of humans with jaguar-like or zoomorphic characteristics expressed mainly in the facial features. It is among the Olmec that we find the first evidence of jaguar shamans and the were-jaguars, the powerful medicine men of the tribe who were able to transform themselves into jaguars at will. Those encountering a jaguar in the jungle could never be sure of what they were seeing: a jaguar or a man.

It is understandable that early peoples worshiped or revered the most powerful animal that shared their living space, and that they expressed such feelings in their art, their carvings, and sculpture. Animals that are part of cultural mythology are always portrayed as more complex and dynamic than what people experience with that same species in the real world. The mythological creature is viewed as separate from the real animal. But ancient cultures viewed the jaguar with a dualism that went beyond simply symbolic-versus-real. The jaguar was viewed as itself having a dualistic nature with a role in both the spirit world and that of everyday reality. So everything about the circumstances of its appearance and behavior in the real world was important and potentially linked to the spirit world.

I wandered among the ruins of La Venta Park, terribly excited at the prospect of virtually stepping back in time, seeing the beginning of the earliest tangible relationship between man and jaguar. When Olmec civilization reached its zenith in around 500 BC, jaguar imagery in stone, ceramic, and metal was common, with numerous sculpted monuments and heads of jaguars in major population centers such as Teotihuacan, near present-day Mexico City. The prevalence of jaguar symbolism and the enduring images of the were-jaguar in the jade and other stone carvings of the Olmec, particularly among the ruling elite, were believed to be a means of linking them to this mythical race of jaguar ancestors and helped legitimize their social position. The impressive monuments at La Venta included three large mosaic masks of ferocious-looking jaguars and were some of the best examples of early jaguar mythology and symbolism. This entire site was built in tribute to the jaguar. With the Caspian Sea home to perhaps the first true jaguars some 2 million years earlier, Mexico, I believe, was the birthplace of the Jaguar Cultural Corridor.

Richard Perry, in his book *The World of the Jaguar*, called the Olmec "jaguar psychotics" who went as far as to deform their own heads to imitate the cat's flattened skull. In 2006, archeologists discovered a 3,500-year-old male skeleton with what was perhaps the oldest-known dental procedure in the Americas: some of the teeth had been filed down to appear, it was assumed, as jaguar fangs. According to the Olmec origin myth, their semi-divine rulers descended from a union between male jaguars and female humans, giving rise to a race of were-jaguars that eventually took on human features to form the Olmec royal families. Interestingly, these beliefs might have had more of a basis in reality than many people suspected.

A fascinating but little-known paper by George Milton and Roberto Gonzalo, published in the 1974 journal *Expedition* from the University of Pennsylvania's Museum of Archaeology and Anthropology, links the Olmec fascination with the jaguar to their interest in human deformities, such as dwarfs and hunchbacks, who were viewed in a mystical rather than a negative sense. Milton and Gonzalo point out the distinctive representation by the Olmec of were-jaguar babies and infants, with sculptures showing a child's face with slanted eyes, a clear epicanthic fold, a round and puffy face, a chubby body, and an open mouth, sometimes with fangs. It is possible, they purport, that these Olmec were-jaguar infants were actually representations of children affected by Down syndrome, who might have been viewed as the result of sexual union between a woman and a jaguar. The authors also consider the idea that the were-jaguar cult among the Olmec could have been the product of a deep concern for individuals with Down syndrome due to a physical resemblance between them and the totemic jaguar.

I finally reached the site I'd been looking for, Altar 4. Almost two meters (six feet) high and at least twice that wide, the altar, now believed by archaeologists to be a throne, was carved as a jaguar's head containing a human figure sitting inside the jaguar's wide, gaping mouth. The carved figure of a man held a knife in one hand and was grabbing an umbilical-like rope that circled around at least part of the base of the stone. The physical and spiritual connection depicted between man and jaguar in this carving was unmistakable. I looked around to make sure no one was close by, and then I climbed atop the stone altar, lay down, and closed my eyes.

I must have dozed a bit before I heard Jane calling my name in the distance. I climbed down off the throne reluctantly. There had been no visions, no epiphany, simply a restful respite from human contact. I felt something was missing from this site, something I had hoped to find. I caught up with Jane and Ed at a little zoo that was maintained as part of the park. The sounds of the animals were comforting, a welcome contrast to the quiet, empty atmosphere of the ruins. And then I heard the distinctive grunting sound that had so often made my heart skip a beat in the dark jungles of Belize.

I made a beeline for the grunts and came upon a large open pit with a lone female jaguar that was being taunted by tourists from the safety of their perch above the pit. From the way she held herself, and the way she vocalized, I could tell that this jaguar was still wild, even before the guard confirmed her recent capture. She had been hanging around a local village, we were told, probably due to a lack of sufficient prey for her to catch in the forest. Now she would spend the rest of her life in this dungeon-like pit, gawked at and harassed by humans. Her days of lying on a rock outcrop to feel the sun warming her body or bearing young in the hollow cavity of some fallen dead tree were over. This magnificent creature was already one of the walking dead.

I headed for the exit of the park, not caring whether my friends were following me or not. Something felt very wrong here. I thought of what my Mayan assistant, Cirillo, had said to me less than a month earlier when we were measuring the fresh footprints of a large male jaguar in Cockscomb that had walked the trail only hours before us. I was telling him the Maya creation story and when I finished with God saying, "Go away and live in the bush," Cirillo immediately retorted: "There is no place for the jaguar to go. All the land is needed by people, and the people will not live with jaguars."

I had left the jungles of Belize to come here, seeking knowledge and understanding about the Maya, their ancestral roots, and the early cultural linkages with the jaguar's world. But my mood had shifted from excitement to depression. The Olmec site, the potential birthplace of so much rich culture that was to follow in subsequent civilizations, was another mausoleum, just like the excavated Mayan sites I had visited. The only living jaguar nearby was locked up in a zoo. Was this what the future held, I wondered? Did ruins and zoos represent all that would be left of wild jaguars and the jaguar culture?

By 400 BC, major parts of the Olmec lands, particularly the large residential centers, had become unsustainable due to overpopulation and overuse of the land. The civilization was fading. But other cultures were already taking its place, maintaining the ideas, beliefs, and practices relating to jaguars that had originated and been perpetuated by the Olmec. The Zapotec culture flourished around the present-day state of Oaxaca in Mexico from 500 BC to AD 1500. They too linked jaguars with the divine and believed that humans not only came from jaguars but returned to the spiritual realm of the jaguar after death. In the Mexican highlands, around AD 900, rose the Toltecs, who were ruled briefly by a leader named Four Jaguar. In Mexico's southern state of Chiapas, the Izapa civilization also appeared to embrace jaguar imagery.

But one remarkable civilization was to span more than 3,000 years, from about 2000 BC to AD 1500, occupying most of the Yucatán and areas into what is now Guatemala, Belize, and Honduras. Regarded as the intellectuals of pre-Columbian America, the Maya created some of the most densely populated areas in the pre-industrial world, deep in the recesses of the tropical rain forests. Never a single empire, but rather a number of autonomous city-states, the ruling dynasties built great cities, mastered astronomy, developed a calendar, and pursued large-scale agriculture. Reaching their peak during the Maya Classic Period of about AD 250–900, the Maya left behind thousands of remains and archeological sites that all depict the jaguar as an important symbol of their culture and a key component of Mayan cosmology.

The Maya represented a new stage in the human-jaguar relationship. No longer simply the realm of the few powerful jaguar shamans, the strength and dominance of the jaguar now belonged also to royalty. As the Mayan priest-kings wrapped themselves in jaguar-skin robes, wore jaguar ornaments, and sometimes sat in limestone seats shaped like jaguars, the boundaries between humans, jaguars, and gods became a bit more indistinct and transitional. Mayan inscriptions indicate that royalty and nobles sometimes used "jaguar" in their official titles, while many of the elite were interred with jaguar pelts, claws, and skulls.

The Classic Maya elevated the jaguar to monumental heights, with Copán in Honduras described as a focal point for jaguar worship. In the 1980s archaeologists discovered a sealed crypt with the remains of 14 large cats, at least six of which were identified as jaguars, making this the largest cache of felidae bones ever found at such a site. The archaeologists speculated that the last ruler of Copán, Yax Pasah, interred the carcasses of these cats during the declining days of the empire in an attempt to use the power of the jaguar to help restore Copán to its former glory. But with evidence from pollen cores indicating massive deforestation around Copán at that time, that number of big cats would have had to have been captured great distances away, raising the possibility that the Maya might have bred jaguars and kept them in captivity for royal funerals.

The jaguar god safeguarded Xibalba, meaning "place of fear" in K'iche' Maya mythology, the surreal underworld where only the most holy and powerful men could enjoy an eternal afterlife. This deity also ruled the night, with a jaguar's fur symbolizing the stars in the sky and its glimmering eyes the shining moon. The jaguar god transformed daily into the sun god, the ruler of light, thus commanding a level of power to which humans could never aspire. In this jaguar hierarchy of the Maya, the jaguar god retained ultimate power, followed by the spiritually powerful jaguar shaman able to roam both worlds. In Guatemala's most impressive Maya archaeological site, Tikal, lintel images portray the "jaguar protector" looming over the priest-king. At Mexico's site of Palenque, explorers found the carvings of life-sized jaguars, back to back, used as a royal throne. One book talked of the priest–kings and special warriors believing they were imbued with "jaguar essence" while still of the human world. This was the first time I'd seen reference to the term "jaguar essence," denoting some special internal quality of the animal itself, as well as the idea that humans could obtain or mimic that quality.

Mayan scholars Stephen Houston and David Stuart believe that one of the common hieroglyphs of the Maya, called T539, has been misinterpreted, and actually depicts the Mayan concept of "co-essence," defined as an animal or celestial phenomenon (such as lightning) believed to share in the consciousness of the person who "owns" it. The placement of what Houston and Stuart call the "Way" glyph changed previous explanations of Classic Maya iconography and beliefs. They believed that many of the supernatural figures or animals once described as gods or underworld denizens, such as jaguars, might instead be co-essences of humans. The jaguar was the most powerful spiritual co-essence of the priests and rulers. This new interpretation of Mayan hieroglyphics linked the Maya and the jaguar even more closely than some scholars had previously thought.

Between AD 800 and 900 Classic Maya civilization collapsed, likely due to causes similar to what brought down the Olmecs and other cultures that built extensive residential centers. With a large non-food-producing populace, resource depletion and agricultural failure were inevitable. Partly a result of their geographic location, the Maya practiced extensive slash-and-burn, a form of agriculture where the forest is completely felled and burned, crops are planted for several years until the soil is depleted, and then the site is abandoned and left to regenerate. With some estimates putting the Mayan population at this time as high as 8–10 million people, slash-and-burn agriculture alone could not fully support the needs of the people.

Around AD 1200, in the Mexican highlands to the north of the Maya, the aggressive and power-hungry Aztecs began to dominate, absorbing the Toltecs, their intellectual and cultural predecessors. While developing a distinct civilization of their own, involving militarism, blood sacrifice, and conquest, they too gave the jaguar a prominent role in their culture and cosmology. The ascension of any new ruler was marked with jaguar rituals and symbolism, and among the military elite was a group called the Jaguar Knights or the Jaguar Warrior Society. Donning jaguar skins and masks in combat, these elite warriors were believed to have participated in human sacrifices and cannibalistic feasts of captured enemies. Upon the arrival of the Spanish conquistadors in 1519, Hernán Cortés noted in dispatches to Spain the great respect accorded jaguars by the Aztec ruler, Montezuma.

While the Aztec culture's focus on the jaguar might further point to Mexico as the heart of the Jaguar Cultural Corridor, other components of the corridor were spreading far to the north and south. Images of jaguars painted on pottery or chiseled on rock have been found across southern New Mexico and other parts of the American Southwest dating from AD 1000–1500. This region was home to the Anasazi, or ancestral Pueblans, who emerged in the Four Corners area of the United States (where New Mexico, Arizona, Colorado, and Utah meet) around AD 500. By AD 1300, they had abandoned most of their cliff dwellings in this region. Two sites in Texas, both attributed to the Mogollon culture (AD 450–1400), include a rock shelter called Jaguar Cave with paintings of what has been identified as a three-foot-long jaguar wearing a collar, and a site called Cave of the Masks, containing a yellow and red painting of a jaguar wearing a conical "shaman's cap."

The earliest record of a potential jaguar "cult" in this northern region was from an excavation by archaeologist Frank Hibben at a prehistoric Pueblo site south of Albuquerque, New Mexico, called Pottery Mound. Painted on the walls of two kivas (round ceremonial structures) dating from AD 1300–1475 were jaguar images, one of which was a seated jaguar alongside other figures of mountain lions and humans that Hibben believed might represent a war council. According to anthropologist Leslie A. White, Pueblo lore told of the *rohona*, a "big cat with spots," that, along with the mountain lion, was a spirit hunter that bestowed power on tribal hunters during the tribe's hunting ceremonies.

Far to the south of Mexico and Central America, across the Panamanian land bridge connecting North and South America that was formed at the end of the Pliocene, about 2.5 million years ago, was the oldest civilization in South America. More than 5,000 years ago, the people of Peru's Chavín de Huántar in the highlands of northern Peru were part of a sophisticated culture with a wide range of craftsmen working with gold, pottery, stone, and textiles. These people also worshipped a jaguar-man god, as depicted in numerous carvings found along the Pacific coast that contain feline composites. Archaeologists believe that there was cultural interchange between the Chavín and their contemporaries, the Olmecs. The repeated occurrence of stylized jaguars among the Chavín led to the theory that they too were a jaguar-worshiping cult who spread their ideas to other cultural groups.

After the demise of the Chavín around 400 BC, the Moche civilization in the fertile Moche River Valley of northern Peru, flourished from about AD 100 to 800, using the jaguar as a godlike symbol. Warriors adorned themselves with jaguar skins and teeth to enhance their courage and strength. More than a dozen other cultures arose throughout Peru between the time of the Moche and the rise of the Inca civilization to prominence in the thirteenth century. Archaeological remains indicate that most, if not all, of the pre-Columbian cultures of this region depicted the jaguar as powerful and godlike.

Among some Amazonian tribes, shamans transformed themselves into spirit-jaguars by snorting powerful hallucinogens or narcotics, referred to as the "jaguar's sperm," through a hollow jaguar bone. As a jaguar, the shaman could now see with "jaguar eyes" and take on the role of "Master of Animals." "Jaguar eyes," of course, referred to the reflective layer of special cells (*tapetum lucidum*) that enhance the cat's night vision. But for the shaman, the all-seeing jaguar could peer at will into the spirit realm, a mirror-image universe existing alongside that of everyday human life. Jaguar masks were often made with mica or glass as eyeballs to represent "jaguar eyes."

Already by the first millennium, South America's vast jungles, mountains, plains and coasts were home to possibly tens of millions of people. The people of the jaguar were thriving, creating a rich, interwoven cultural corridor throughout the continent. But the habitat of the jaguar was diminishing.

The largest empire in pre-Columbian America, the Inca arose in the high Peruvian Andes. In Incan cosmology, the dominant felines were both the jaguar and the puma, with the jaguar regarded as the "master cat." Important members of Inca society wore jaguar skins as symbols of their authority, and the jaguar's image adorned many official emblems as well as warrior attire. The Inca word for jaguar, *otorongo*, was only bestowed upon the bravest soldiers, who often claimed they could turn into jaguars.

Years later, on orders from Christian priests, much of the Incas' recorded material was burned by the Spanish; thus much of our current knowledge of Inca mythology is based on accounts by the Spanish themselves, in addition to depictions found on Incan artifacts. But Richard Mahler, in his book *The Jaguar's Shadow: Searching for a Mythic Cat*, states that not only were jaguar imagery and jaguar adornments used by the Inca as a way of emulating the dominance, beauty, power, and fearlessness of the beast, but also some interpretations of Inca cosmology claim that the jaguar embodied the concept of the ultimate warrior, so powerful it lived without enemies both in this world and beyond. This idea of power that transcended physical confrontation is one I would revisit when trying to understand the essence of the jaguar, as discussed later in this book.

After leaving La Venta, where my hopes of somehow feeling the power of the Olmec had not materialized, compounded by the anguish of seeing the captured jaguar, I felt discouraged, uncertain whether or not this trip had been a mistake. But we continued the journey, taking a short flight to Tuxtla Gutiérrez, the most developed and populated city in the state of Chiapas, Mexico, and now its capital. It was here, according to author Nicholas Saunders, that young men once dressed as jaguars and fought in makeshift boxing tournaments until blood was drawn. Only then would the jaguar deity, considered the Master of Rains, reciprocate and spill his own blood in the form of raindrops for the maize crops.

What struck me most about this story was how the fighters wore their jaguar helmets, or *cascos*, as they entered a sacred ring drawn in the dirt, but they only fastened the cords on the masks when the fight was about to take place. After the fight was over they loosened the cords before leaving the circle, disengaging the helmets from their bodies. The belief, according to Saunders, was that these actions kept violence and evil from leaving the circle with the participants. Though these fights were banned by Mexico's colonial government, they were started up again at the time of the Mexican Revolution (1910–20) and still take place today, in a more ritualistic form, in smaller towns or villages during the Catholic Holy Week (the week before Easter), which also coincides with the beginning of the spring planting season.

My mood started to lighten when we rented a car and drove from Gutiérrez to San Cristóbal de las Casas, the capital of Chiapas until 1892 and the third-oldest city in the New World. Sitting high atop the central Mexican highlands at more than 2,500 meters (8,200 feet), this picturesque location would officially be declared one of the country's "Magical Villages" in 2003. Victor was excited when we reached the town because from here it was a relatively short distance to our ultimate destination, Palenque, a medium-sized Mayan archaeological site, smaller than places like Tikal and Copán, but with some of the best architecture, sculpture, and bas-relief carvings ever produced by the Maya.

But it was not just another set of Mayan ruins that I had come this far to see. Instead, I was excited at the prospect of visiting the Lacandon Indians who, according to Victor, were the most primitive Maya still living. After the feeling of emptiness at La Venta, I was almost desperate to find some evidence of a living link to the past.

When we arrived in Palenque, no one had to tell me that jaguars were long gone from the area. The remaining forests around the site were extensively timbered, burnt, and degraded. But when I saw the first Lacandon—dressed in simple white cloth, with bare feet and long, uncut hair—I was hopeful. Then I saw that they were there selling trinkets to tourists, taking breaks to go sit in their pickup trucks or listen to music on their boom boxes until the next group of tourists came and it was time to hawk their wares again. Victor asked after the whereabouts of Chan K'in, the spiritual leader of the Lacandon, from his son, whom Victor recognized selling little toy bows-and-arrows at the entrance to Palenque. The young man pointed us in the direction of their village, Naha, not far from the ruins, and then decided to accompany us. To Victor's surprise, we could drive there on a road that had only been completed in 1980. Electricity still didn't reach the village until a decade later.

When I first met Chan K'in, two things struck me: first, his pleasure at seeing Victor was clearly genuine, and second, it was clear that rumors of his imminent demise were greatly exaggerated. He laughed when we told him of such rumors and our expectations of seeing him on his death bed. While he had been feeling unwell a while back, he said, he was as strong as ever now. After inviting us into his home, he called over a young woman whom he introduced as his new wife (he would have four wives and 17 children before his death). I looked around the simple hut with its meager possessions as Victor introduced each of us to Chan K'in. When the word *jaguar* was spoken in reference to myself, Chan K'in's eyes lingered on me a while longer than on the others.

After several years working in the jungles of Belize with jaguars and the Maya, I felt that, by comparison, I could already draw some conclusions about what I was seeing. It was clear to me that the forest and people here were all but dead already, like the jaguar in the pit at La Venta, with dull, vacant eyes living as symbols of a richer but long lost past. The exception was Chan K'in—I knew Victor was right when he had told me I could learn something from this man. When Chan K'in spoke, the eyes in his leathery face lit up, and when he moved, it was with the inner energy of a man still young in spirit though old in years. There was knowledge in that head of his, I believed, and everything about him seemed to transcend the decrepit surroundings. Perhaps he was the link I was searching for.

We sat that night in his darkened hut, eating a dinner of black beans, rice, and corn tortillas, with Chan K'in's strong, cavernous face mostly obscured by the smoke of the big Valdez cigars that we had brought for him. When the mood was right, we started telling jaguar stories. Chan K'in listened with great interest as I told him of my work in the jungle. I told him the story of tracking down a jaguar hunter by following the signal of one of the special radio-collars I put around their necks. The hunter didn't know what it was and hung it in his hut as a trophy, alongside the jaguar skin. I saw an opportunity and told the hunter that the special radios on these jaguars allowed me to talk to them when they roamed the forest. If anyone shot them, the jaguar would tell me who it was before it died. That was how I had found him, I said. I thought that even if people didn't know whether to believe me or not, perhaps they would be less likely to hunt around Cockscomb.

Chan K'in fell back laughing as my story was translated for him by Victor. Then he turned his big smile on me, puffed away on what was now just a stub, and rasped: "You told a good story. And I am sure they believed you because what you told them was true once. They knew that even if you didn't." He laughed again, then shook his head as if explaining something to a child. But his expression was serious.

"Jaguars do not want to hurt man, because they are of man," he said to me. "Most people no longer understand this. We forget that they are of this world, and they are not of this world. Jaguars used to talk to man until man betrayed them. Now they no longer talk to man. They stopped in my grandfather's time. There is little time left. Jaguars are dying. We are dying."

Chan K'in looked out the window of his hut and talked of still communing with the spirit world, but he said that the voices of the spirits could barely be heard these days. He told me of the last jaguars killed around Palenque and how the spirits were much quieter after that. "As more trees are cut in the forest," he said, "they take part of the heavens down with them. Now the stars are mostly gone."

When he spoke of the sacred God house on the outskirts of the village where few ventured anymore, my interest was piqued. It was there that Chun K'in went to burn resin of the copal tree in clay pots and commune with the spirit world. This was not completely unfamiliar to me. I knew of the practice of Obeah in Belize, a kind of folk magic similar to voodoo, which had originated in Africa. An old mestizo, claiming to be an Obeah practitioner, had told me he could summon the master animal of every species if he so desired. At my request, he visited me one night at my camp in the Cockscomb Basin to practice his craft, which also involved burning copal resin. The next morning, I had a jaguar in my trap.

I asked Chan K'in if I could visit the God house that night. He smiled, then agreed. But I would need to go alone, he said.

After the others went to bed, I was led along a path to the edge of the village and then was left alone at a simple thatched-roof structure that was partly walled. A little nervous at first, after having been admonished not to touch or disturb any of the sooty clay pots or sacred figures at the site, I lay down in the center of the hut and closed my eyes, hoping to feel a vestige of the energy that once must have permeated this place and these people. I heard murmurings from distant huts, then dogs barking.

Several hours passed before all village sounds died away. Then there was nothing. And more nothing. I thought of lying on the cold altar stone at La Venta, I heard the voice of the young female jaguar in the pit, and I pictured Chan K'in's son selling trinkets amid the starkness of Palenque. If they were ever here, the spirits have long fled this place, I thought. I start to doze off, remembering the eyes of Xamen Ek and the intense feelings I had had while sitting at the round altar stone of the ancient Mayan ceremonial site deep in the jungles of the Cockscomb Basin.

Hours later I awakened to sounds of village activity and chickens walking around my head. I felt incredibly rested and, for the first time during the trip, clear-headed. The trip to the Olmec ruins at La Venta and to the Lacandon at Palenque had, I realized, given me exactly what I had come here for, just not in the way I had expected.

I had left the rich jungle of Belize to seek answers that had perhaps been in front me the entire time. In the Cockscomb Basin and elsewhere in the country, it was not too late. The future was not yet written. I thought of the indescribable power of the jaguars still trying to keep their home, and of young Xamen Ek, the jaguar I'd captured who had never seen a human, crouching in the corner of the trap and watching my actions rather than attacking, and of Cirillo, whose uncertain gaze upon the Mayan temple in the forest showed me that the link to the past was indeed still there. There was still a place where jaguars spoke to man. But it was not in a voice or sound that I was used to. If I wanted to understand what the jaguar was saying, I needed to look, listen, and think differently. I needed to understand jaguarness.

After leaving Mexico, I was never again to meet or speak with Chan K'in or Victor Perera. Chan K'in died on December 23, 1996. One of his sons said he was 104 years old. Victor passed away on June 14, 2003, at age 69. I would remember both of these men throughout my life with great fondness, and reflect on our times together.

Chapter 5

The Conquest of Jaguar Land

*I*N FOURTEEN HUNDRED NINETY-TWO *Columbus sailed the ocean blue.* I
memorized that rhyme in grade school, to imprint in my memory
the date of the seemingly indisputable fact that when Christopher
Columbus and his small fleet of Spanish ships, the *Niña*, the *Pinta*,
and the *Santa María*, set out to prove that the world was not flat,
they discovered America. I think my teachers believed much of the
myth. Only much later would I would learn that the world was
already known not be flat by that time, and that Columbus had no
idea where he was when, seeking a new route to India and China,
he bumped into a small island in the present-day Bahamas. Before
he could return to Spain, his flagship, the *Santa María*, sank. Despite
failing at what he set out to do, Columbus was still hailed as a hero.
It was an Italian explorer and cartographer, Amerigo Vespucci, who
soon afterward demonstrated that Brazil and the West Indies weren't

part of Asia, as Columbus believed, but part of an entirely separate landmass that came to be named "America" after Vespucci. And it was Vespucci who first used the word *panther* to describe the jaguar during his exploration of Venezuela in 1500.

In the years that ensued after grade school, I would periodically read of new "discoveries" that would further destroy that cherished myth of Columbus and add to the growing list of evidence that other early explorers from Africa, Asia, Europe, and even Oceania had made transoceanic voyages and contacted the indigenous peoples of the Americas long before Columbus accidentally bumped into the New World. Some of the other evidence for pre-Columbian voyages to the Americas made for good storytelling: skulls found off the coast of Chile and the presence of sweet potatoes in Polynesia indicating early Polynesian contact with the New World; traces of coca and nicotine found in Egyptian mummies, implying travel to the New World by ancient Egyptians; a memorial tablet erected in Mobile Bay, Alabama, stating that Welsh explorer Prince Madog landed on the shores of Mobile Bay in 1170; Roman coins found in North America; Carthaginian coins inscribed with maps of the ancient world, including the Americas; African plant species in the Americas and Olmec carvings with Negroid features; stylistic similarities between the decorative motifs of ancient China and those of the ancient Maya; an image in a southern Indian temple of a goddess holding maize from the New World; genetic links between Native Americans and Icelanders, proving that the Viking explorer Leif Ericson reached the Americas 500 years before Columbus.

The list of contenders for the discovery of America was all-inclusive: the Norse, the Polynesians, ancient Egyptians, the Chinese, Africans, Indians, early Muslim expeditions, Semitic groups, an Irish monk, a prince from Wales, the Carthaginians, the Romans, and the Japanese. So far the only verifiable site of pre-Columbian European settlement anywhere in the Western Hemisphere is L'Anse aux Meadows, near the northern tip of the Canadian island of Newfoundland, which was settled by the Norse near the end of the tenth century.

There was one transoceanic pre-Columbian contact story, however, that grabbed my attention more than others—the origin of the parasitic hookworm in the New World. One of the most widespread human ailments in tropical America, hookworm infects an estimated 600–700 million people worldwide. Thought to have originated in Asia, the predominant hookworm species in the Americas was likely introduced by slaves brought from Africa. But the hookworm's pre-Columbian presence in the Americas was established beyond doubt when evidence of the parasite was first found in a Peruvian mummy dated AD 900, and then later confirmed in other mummies and human coprolites. In 1988, Brazilian scientists identified the parasites in excavated remains 7,200 years old.

The speculation that this parasite was brought over by early hominid migrations was challenged by microbiologist Samuel Darling who, in 1920, indicated that the life cycle of the hookworm meant that immigrants to the New World via Beringia would have had to arrive hookworm-free, due to the cold ambient conditions that would have killed the parasite in the soil. The only other feasible alternative would be the arrival of hookworms via early transpacific migrants, presenting a strong argument that pre-Columbian contact with indigenous people of the Americas, while probably involving relatively small numbers of humans, might have had a significant and disproportionate impact on future populations of both people and jaguars.

The Mopan Maya that I lived with in Belize suffered from lots of maladies and a shopping list of intestinal parasites, with hookworm topping the list. Hookworm eggs leave the body of an infected person through the feces, then hatch in moist soil. The hatched larvae then penetrate the skin of a person's bare feet, burrow their way into the vascular system, and are carried by the blood to various parts of the body, resulting in coughing, weakness, and anemia. When I lived in the Cockscomb Basin, the Maya had no toilet facilities, they used corncobs to clean themselves after defecating, and they walked around with bare feet. Nearly every Mayan family had domesticated pigs roaming freely that both consumed and stepped in their own feces, spreading it around the living area.

The cycle of infection and re-infection by hookworms was guaranteed, causing chronic debilitation and, in some cases, intellectual, cognitive, and growth retardation among the Mayan children.

While hookworm was easily treatable, the Maya had no means of getting such treatment. And while I tried my best to avoid getting this insidious parasite, I too was eventually infected. So on periodic trips back to New York, I would visit the chief veterinarian at the Bronx Zoo to receive my three-day dose of anti-worm medication.

Interestingly, I also encountered hookworm, at least two different species, while collecting jaguar feces in the Cockscomb Basin. While the hookworm species that infected jaguars did not infect humans internally, they would burrow below a person's skin, causing a creeping eruption known as cutaneous larva migrans. One morning I woke up in a panic, scratching furiously at what appeared to be a network of tunnels running up and down my arms. The local doctor in the nearby Belizean town of Dangriga had, in fact, seen this often in children, and he injected the tunnels with a weakened solution of formalin, a procedure that horrified my doctors in New York when I relayed the story afterward. But the treatment was effective and the scarring only temporary.

While humans could be treated, there was no treatment or natural remedy in the environment available to jaguars. Hookworm in cats causes anemia, intestinal bleeding, diarrhea, and possibly death. And as just one more contributor to the relatively heavy parasite load we were seeing in wild jaguars, this was yet another challenge in the species' fight for survival. I was certain that the parasites infesting wild jaguars, and hookworm in particular, played a role in jaguars living only half as long in the wild (10 to 15 years) as they did in captivity (the record is 29 years).

By the time that Columbus, or any of the intrepid adventurers that might have preceded him, reached the New World, there were already millions of indigenous people in North and South America, with broad estimates ranging from 10 to 100 million people, most of whom lived in Central and South America. Some estimate that there were 8–10 million people in the Mayan domains alone 1,000 years ago and perhaps 5 million people in the Amazon region at the onset of European colonization. Some of the North American natives were still seminomadic hunter-gatherers, while others were more technologically advanced sedentary agriculturalists. The notion that Europeans arrived in the New World to find a rich, pristine landscape with indigenous peoples living in harmony with nature was never true. Indigenous groups were already heavily exploiting the environment: large areas of forests had been cleared, many hillsides were eroded, populations of certain wildlife like migratory birds and ducks had been dangerously depleted.

More than 15 percent of the once-forested land on the Central Plateau in Mexico alone was under cultivation by the Nahua people (an ethnic group of Aztec origin) when the Spanish arrived. Mayan murals depict marketplaces filled with live and dead animals, including skins of jaguars. The Aztec were expert hunters with bows and arrows and expert fishermen with nets. In addition to using wildlife as food, merchants sold the pelts of jaguars, puma, otters, and deer. Large food surpluses were necessary to sustain the non-food-producing members of indigenous societies: porters, masons, sculptors, toolmakers, carpenters, painters, laborers, priests, diviners, and many others. The image of "the ecological Indian" or "the noble savage," terms referring to the inherent goodness of indigenous people who were thought to live in balance with their environment, is more myth than reality. Anthropologist George Collier, who has conducted extensive research in the Chiapas region of Mexico since the 1960s, describes native people living in "obvious disequilibrium" with the natural world long before the arrival of the Spanish.

An oft-used example of precolonial ecological imbalance is the fact that some of the most densely populated, technologically advanced civilizations and indigenous centers were abandoned by the time the Spanish arrived. The Anasazi and Hohokam of the American Southwest left behind extensive cliff dwellings and the largest canal system in pre-Columbian North America, respectively; the Cahokians in the area of modern-day St. Louis, Missouri, abandoned the largest pre-Columbian site with some of the most extensive earthworks; the Olmec, Maya, and Aztec of Mexico and Mesoamerica abandoned their temples and cities to the jungle.

While historians are not certain what happened in these places, the most prevalent hypotheses involve unexpected environmental catastrophes, such as floods or droughts, combined with the over-use and overexploitation of lands and wildlife that made these large population centers unsustainable. The abandonment of these heavily populated and exploited areas allowed some forests and wildlife to recover but, by the time of European settlement, the jaguar's world, particularly in North and Central America, was already gravely threatened due to hunting and habitat conversion to meet the needs of long-standing, burgeoning indigenous populations.

After Columbus, the initial exploration and conquest of the New World was carried out by the Spanish and the Portuguese, the two great maritime European powers. In 1494, anticipating more riches and still more lands to be discovered in the West, Pope Alexander VI supported an agreement that all newly discovered lands outside of Europe would be split between these two countries alone. The Treaty of Tordesillas established an imaginary line, running north-south, west of the Cape Verde Islands (off the west coast of Africa), giving Spain virtually all of the Americas, but allowing a foothold for Portugal into what is now Brazil.

Just as Hernán Cortés de Monroy y Pizarro overthrew the Aztecs in Mexico, his distant cousin Francisco Pizarro González conquered the Inca Empire in Peru, and Francisco Vásquez de Coronado conquered and became governor of the Kingdom of New Galicia (a province of New Spain in modern-day northwest Mexico and the American Southwest). In 1542, as part of the quest by Pizarro to search for the legendary "golden" city of El Dorado, Francisco de Orellana led an expedition down the Amazon River and along the South American coast to Venezuela. This early exploration helped open up the interior of South America for later conquest.

By the mid-1500s, the Spanish controlled much of western South America, Central America, and southern North America, as well as some of the Caribbean. In 1540, Spain established the Captaincy General of Guatemala, extending their control from southern Mexico to Costa Rica—most of present-day Central America. Meanwhile, Portugal colonized much of eastern South America, naming it Brazil. The conquest of such vast, rich empires by relatively small numbers of conquistadors facing millions of indigenous people was accomplished not only through the use of firearms and cannons but, sadly, with the help of the indigenous people themselves. The already existing divisions among the many different indigenous communities was often intense and was used by the Spanish, who enlisted tens of thousands of native people to help them in their conquests of other tribal groups.

Other European nations eventually disputed the terms of the Treaty of Tordesillas, as England and France tried unsuccessfully to gain a foothold in the Americas in the sixteenth century. By the seventeenth century, though, England, France, and the Dutch Republic succeeded in establishing permanent colonies on Caribbean islands and in areas of eastern North America that had not already been colonized by Spain. Other European possessions in North America at this time included Spanish holdings in Florida and New Mexico, the English colonies in Virginia and New England, the French colonies of Acadia and Canada, the Swedish colony of New Sweden, and the Dutch New Netherland, centered on New York City and the Hudson River Valley but taken over by Britain in 1664. By the eighteenth century, Denmark and Norway had colonies in Greenland, while the Russian Empire gained a foothold in Alaska.

While the jaguar was, by this time, gone from most of what is now the United States, the colonization and development of the North American continent played a major role in the future economies of Central and South America, thus greatly affecting the jaguar's remaining habitat, its distribution, and its chances for survival.

Whether by accident or not, Columbus helped set in motion nothing less than the domination and control of much of the Western Hemisphere by European governments, accompanied by drastic changes to the landscape and all the life that lived there. Historically termed "the Columbian Exchange," what followed Columbus was a widespread exchange of animals, plants, culture, humans (including slaves), ideas, and diseases between the Old and New Worlds. This was to impact the jaguar and the people of the jaguar in very different and unexpected ways. Indigenous Amerindians experienced two distinct episodes that contributed to their eventual genetic makeup: the first with the initial peopling of the Americas by crossing Beringia in the late Pleistocene, and the second with the European colonization of the Americas. It was the former that created the gene lineages present in today's indigenous Amerindian populations. But it was the latter that was to dominate the future genetic makeup of the population and relegate the Amerindian to a new and arguably lesser place in history.

The jaguar, the super-carnivore that had forged the Pleistocene Jaguar Corridor to the Americas, survived the major Quaternary extinction event, and radically shifted its distribution and size as it moved from Eurasia into North America and south to warmer habitats in Mexico, Central America, and South America, would also experience a radical change to its environment. Ironically, the change that decimated and changed forever the indigenous peoples of the Americas was to be a major lifeline for the jaguar.

Early in this chapter we learned of the likely introduction to the New World of hookworm, a devastating parasite that continues to affect the lives of humans and animals to this day. While this introduction of various hookworm species, as evidence suggests, predates Spanish colonization, other parasites and diseases that were introduced into the New World by the Columbian Exchange were to have devastating results (the only reciprocity being the possibility that Columbus and his crew brought syphilis back to Europe from the Americas). In many cases, the Old World diseases spread to the indigenous populations along local trade routes, reaching remote areas before the Spanish conquerors even arrived there themselves. Smallpox spread into South America from other infected colonized areas of the New World, killing 60–90 percent of the Incas, including the Inca ruler Huyana Capac and his heir, before Pizarro arrived in the weakened empire and took control. The smallpox pandemic was followed by successive waves of disease, killing the Incas and other indigenous groups in the region: typhus in 1546, influenza and smallpox in 1558, smallpox again in 1589, diphtheria in 1614, and measles in 1618.

The indigenous peoples had no immediate defense for what amounted to the biological weapons of the European conquerors. While the loss of so many lives and the resulting cultural and political instability accelerated the Spanish conquest of Mexico and Central America, it also averted invasion in parts of the Amazon because too few people were left to attract major expeditions seeking cities to conquer and gold to carry away. Compared to a population of perhaps 5 million Indians living in the Amazon 500 years ago, before the introduction of European diseases, now only about 250,000 Indians, just 5 percent of the pre-Columbian population, still survive. Such devastation "helped" large areas of the extensive Amazon region to remain relatively unscathed by more direct foreign influence until the latter part of the twentieth century.

The massive loss of life that began in 1492 continued well into the seventeenth century with the deaths of tens of millions of people, as much as 90 percent of the indigenous population at the time. The descendants of the Paleo-Indians who had followed the jaguar across Beringia were now being replaced by Europeans. But over the three centuries following colonization, Spanish arrivals still numbered only 700,000, most arriving during early silver booms, and the Portuguese immigrants numbered only 525,000, mostly from the early eighteenth-century gold rush.

The Spanish were quick to exploit the land and resources of the New World. In addition to bringing guns that could easily kill wildlife, horses were brought over for better transport (native horses went extinct in North America in the Holocene, about 8,000 years ago). Through the use of the plow and livestock, new land-use practices eroded soils more rapidly and degraded the environment quickly. With the massive declines in indigenous populations, extensive grazing replaced intensive cultivation, and domesticated or semi-feral Eurasian livestock replaced humans. While ranching was a far less efficient use of the soil, it was also far less labor intensive. As a result, meat became a predominant staple in the diets of both the Spanish and the remaining indigenous peoples.

By the end of the sixteenth century the Roman Catholic Church was the sanctioned religion of the Americas, mandating evangelization of the natives and overruling the traditional beliefs and customs. The Spanish conquerors didn't believe in the mystical powers of either the forest or its wildlife. With a strongly anthropocentric tradition that assumed a duality between humans and nature, the Spanish did their best to demystify and disempower nature, with particular focus on any form of jaguar worship. Indigenous peoples were told how "cowardly" jaguars were because they ran up trees to escape dogs. The Spanish were confident that it was God's will for humans to multiply freely and exploit nature for society's self-determined goals, with few adverse consequences. Columbus, and many of those who followed, saw religious conversion as one of their mandates for conquest. The jaguar was simply one among many threats that needed to be controlled or wiped out. Those indigenous people who survived the disease epidemics found their cherished mythology and folklore further under attack by the Franciscans and other Spanish clergy who wanted to destroy all native religions and convert the natives to Christianity by any means possible.

As increasing numbers of settlers arrived in the Americas and began clearing land for farming, cutting forests for ship building, and trapping and hunting for the market, there was less tolerance for predators, fewer prey for jaguars to feed upon, and more fragmentation of wild habitat. In 1541 Carlos V, king of Spain, declared that all forests, pasturelands, and waters in the New World were to be held in common, with Indians having unrestricted access to resources in those areas. But by 1813, in an effort to control rampant forest destruction and resource depletion, the Spanish parliament changed course, converting all lands in the New World, except some essential communal lands, to private property. While new laws and prohibitions were put in place to protect and restore wildlife populations, wildlife conservation efforts did not extend to animals deemed harmful to people or their livestock, and the killing of predators was still encouraged. Since the Spanish conquest, the status of the jaguar had fallen from godlike to vermin. The eighteenth-century Spanish naturalist Felix Azara recorded as many as 2,000 jaguars being killed annually in the valley of the La Plata in Argentina.

Spanish historical documents continued to record the jaguar as far west as Baja California and as far east as Louisiana during the colonial period, from 1540 to 1821. When the Spanish explorer

Coronado led European expeditions into Arizona and New Mexico in 1540, hoping to find and conquer legendary cities of gold, he visited the Zuni people and recorded the presence of both "tigers" and "leopards" in the area, one or both of which were presumably jaguars. By the 1700s there were still reports that Native Americans in the Southwest, including the Apache, Comanche, Hopi, and Navajo, all prized jaguar skins for making arrow quivers and horse blankets. Other jaguar parts were also used or worn to bestow status and power on their owners. The level of contact these tribes had with groups in Mexico and farther south is unknown, but clearly the jaguar was a natural inhabitant of their lands and a part of their culture.

But the jaguar's northern range in what is now the United States was steadily contracting, and those relatively few jaguars still roaming north of the Mexican border were aggressively persecuted. A Jesuit priest in the early seventeenth century who was serving at missions in the borderlands to convert native populations to Christianity describes a hunting scene (*tigre*—that is, "tiger"—is the Spanish word for jaguar):

> Tiger skins are prized above all others by the Indians. . . . They search indefatigably for the track of the tiger, pursue the animal until they come upon it, and slay it with their arrows. At times the tiger gives them much trouble, for he may hide himself in a cave to escape death. . . . They light a fire at the cave's entrance and thus force the animal to emerge. Upon its appearance, it is met with arrows. . . .

By the 1800s, the northern perimeter of jaguar range had constricted considerably. While reports by trappers, surveyors, and hunters claimed that the jaguar was still common along the border area with Mexico, a report published in 1867, *The Quadrupeds of Arizona*, lists the jaguar as possibly existing only in the southwestern portion of the United States. The Apache of southwest New Mexico, southeast Arizona, and northwest Mexico were still hunting jaguar, eating the meat, and using the skin. But by now, the Spaniards had also introduced thousands of domestic cattle, sheep, goats, and pigs into the region, which degraded habitats and consumed the food sources needed by grazing wildlife. The founder of Texas, Sam Houston, had a favorite vest made of jaguar skin, which he proudly wore in the 1840s and 1850s. The last stand of the jaguar in the United States was close at hand.

With the ravaging of the indigenous people by diseases brought over by the Europeans, and with initial Spanish settlement focused on the Pacific slopes and central highlands of New Spain and Peru, lowland jungles rebounded and jaguars repopulated large areas of Mexico, Central, and South America that had been taken from them by the Maya and other early civilizations. This was a respite unlike anything experienced by any other big cat species, either before or since. Most of the lands emptied of humans by death and disease would not be repopulated in large numbers for many years.

The Americas were more heavily forested in 1800 than they had been in 1500. Even those who came to the New World a century or more after conquest found a greener, wilder place than it had been before 1492, with more forest, more wildlife, and fewer people. Evidence suggests that so much deforestation and degradation of natural habitat had taken place, due to the large numbers of indigenous peoples, that when the massive human die-off occurred, the subsequent reforestation of denuded landscapes and the resulting carbon sequestration pulled billions of tons of carbon dioxide from the atmosphere, diminishing the atmosphere's heat-trapping capacity. This event contributed to centuries of modestly cooler temperatures in the Northern Hemisphere during the years after the Middle Ages: climatologists call this Europe's "Little Ice Age."

Genetic data indicate that jaguars now living throughout Mexico and Central America in areas from which they had been extirpated in pre-Columbian times came from northern South American jaguar populations. It is likely that without the massive human die-off resulting from Spanish conquest, there would be far fewer jaguars alive today, with a likely range restricted primarily to South America. That was the good news. Sadly, the Jaguar Cultural Corridor was decimated along with the indigenous communities and was further weakened by European missionary efforts. But while the strong cultural bond that had existed between indigenous people and jaguars became gravely threatened, native beliefs often survived behind a thin veneer of Christianity. The complete spiritual and cultural conquest that was sought by the missionaries never occurred. The Jaguar Cultural Corridor was tenuous and diffuse, but still alive.

Another big change was coming, though. European powers were about to be dethroned as rulers, and the emerging native-born leaders in Central and South America, often spurred by a sense of both ownership and entitlement, identified more with their home in the New World than with Europe. Mounting frustration with the colonial overlords resulted in a series of revolutions from the late eighteenth to the mid-nineteenth centuries. Starting with the United States Declaration of Independence in 1776, the decolonization of the Americas was underway. In 1808, for the first time after 300 years under the Spanish Crown, Spain and her colonies were suddenly without a king, further fostering armed revolts both at home and abroad. Men such as Simón Bolívar and José de San Martín played key roles in the fight against the Spanish Empire, leading the countries of Colombia, Venezuela, Ecuador, and Bolivia to independence and helping to lay the foundations for democratic ideology throughout much of Latin America. With most of the original people of the jaguar already gone, the European reign over the Americas was now about to come to a close. And the respite for the jaguar was over.

In many ways, the modernized interpretation of the Mayan creation myth that had been told to me in Belize had come to fruition. God had put guns into the hands of the people to use as they liked against the jaguar and other animals. The jaguar, despite its strength and resourcefulness, was no match for the humans. And as the jaguar's land was increasingly taken over by people, the jaguar was relegated to the remaining jungle areas.

Had the story ended there, however, the jaguar would likely now be as endangered as its two larger cousins, the tiger in Asia and the lion in Africa. But the Mayan myth had not foreseen the events recounted in this chapter, the European colonization that was to wipe out most of the descendants of those who had created the myths in the first place, giving more of the jungle back to the jaguars. And while the jaguar would still have to fight for its own survival, it now had the opportunity to forge a new future for itself, in a way that no one predicted—the modern-day Jaguar Corridor.

Chapter 6

The Killing Grounds

I WAS TAKING THE WEEKEND OFF, a rare break during my two-year jaguar project in the Cockscomb Basin, and was staying with wildlife filmmaker Richard Foster at his house south of Belize City. While I was telling Richard about all the events that had transpired with the jaguars since we'd last met, one of his workers rushed into the house. A jaguar had just been hit less than a mile away along the Western Highway, a stretch of broken and buckled asphalt connecting Belize City with the small inland capital city of Belmopan, surrounded by hundreds of square kilometers of wild, scrubby jaguar habitat. I was surprised. Jaguars were not usually active during the day and they didn't like moving through the kinds of wide open spaces that surrounded the highway. But the strangest thing about the news was that a jaguar was hit by one of the few cars that traveled that narrow strip of road.

Reality was often stranger than fiction in Belize. When I got to the Western Highway on my motorcycle, the jaguar was lying in the middle of the road with two cars at the scene. The first car, I was told, had broken the jaguar's front leg, while the second car, accompanying the first, swerved intentionally and hit the jaguar again, presumably killing it. To make sure the jaguar was dead, the car backed over it. One of the occupants of the second car, it turned out, was the chief of police of Orange Walk District in northern Belize. Normally that piece of information would have made me approach the situation with a little more political finesse than I did this time. But the sight of that big male jaguar lying crushed in the middle of an otherwise empty stretch of road was infuriating.

Angry and indignant, I stated in no uncertain terms that this jaguar was government property and that since I was authorized by the government to study jaguars in Belize, ipso facto the jaguar was mine to confiscate. The police chief thought otherwise and had no qualms, he said, about taking both the jaguar and me into custody. Not wanting to test his resolve and end up inside a Belizean jail, I calmed down and explained about my jaguar research in Belize and how much information I could garner from a newly dead jaguar. He had read of my work in the local newspapers, he said, and after we talked for a while, still standing beside a dead jaguar in the middle of the highway, he became somewhat conciliatory.

I could have the jaguar's body sans skin, he said, which was valuable and which he intended to keep. The fact that jaguar hunting and the sale of skins had been banned in Belize for almost a decade was of little consequence to him. We both knew that, despite the laws, there was still a brisk illegal market in jaguar skins. But this was not the time and place for me to take a stand. The second caveat to his bargain was that if I wanted the body I had to skin the jaguar myself—right there in front of him! I agreed, on condition of being allowed to bring the body back to Richard Foster's house and getting the jaguar off the highway and out of sight.

The split of the New World's colonies from the ruling powers of Europe made the nineteenth century a time of political, social, and economic transition. In 1821, General Agustín de Iturbide declared Mexico's independence from Spain and demanded that Guatemala join the new federation. The Captaincy General of Guatemala, also known as the Kingdom of Guatemala, in turn, declared Central America independent of Spain and annexed itself to Mexico without consulting the other provinces, including Chiapas (now a part of Mexico), Guatemala, El Salvador, Honduras, Nicaragua, and Costa Rica. Thus, from 1821 to 1823 the First Mexican Empire included much of Central America. Panama, after declaring its independence in 1821, joined the Colombian Confederation, which included Venezuela, Ecuador, and Peru, and remained a part of Colombia until 1903. In Bolivia (then called Upper Peru), the fight for independence which started in 1809 finally came to fruition in 1825. Argentina fought its war of independence from 1810 to 1818, while present-day Uruguay, Paraguay, and Bolivia also pushed for their autonomy. In 1822, Dom Pedro I, son of the Portuguese king Dom João VI, proclaimed Brazil's independence from Portugal and became its first emperor.

In 1823, the countries of Central America broke from Mexico to become the Federal Republic of Central America. The Venezuelan military leader Simón Bolívar tried to keep the Spanish-speaking parts of the continent politically allied, but by 1840 rivalries and competition for control led to civil war and the eventual breakdown of the Republic. As the separate governments of Honduras, El Salvador, Nicaragua, and Costa Rica strove for political legitimacy and material prosperity, a newfound sense of nationalism took hold. But with the fledgling governments in no position yet to compete in producing industrial goods, the path to prosperity was through commerce in agricultural, mineral, and forest products.

Latin America's new leaders, striving for economic growth, abandoned any idea of conservation or of common lands, policies put into place under the kings of Spain and Portugal. One of the most significant manifestations of this change was the widespread cultivation and exportation of coffee. Large expanses of former jungle

habitat had to be cleared. And the control of such large-scale cultivation required the transfer of public and indigenous lands into the
hands of private individuals, leading to the emergence of a coffee
oligarchy that came to control the economy and the politics of each
country in the region.

Though forest habitats and jaguar numbers had rebounded as a
result of the disease epidemics that decimated indigenous peoples
after Spanish colonization, development was now advancing rapidly
in these newly formed nations. Activities such as livestock breeding, agriculture, mining, and road building were rapidly altering
the physical environment. Jaguar populations continued to decline
through the mid-1800s as a result of shooting, trapping, and poisoning, as well as extensive land clearance and further habitat degradation. In El Salvador, described as having "many jaguars" in the
1600s, the combination of rapid population growth and forest loss
removed any refuge for this top predator. By the early part of the
twentieth century, the jaguar was extinct in El Salvador.

But it was not just the physical environment and jaguar populations that were undergoing rapid changes. Rapid development in
the New World was also altering the traditional cultural beliefs of
remaining indigenous communities. The link between earlier indigenous cultures and the jaguar had to do, in part, with the jaguar's
strength and ferocity, its domination over the wild jungle in which
the earliest human communities lived, and the perceived supernatural abilities of the species to link shamans and priests to spiritual
realms not accessible to ordinary humans. But as the role of nature
became completely utilitarian, remnants of the original Jaguar Cultural Corridor were further weakened.

In the United States, a growing conservation ethic that first
emerged in the nineteenth century, earlier than in most parts of
Mexico or in Central or South America, could do little to save
the jaguar. By the turn of the twentieth century, there was no evidence of a viable resident population of jaguars north of the Mexican border. A number of jaguar kills were recorded for southern
New Mexico in the early 1900s, including at least one killed and
photographed by Hopi hunters in 1908 and another presented as a
rug to New Mexico governor Miguel Otero in 1902. In Arizona,

jaguar killings were recorded on or near the Fort Apache Reservation around 1907. By 1922, Aldo Leopold, working as a forester in Arizona and New Mexico, searched unsuccessfully for jaguar sign on the delta. His famous lamentation from *A Sand County Almanac* on the disappearance of the jaguar from the area bears repeating:

> We saw neither hide nor hair of him, but his personality pervaded the wilderness; no living beast forgot his potential presence, for the price of unwariness was death. No deer rounded a bush, or stopped to nibble pods under a mesquite tree, without a premonitory sniff for El Tigre. No campfire died without talk of him. No dog curled up for the night, save at his master's feet; he needed no telling that the king of cats still ruled the nights; that those massive paws could fell an ox, those jaws shear off bones like a guillotine. By this time the delta has probably been made safe for cows, and forever dull for adventuring hunters. Freedom from fear has arrived, but a glory has departed from the green lagoons.

I knew what Leopold was talking about. While Leopold decried the loss of jaguars from the region, what his writing inferred was the continued power of the jaguar, the jaguarness that pervades the environs, even though the chances of encountering a jaguar had become slim to none. After years in the jungle, I knew when jaguar habitat no longer had jaguars. Leopold himself recognized the biological basis of what to others seemed almost mystical. When the top predator no longer walked the land, no longer vocalized in the night, no longer left sign of its passing in the form of scrapes, tracks, scent, urine, or feces, the behavior of wildlife and thus the energy of the forest changed. Big prey animals were not so skittish, offspring could be left alone for longer periods, and the tracks of smaller animals were more obvious along trails or in open areas. But while the animals in an area realize quickly when a large predator is no longer around, the same could not always be said of people. Myths, stories, and folktales often lived on long after the animal that the tales were based on was gone. Research has shown consistently that human memory, the way we incorporate experiences into the human psyche, can be unpredictable, unreliable and, in some cases, chimerical. We are often convinced of something even when all the evidence points otherwise. This is seen particularly with incidents or stories that have a powerful effect on our thinking and behavior.

In the early decades of the 1900s, anthropologist Alfred L. Kroeber pointed out that members of certain tribal groups such as the Mojave, indigenous to the Mohave Desert region of California, Nevada, and Arizona, rarely if ever even saw a jaguar, yet they maintained traditional myths and storytelling about the animal among the tribe. The jaguar was also well known by the Northern Pimans of southern Arizona, some of the Yuman tribes, the Comanches and the Yaquis, all living—at least in modern times—in areas of few, if any, jaguars. No jaguar has ever been documented in Navajo country, occupying northeastern Arizona, and parts of northwestern New Mexico and southeastern Utah, yet the knowledge of and respect for the jaguar by Navajo is clearly evident in their stories. In their long, ongoing relationship with the Pueblo people, there was an apparent willingness by the Navajo, according to oral history, to adopt Puebloan ideas and myths into their culture.

Many present-day folklorists believe that "historical memories" can have a life span of a century or more. When a cultural icon like the jaguar so deeply influences and is embedded in the lives and behavior of the people among whom it once lived, the knowledge and mythology of that animal can persist not only among the descendants of those people, but might also persist in the minds of people beyond the boundaries of the animal's historical range. Memories or stories of species among whom people have never lived in recent times might, in fact, be something other than historical memory.

There has long been speculation that other kinds of memory might exist alongside historical or conscious memory, particularly when a culture or tribe has myths that feature animals that never even occurred in their region. Native American folktales abound with recurring themes and lore involving big hairy beasts, which has led to ongoing debates about whether or not humans have retained memories of long-extinct Pleistocene megafauna. Across the globe there are dozens of folktales and myths describing a hairy, apelike man of the forest. I remember being told such stories while traveling in remote forested areas of the Americas and Asia. Yet no ape species resembling the mythical beast of the stories (other than the relatively small Asiatic gibbons that rarely travel on the ground) ever lived in those places. In medieval Europe, Christians told tales of large wild cats, often black, that stole away and ate children. But wild cats didn't exist in Europe, not even in the zoos that did exist at the time.

Famed psychotherapist Carl Jung believed that human consciousness contained much more than just our immediate, personal experiences that could be seen, touched, or smelled. He proposed the existence of a second psychic system of a universal and impersonal nature that was identical in all individuals. This "collective unconscious" was inherited, he believed, but played only a secondary role in conscious thought or behavior. Jung's peer and sometime collaborator, Sigmund Freud, described a similar concept he called "archaic remnants," which he said were aboriginal and innate and could not be explained by anything in an individual's own life. What Jung and Freud tried to describe is similar to what would later be termed *genetic memory*, defined as a memory present at birth that exists in the absence of sensory experience and is incorporated into the genome over long spans of time.

Jean-Baptiste Lamarck, an eighteenth-century French naturalist who predated Charles Darwin by more than half a century, was ridiculed for his argument that a living being's own environment, choices, and efforts could cause changes to the next generation, popularly called the use/disuse theory, or "soft inheritance." More simply put, Lamarck proposed that individuals' efforts during their lifetime allowed them to acquire needed adaptive changes which could then be passed on to their offspring. One of the most oft-cited examples of his theory was the explanation that giraffes have long necks because of stretching them to reach the highest leaves on trees, with a generation-by-generation cumulative effect on the species.

The concept of genes was unknown to Lamarck at the time (and, later, to Darwin as well), so a mechanism for such theories was lacking. For many years, the idea that memories might be stored in our genome remained controversial. Yet even Charles Darwin's theory of evolution by natural selection, as documented in his book *On the Origin of Species*, gave credence to some of Lamarck's theories, acknowledging that the inheritance of acquired characteristics might be an alternative or parallel, albeit more minor, means of evolution. While Lamarck was never appreciated in his time, some of his ideas, loosely grouped under the heading of "neo-Lamarckism," were used by nineteenth-century biologists trying to better understand and explain genetic memory.

The modern view is that common experiences of a species become incorporated into the genetic code, not by a Lamarckian process that reacts to specific memories, but by a process that encodes a more general reaction to certain stimuli. One of the most famous tests of genetic memory involved mice taught to maneuver through a maze. While the first generation of mice took weeks or months to learn to get through it, their offspring a year later got through the maze in half the time. The third generation was even faster, and after several more generations, mice were getting through the maze in less than 30 seconds upon their first try.

There are myriad other well-known phenomena that support the idea of genetic memory. Cattle that learn to restrict their movements across cattle guards can give birth to calves that have never seen a cattle guard but won't cross lines painted on a road to resemble a grid. A newborn chick that is completely comfortable when introduced to another chicken for the first time frantically tries to find cover when placed in a room with a hawk. The long-held paradigm that our genetic code is fixed at the beginning of our lives and remains virtually unalterable is being rethought. Our genetic code may in fact be getting rewrites on a daily basis. There is evidence to suggest that certain DNA molecules in the brain may be getting rearranged in response to each new experience, and that this altered DNA creates "memory molecules" that can take up specific positions in synapses, making the memories stable without disturbing other synaptic structures. This theory, if proven true, means that what we experience in our lifetime and who we become as individuals might leave a permanent mark on our genome that can be passed on to our descendants. Behaviors categorized as "instinct"—e.g., an infant placed in a pool of water immediately begins to paddle and kick in a swimming motion instead of simply sinking and drowning—may in fact be the result of genetic memories.

Recent discoveries in the field of epigenetics are taking us far beyond the traditional "nature versus nurture" arguments of whether genetics or life experience has the greater effect on making us who we are, and these findings are also giving credibility to the theories of Jung, Freud, and other proponents of genetic memory. The term *epigenetics* was first coined in 1942 by biologist C. H. Waddington, who believed that the way genes interacted with their surroundings, what he called the "epigenetic landscape," led to differences in the way both cells and animals developed, and that such changes could be passed on to other generations. But it was only in the 1990s, almost half a century after the actual structure of DNA was revealed by James Watson and Francis Crick, that the term *epigenetics* was used widely to describe changes in gene activity that don't involve alterations to the genetic code. Such changes, influenced potentially by activities such as overeating, smoking, and exercise, involve alterations that can get passed down to at least one generation and can even become permanent if the environmental pressure remains.

One particular experiment in epigenetics was of particular interest to me. Chickens from the same genetic stock were raised in two different environmental conditions: one group was raised with predictable light rhythms of 12 hours of light and 12 hours of darkness, and the second group was raised with random, unpredictable light patterns during a 24-hour period, necessitating unpredictable eating patterns among this group of chickens. The researchers then examined the eating patterns of the offspring of both groups, all of whom were raised uniformly in the predictable-light environment. Chicks from parents raised in the unpredictable light environment had a more efficient and aggressive eating behavior, resulting in greater weight gain than their genetically identical mates from parents raised in the comfortable, predictable environment. Researchers actually found epigenetic changes in the offspring from the more-stressed parents that they believed affected immune and hormonal genes. Experiments such as this suggest that epigenetic changes from environmental stresses could actually provide survival advantages to future generations—a Lamarckian form of short-term evolution.

These ideas are extremely relevant in gaining a better understanding of the survival abilities of species like the jaguar. The
struggles and learning experienced by jaguars as they navigated the
Pleistocene Jaguar Corridor could very well have imbued important
behavioral characteristics that they passed along to future progeny
in the New World. In other words, part of the jaguarness that exists
today could be a result of genetic or epigenetic memory, created
through the trials and tribulations of the fittest surviving Pleistocene
jaguars.

Despite the survival abilities, structural and behavioral, that the jaguar had developed by the late nineteenth century, it became increasingly difficult for the species to survive the relentless destruction and
manipulation of the natural environment by *Homo sapiens*. One of
the biggest changes to the landscape of the early twentieth century
was that extensive areas that had once been densely populated with
indigenous peoples before they died off from disease, then refor-
ested and repopulated with jaguars, were now home to large herds
of livestock. With domestic cows, pigs, and other livestock appearing as new potential prey to a jaguar, jaguar–livestock conflict was
inevitable.

Despite numerous other causes of livestock deaths on ranches,
death by jaguar was taken quite seriously, often resulting in retribution killings. Many ranchers had a shoot-on-sight policy or hired
hunters just to go after jaguars. Stories told around the campfires
were no longer about the jaguar as a central figure in human cosmology or as a protector of the underworld, but as a villain—with
the heroes being the intrepid hunters who stalked and killed the
jaguars, as related in exaggerated accounts of their encounters with
this dangerous beast.

One of the most infamous and daring popularizers of the jaguar
hunt was Sasha Siemel, Brazil's "Tiger Man." Born in Latvia in 1890,
this onetime mechanic turned adventurer gained fame for learning to hunt jaguars with a more than two-meter-long (7-foot-long)
spear called a *zagya*. During his hunts in the 1920s and '30s, mostly

in the Brazilian state of Mato Grosso, he reportedly killed over 300 jaguars—a few of which, he claimed, topping 160 kilograms (350 pounds). It was in this same region that Theodore Roosevelt in 1914 killed a jaguar on one of his hunting expeditions.

Starting in the 1950s, the jaguar became a popular trophy of big-game hunters, and the so-called sport of jaguar hunting gained popularity. The Lee Brothers of Tucson, Arizona, were the most famous early puma-, bear-, and jaguar-hunting guides in the American Southwest. Having started out as hunters for the Predator and Rodent Control Branch of the United States Biological Survey in the late 1920s, the Lee Brothers were responsible for the deaths of at least 124 jaguars, mostly in the United States, Mexico, and Central America, from 1930 until the 1960s. The last jaguar hunt they organized was in Belize (then British Honduras) in 1964, a decade before jaguar hunting was banned and almost 20 years before I first set foot in the country to try to study and protect the animal.

The biggest jaguars and some of the densest populations were always reported to live in the Brazilian Pantanal, the world's largest wetland area and now the most famous area of jaguar range, thanks to the exploits of Roosevelt and Siemel. It was here that other famous jaguar hunters, Alberto Machado, Richard Mason, and Tony de Almeida, led hunts that killed hundreds of jaguars in the 1960s and '70s. Many of these professional hunters had more experience and understanding of the jaguar than any biologist of the time. One of them, Tony de Almeida, in his 1975 book *Jaguar Hunting in the Mato Grosso and Bolivia*, meticulously records some of the most extensive and important behavioral and measurement data for jaguars that exist today. In the second edition of his book, he revealed feeding behaviors of Pantanal jaguars that few people had ever observed in the wild, also noting differences in the behaviors of jaguars and those of lions, leopards, and tigers:

> Jaguars always begin to feed on the foreparts of their (large) kills, usually starting with the face, then going to the neck and breast, down to the tips of the ribs. . . . The cats will not normally touch the hindquarters of larger animals, except for the udders of cows, to which they are partial. . . . Usually, they feed only once . . .

[and then] walk away from the vicinity, abandoning more than half of the animal unconsumed. Sometimes the jaguars will just lap the blood oozing from the fang marks on a victim's neck and leave the carcass otherwise untouched. . . . Jaguars will not touch tainted meat. . . . Jaguars practically never draw out the entrails or cover their kills.

Jaguar trophy hunting was, in many ways, simply an extension of practices dating back at least to precolonial times. As mentioned in earlier chapters, jaguar skins, teeth, and claws were used extensively by royalty and warriors of the Olmec, Aztec, Maya, and other pre-Columbian civilizations along the Jaguar Cultural Corridor. Later, cowboys, settlers, and politicians valued jaguar rugs, wall hangings, and articles of clothing such as vests or chaps made of jaguar skins. Whether a Mayan king, an Apache warrior, or the first governor of Texas, a person possessing parts of this strong, fearsome animal could feel as if he possessed some of the power of the animal, thus making him more capable of overcoming adversity and dominating the world around him.

Until the 1960s, the decline in jaguar numbers throughout their range was primarily a result of large-scale habitat destruction around urban centers and along agricultural frontiers, as well as from local hunting of jaguars and their prey. This had a significant impact on population degradation and fragmentation, and hunters had already started reporting declines in jaguar numbers south of the United States border. Still, for the most part, the jaguar was able to adapt to hunting pressures by humans as long as adequate habitat and wild prey remained available. But that was about to change. The jaguar was to suddenly become a hugely valuable commodity.

In 1962, the First Lady of the United States, Jacqueline Kennedy, appeared in public wearing a leopard-skin coat designed by Oleg Cassini and purchased in New York City. With Mrs. Kennedy a fashion icon at the time, this ignited a craze for high-priced spotted-cat fur coats, as well as other spotted-cat accessories. Though Cassini would later deeply regret his creation, the fashion industry was quick to react, with middlemen helping to provide hunting and field supplies to thousands of cowboys south of the border in order to help them bring in spotted-cat skins. Although U.S. president William McKinley had in 1900 signed the Lacey Act, prohibiting trade in animals and plants taken or sold illegally, it wasn't illegal at the time to kill or sell jaguars and other spotted cats.

The killing of spotted cats became so rampant that the International Union for the Conservation of Nature (IUCN), created in 1948 by the United Nations Education, Scientific, and Cultural Organization (UNESCO) and signed off on by numerous governments and nongovernmental organizations, issued a statement at its 1963 General Assembly that "the present fashion . . . of spotted cats is a threat to the continued existence of these kinds of animals," referencing the leopard and jaguar in particular. The jaguars and other cats killed during this period numbered, at the very least, in the tens of thousands. One report cited 13,516 jaguar skins in 1968 and an additional 9,831 jaguar skins in 1969 that were imported into the United States from Brazil, Colombia, Mexico, Peru, Bolivia, Paraguay, and other countries. In 1969 Brazil reported exports of nearly 50,000 kilograms (110,000 pounds) of jaguar skins to the United States, West Germany, the United Kingdom, Switzerland, France, Canada, and Austria—more than a tenfold increase from prior years. A pair of scientists in Brazil reported jaguar skins in every curio shop of every major town they visited, with many skins appearing to have come from young, immature animals. In 1966 a wildlife advisor to the Peruvian Government reported the numbers of skins traded at Iquitos: 891 jaguars, 15,000 ocelots, and 4,000 margays. Prices paid for raw jaguar skins reached a high of $130–180 in the early 1970s. One fur manufacturer said it took eight leopard skins or the skins of at least 25 smaller cats to make a coat, and also that skins were being rushed to market so quickly that he was getting pelts with the blood still on the fur.

By 1969, the fur industry had pushed many species of spotted cats, especially the jaguar, to the verge of extinction. A jaguar coat fetched up to $20,000 in a fur boutique in New York in 1975, and ecologist Norman Myers estimated the value of the international trade in spotted-cat skins at approximately $30 million at this time.

West Germany was the world's largest consumer of spotted-cat skins for more than a decade, importing an estimated 220,000–370,000 skins a year until 1984, when imports dropped to 90,000 skins. An advertisement in the 1970s read as follows:

> Untamed . . . the Snow Leopard, provocatively dangerous. A mankiller. Born free in the wild whiteness of the high Himalayas only to be snared as part of the captivating new fur collection . . . styled and shaped in a one-of-a-kindness to bring out the animal instinct in you.

This was a new level of threat to the jaguar's survival, far different from the threats posed by the warrior cults, the shamanistic practices, and the other beliefs of the numerous tribal groups of the Jaguar Cultural Corridor that worshipped jaguars even while killing them for their skins and for their use in rituals. The respect and the fear that had moderated indigenous practices involving the jaguar had been severely degraded with the decimation of indigenous peoples and cultures resulting from the Spanish conquest. As more and more Europeans settled Latin America, their Judeo-Christian values led to a more utilitarian view of the natural world. The jaguar, having at first benefited from the devastation of native peoples by being able to reoccupy formerly human-occupied lands, was again finding itself fighting against human attitudes and practices that were becoming as widespread and potentially unsustainable as those of the early occupiers of the land.

Already by the early 1900s, the jaguar's home was shrinking and its prey was becoming scarcer as local people targeted deer, peccaries, caiman, and other species that could be sold or eaten. Until then the jaguar had still been able to adapt and re-adapt in remaining forested areas, despite occasionally being killed as a trophy or to mitigate livestock conflict. But with the highly profitable commercial opportunities created by the new fashion trends, the killing was happening too quickly. Every jaguar had a dollar sign next to the bull's-eye on its back.

By the end of the twentieth century, reproducing populations of jaguars could only be found from northern Mexico to northern

Argentina, and the species had become extinct in El Salvador, Uruguay, and Chile. Having been forced from Europe, Asia, and now much of North America, the jaguar's range was reduced to only certain forested regions of Latin America, with its back against the sea and nowhere else to go. What the Ice Age, Pleistocene extinctions, and European invasions had failed to accomplish might now come to pass. The jaguar was on a potential path towards extinction.

Chapter 7

Into the Jaguar's World

THE MASSIVE TRADE IN JAGUAR SKINS and the clear threat of extinction, not only of jaguars but of all the spotted cats, finally spurred international action. The same nationalism that had precipitated rapid development and decades of intensive exploitation of the land throughout the Americas following independence from colonial rule was now resulting in a growing awareness of the need to better manage and conserve limited natural resources. Although the desire to protect native wildlife species was a low priority, the death of so many spotted cats in a short period of time brought the issue to a head. By the late 1960s and early '70s, many South American countries had already prohibited trade in their native cats: Brazil in 1967, Venezuela in 1970, Chile in 1972, Colombia in 1973, Peru in 1975, and Argentina in 1976.

In 1966, the United States passed the Endangered Species Preservation Act, authorizing the secretary of the interior to create a list of endangered domestic fish and wildlife species and to spend up to $15 million a year to purchase suitable land for listed species. This act was amended in 1969 to provide additional protection for species in danger of worldwide extinction. Two separate lists of endangered wildlife were created, one for foreign and one for domestic species. The jaguar was on the list for endangered foreign wildlife. This 1969 act was the precursor to the more substantive Endangered Species Act of 1973, which then merged the foreign and domestic lists. The jaguar was not on this new list, and thus not included in the United States Endangered Species Act. This was an oversight that would take nine years for the United States Fish and Wildlife Service to acknowledge and 24 years to rectify. Still, this 1973 landmark legislation served as an important model for conservation legislation that was being debated south of the border.

In 1970, in response to widespread public outcry about the decimation of species such as jaguars resulting from the fur and skin trade, New York State passed the Mason and Harris Acts, and other states passed similar laws, banning the sale of various specific endangered animals as well as any products containing their skins. While such actions helped curtail the trade, it continued unabated in many places, supplying the markets of Paris, London, Rome, and Tokyo. On a trip into the Amazon in 1976, writer and naturalist Alex Shoumatoff asked a trader about the effect of the new laws on his business. "Skins still move—jaguar, ocelot, caiman," answered the trader. "You just pay off the police, and they look the other way."

Traders continued to smuggle skins out and sell them on international markets until 1975, when the Convention on International Trade in Endangered Species of Wild Fauna and Flora, or CITES, finally came into force, making commercial skin trade illegal on a global scale. CITES was a significant step forward, an international agreement between governments meant to ensure that trade in wild animals and plants did not threaten the survival of species such as jaguars. But implementing it took far too long. First drafted at the 1963 IUCN meeting, it took another 10 years for the text of the resolution to be agreed upon and another two years to achieve formal passage, in 1975. The jaguar was placed in Appendix I of CITES, meaning that all commercial trade in the species was prohibited. Sadly, in the 12 years it took for the convention to be put into place, untold thousands more jaguars and other spotted cats were killed and traded.

Jaguar-range countries such as Costa Rica, Peru, and Brazil, with some of the healthiest jaguar populations existing today, were three of the earliest countries to join the convention in 1975, while Mexico was the last, waiting until 1991. There were myriad problems and violations of the convention from the onset: countries failed to accurately report animals that were taken in violation of the treaty; there was a great deal of laundering of animal skins through other countries; too few customs officials were trained properly to identify endangered species parts; and the sanctions for violating CITES were inadequate. In fact, CITES was little more than a gentlemen's agreement among the signatories, with all the weaknesses inherent in such an agreement. Still, this was the first such initiative of its kind, actually promoting international pressure and sanctions against countries that violate the agreement and fail to properly protect their endangered animals and plants. Over subsequent decades, it remained the largest and arguably the most effective international wildlife conservation agreement in the world. Despite its flaws, CITES played a significant role in curtailing the killing of jaguars and putting the brakes on the spotted cat trade throughout the Americas.

The 1970s was a stellar decade for the political, social, and economic awakening of conservationism and environmentalism in the United States. In addition to CITES, this decade saw the creation of the Endangered Species Act, the establishment of Earth Day, the creation in Greenland of the largest national park in the world, and, towards the end of the decade, the Gaia Hypothesis, proposing the earth as a single interconnected organism. One of the greatest influences on this decade was the publication eight years earlier of Rachael Carson's *Silent Spring* (1962), which painted an image of a barren world where many of the animals had vanished.

Governments south of the border took notice of the actions of their neighbor, the United States, and Rachel Carson's book was translated into both Spanish and Portuguese soon after its initial American publication. Still, the environmental movement did not take hold in Latin America as quickly or in the same way as it gained ground in the United States. Beginning in the 1970s, Latin American deforestation rates were among the highest in the world, largely due to the booming cattle industry as well as the use of tropical hardwoods for pulp, paper, and paperboard. Dam building for large hydroelectric power projects flooded thousands of square kilometers of forest. The prevailing attitude was that tropical forests were unlimited and that land conversion was a symbol of progress. At the United Nations Conference on the Human Environment held in Stockholm in 1972, Latin American attendees were surprised by new laws and attitudes by the United States and other more developed nations on issues such as wildlife protection and pollution. They viewed such actions as obstructionist. One Brazilian official argued that Brazil wanted more pollution because pollution was an excellent indicator of development.

In the United States—a relatively new, expansive country of seemingly infinite possibilities—the environmental movement started from the ground up, with the people forcing the government to respond. But throughout the late nineteenth and early twentieth centuries in Latin America, the prevalent thinking was that forests and wildlife had to be utilized for economic gain. Despite a growing awareness that resources were not inexhaustible, the jungle was viewed as the antithesis of civilization, and protection of resources was given scant attention.

There were some notable exceptions. In 1861, the Mexican government enacted laws to conserve forests on national lands. In 1894, Mexican President Porfirio Díaz expanded existing forestry laws to include wildlife protection, though little was done to protect animal species that had no economic importance. Some early-twentieth-century conservationists, such as Miguel Ángel de Quevedo, called "the Apostle of the Tree," linked healthy forests to human health issues. He was instrumental in creating the Mexican Forestry Society, establishing schools for the training of foresters, creating forest zones around cities and ports, and pushing to include conservation in the Mexican constitution.

But in the 1980s, Latin America's "lost decade," the regional debt crisis put the economic stability of Latin America in a tailspin. Prices for leading exports such as coffee, sugar, and bananas declined drastically in international markets, causing declining incomes, rising unemployment, and a general decline of the quality of life. So as many smaller nations in Latin America struggled to compete and gain a foothold in global economic markets, intense political differences continued to obstruct economic cooperation among countries in the region. Despite general agreement on the need for a strategic environmental agenda to stem the tide of deforestation and biodiversity loss, the general populace was concerned mostly with bettering their own lives. Unlike in the United States, the environmental mandates of this period were initiated by the government and pushed downward.

But despite the lag in environmental consciousness in Latin America, the later part of the twentieth century was a positive period for wildlife protection from Mexico southwards. Beginning in the 1970s, international pressure such as the CITES agreement, and the growing realization that uncontrolled environmental destruction was ultimately detrimental to economic growth, prompted Latin American governments to enact new laws and institute new agencies to protect the environment. The most important result of this top-down approach was a veritable boom in the creation of new parks and reserves, many of which contained jaguar populations.

As deforestation, hunting, and land development continued throughout Latin America, protected areas were to become some of the only remaining inviolate homes for jaguars—and the core components of what we would later recognize as the Jaguar Corridor. Despite limited funds and a lack of trained staff, the surge in new protected areas, improved management practices, and some clear enforcement mechanisms for the new laws all combined to give the jaguar another respite from the rampant hunting and loss of habitat that had been surging throughout the Americas during most of the twentieth century. Only this time, the benefit to the jaguars was not the result of a massive loss of human life but came instead from national dictates that better protected both the natural environment and the remaining indigenous cultures that had been the backbone of the Jaguar Cultural Corridor.

By the start of the twenty-first century, nearly 70 percent of the more than 1,000 protected areas now found throughout Mexico, Central, and South America had been created during the 1970s and '80s. In Brazil and Colombia, the two countries that contained the majority of the remaining Amazon forest with areas of prime jaguar habitat, more than 500 special reserves for indigenous communities were also created. The number of protected areas set up during those two decades alone (N), and the percentage of the total that this number represents in each country, are listed below (not including indigenous and extractive reserves):

Mexico: 40% (N=80) Another 40% of the protected areas in Mexico were created during the 1930s and '40s.

Central America: Belize 48% (N=23), Costa Rica 68% (N=87), Guatemala 50% (N=28), El Salvador 100% (N=5), Honduras 90% (N=40), Nicaragua 48% (N=41), Panama 64% (N=28).

South America: Colombia 80% (N=89), Brazil 69% (N=231), Bolivia 67% (N=43), Venezuela 81% (N=108), Surinam 50% (N=14), Peru 78% (N=41), Ecuador 88% (N=67), Chile 35% (N=66), Paraguay 80% (N=15), Uruguay 9% (N=11), Argentina 49% (N=134).

And as the sun set on the twentieth century, there were more legal protections and more protected areas for the jaguar than ever before. Still, the largest cat in the Western Hemisphere, an iconic species to indigenous cultures throughout much the Americas, past and present, was now confined to a fraction of its post-Pleistocene range, with remaining populations having become increasingly fragmented. Surprisingly little was still known of the jaguar—a cat that relatively few people had ever seen other than as a skin. Richard Perry's

The World of the Jaguar, published in 1970, was the first attempt to explain the life of this species through mostly anecdotal accounts from hunters, explorers, and naturalists along with what little data was available at the time. The First International Symposium on the World's Wild Cats was held in 1974. Not one of the more than 26 papers presented discussed jaguars.

It was this lack of data and the lingering mystique surrounding the species that caught the attention of the world's pre-eminent wildlife biologist, George Schaller, in 1976. After conducting seminal work on tigers, lions, and leopards, Schaller decided to delve into the secretive life of the jaguar, choosing as his study site the mecca for jaguar hunters—the Brazilian Pantanal. This corner of southwestern Brazil, the world's largest wetland extending into Paraguay and Bolivia, reportedly contained the biggest and fiercest jaguars on the planet. Part of the reason that these jaguars grew heavier was because of the thousands of cattle in the region, and some of the biggest jaguars on record were cattle killers that were hunted in the Pantanal by people such as Sasha Siemel, Tony Almeida, and Theodore Roosevelt.

Dating back to the colonial era, cattle ranching had long been a traditional livelihood in the Pantanal. With large numbers of livestock ranging freely over extensive areas until they were rounded up once a year, this made for easy pickings for jaguars, despite the abundance of wild prey. Cattle died from a variety of causes while roaming far afield—disease, snake bite, starvation—but the blame for most deaths was pinned on jaguars, giving ranchers and cowboys a good excuse to hunt and kill them. (The next chapter will provide more detail regarding the livestock-conflict issues that came to characterize the jaguar.)

Schaller wanted to try something far more difficult than simply chasing and killing a jaguar. In the late 1970s Schaller was the first person in this region to capture and radio-collar jaguars, and then follow them to obtain basic natural history data on the species. He was assisted in his efforts by two young, aspiring field biologists, Howard Quigley and Peter Crawshaw, who would eventually help mentor future generations of jaguar biologists for Brazil and elsewhere.

As noted in chapter 1, it was into this arena that I entered the picture after meeting George Schaller at the University of Tennessee while I was completing my PhD. He had come down to visit with my professor, and I was asked to take him for a hike in the Great Smoky Mountains National Park. We raced each other up Mount Le Conte, the third-highest peak in the park, competing in a test of wills while engaged in animated conversation about people and wildlife. It was a scene I was to repeat with Dimitri Pikinov in the Russian Far East many years later while searching for the Amur leopard. When we parted late that afternoon back at the university, I never thought I would see George Schaller again.

It was at my going-away party, a few days later, that my professor arrived unexpectedly and asked to speak with me outside. There were no further preliminaries. "Schaller called," he said. "He wants to know if you're interested in going to Belize to survey the country for jaguars."

My professor was smiling.

"Tell him yes," I answered immediately, feeling a tightness in my chest. I had no idea where Belize was.

"He wants you to take a week to think about it, and then call him," my professor said.

"I don't need a week," I said. "I need a phone."

I was to learn later that George had become intrigued with Belize, as he kept hearing stories about a land filled with jaguars, a "sportsman's paradise," in this tiny Central American nation described at that time by *Doubleday's Encyclopedia of World Travel* as "distinguished by emptiness and forests." Despite what he was learning in the swamps of Brazil, no one had yet attempted to find out how jaguars lived in the dense jungle habitat encompassing much of their range. Belize seemed a perfect place for such research.

After just a few hours of getting to know me while hiking in the forests of Tennessee, George was offering me the chance of a lifetime in a field with few such opportunities. He was not doing me any favors—of that I was certain. He wanted this research done and I believe he saw in me something that I had yet to discover in myself. It seems almost comical to me now that I didn't even consider at the time what it meant to go by myself into a remote jungle and search for the Western Hemisphere's most powerful predator. I just knew that this was to be the start of my career and the start of a life I needed to live. It was also the continuation of my journey with the iconic animal of my dysfunctional childhood.

My first stop on the journey was Brazil, after Schaller decided in August 1982 I should spend time with Howard Quigley and Peter Crawshaw in the Pantanal to learn some of the basics of jaguar research and behavior. With its abundant jaguar prey, large open grasslands, and seasonal flooding, the Pantanal offered me the ideal training ground. Described variously as *vibrant, steamy, beautiful, deadly*, and *unforgiving*, the Pantanal is, according to Julian Duguid in his book *Green Hell*, "that vast primeval sponge absorbing the Rio Paraguay's perennial floods—trackless for the most part to all but the few Indians whose numbers are still unknown."

For me, those early days in the Pantanal were everything I had hoped for and needed—adventure, solitude, and challenge. The mandate for Howard and Peter in the Pantanal was the same as the directive that Schaller would later give me in Belize: by whatever means possible, figure out how to capture jaguars that didn't want to be captured, follow jaguars that didn't want to be followed, and document the behavior of jaguars that didn't want to be seen. Each morning before sunrise, the three of us would leave the cabin or campsite to walk, boat, or ride horses while trying to track or capture jaguars. Our base of operations was a small cabin built on the grounds of one of the largest cattle ranches, or *fazendas*, in Brazil.

Every part of the Pantanal was an assault on the senses. With field guides in tow, I could identify only a fraction of the colors, sounds, and flight patterns of the more than 500 bird species recorded in the region. Every pool of water we passed and every stream we waded had multiple "eyes" floating on the surface. Usually those eyes were attached to bodies up to three meters (10 feet) long belonging to one of the estimated 10 million Yacare caimans living in the seasonal waters of the Pantanal—the highest concentration of crocodilians anywhere in the world. I marveled at each new encounter with caiman, anacondas, boa constrictors, and tarantulas, on top of the hundreds of ticks, mosquitoes, and biting black flies. In fact, the bugs were almost unbearable at times, as I recorded in my field notes:

> If I get any more insect bites on my poor body, I'm going to start ripping at my skin so that the pain of self-mutilation overwhelms the constant itching that is driving me crazy. I feel like a leper who wakes each morning to find his body a little more diseased than the day before.

In the weeks that followed, I learned how to set snares, calculate proper drug dosages, shoot dart guns, and fit special radio collars on the big cats. The snares were wire cables that, if properly placed, would catch the jaguar around its leg. But jaguars could potentially hurt themselves while struggling to escape these snares if we didn't get to the animal soon after it was captured. And sometimes the snares caught other animals besides jaguars. Another way to catch jaguars was by following the techniques of hunters, using trained dogs that would follow a jaguar's scent and then chase it up a tree, at which point a hunter following behind would come up to the tree, calmly take aim, and kill the jaguar. But in our case, we would shoot it with a tranquilizer and then lower it from the tree—alive, healthy, and, if all went well, fast asleep.

Nothing I had done in my life or read beforehand about jaguar hunts prepared me for what I experienced, first in the Pantanal and later in Belize—a hunt that started with a team of yapping hound dogs filled with bloodlust racing through the bush and across rivers to try to sink their teeth into a jaguar. Once they were on a scent it was almost impossible to call the dogs back, and we raced behind them on horseback, in boats, and on foot, chopping through the bush, trying to keep within hearing distance of the dogs. But whatever adversity we endured during the chase, it was a small price to pay compared to the finality of the hunt, when the jaguar scaled up a tree, believing itself safe. I described one such encounter in my first book, *Jaguar*:

> The foliage was thick, but through that mass of green there was no mistaking the large spotted head and the green piercing eyes that shone golden when the light hit them. I was looking into

the face of the animal I had sought for so long. I heard nothing but my heartbeat. I felt naked and alone, as I confronted wild, untouchable beauty. Those eyes were watching me with no trace of fear or anger, but with thoughts I'd never know, and listening to voices I'd never hear. A voice in my own mind told me to leave, that I had no right to interfere, to do what I was spending so much time and effort to do. . . . The mouth opened, canines flashed, and a low growl brought me back to the matter at hand. It was time to get on with my work.

It was in Brazil that I first wondered what was going on in a jaguar's mind. It seemed almost embarrassing that this huge, magnificent predator would run from dogs that it could simply turn and kill, then try to hide high among the branches of a tree as a human calmly strode up and ended its life. If a jaguar was cornered before finding a tree to climb, it would often kill or maim the dogs that were chasing it. But it rarely harmed the hunter with a gun who stood nearby to kill it. I understood why some early Spanish clerics called the jaguar "cowardly" when they tried to dissuade the indigenous peoples from some of their mystical beliefs. Only later would I understand how this behavior, detrimental to the jaguar's survival under these particular circumstances, was in fact a key facet of the jaguar's ability to survive, a part of its jaguarness.

Whether we used snares or dogs, the end result of our efforts was never a dead animal, but a sleeping, drugged jaguar that would awaken with a radio collar around its neck. In the days, weeks, and months to follow, that jaguar would provide us with a stream of data on its activity, movement, and behavior. Difficult as it was to capture jaguars safely, it took far more effort to actually follow the collared animal afterwards. These were not yet the days of GPS or satellite telemetry, where large amounts of location data could be stored in the collar or collected remotely. With our simple radio collars, developed in the 1960s and first used on grizzly bears in Yellowstone National Park in the United States, we had to be on the ground and relatively close to the collar to pick up the signal from the animal and try to locate it. Trees, hills, bad weather, a shaky hand holding the antenna—almost everything affected the quality of the signal. Sometimes radios would simply go dead or batteries would fail prematurely, negating months of effort.

Once the unique signal from a collared jaguar was heard, we knew whether that animal was moving or stationary but not where it was located. For that piece of information we had to "triangulate" by covering enough ground, on foot, on horseback, or by vehicle, to get compass bearings or azimuths on the signal from at least three locations that, when plotted on a map, intersected to give the approximate location of the animal. Since any kind of topographic feature could throw the signal off, usually more than three azimuths were taken. Hundreds or even thousands of such locations, collected over months or years of work, would give us the movements and ranging patterns of the jaguar. Once we had such data for several individuals, male and female, we could start to understand the habits and behavior of the species.

We tracked and calculated locations by day, when the jaguars were mostly resting, and then camped close to where a particular animal was and listened to the activity patterns at night, often staying up 24–36 hours at a time, trying to understand how often the animal rested or fed, and how far it traveled in a day. When possible, I walked in on a jaguar's resting area after it had left, in order to figure out what kind of shelter or cover it preferred—a rock overhang, perhaps, or the shelter of a dead, fallen tree, or a brushy thicket. If we couldn't find an animal for a few days, and there was extra money in the budget, we would hire a small Cessna 156 single-engine airplane, attach our antennas to the wing struts, and radio-track the cats by air.

But the real beginning of my ability to understand jaguars came through the days and nights of tracking them in the field—examining their pugmarks, scrapings, scent marks, and feces. With help from Howard and Peter, I learned to recognize the subtle, musky smell of scent sprayed from a jaguar onto a tree or a bush, to identify different individual jaguar's tracks, and to recognize scrapes in the dirt or scratches on trees made by jaguars to mark their territory. We'd collect any jaguar feces we found in order to figure out what the cats were eating. Sometimes the feces contained just a few scales or strands of fur that we couldn't identify; other times we found the crunched remains of bones, hooves, claws, and teeth of a peccary or a capybara, all wrapped in thick balls of hair, presumably to make passage through the gut easier and safer. If there was nothing identifiable in the feces, it indicated that the jaguar might have feasted on large, meaty prey like cattle.

When I was comfortable enough to start going out alone in the field, I really started to feel the jaguar's world around me and to experience it in its entirety. I would follow the tracks of jaguars for hours along trails or dirt roads. Sometimes the tracks would veer off into the jungle and disappear but then reappear farther up the trail. Eventually I could tell by the tracks when the jaguar had walked, then run, then pounced upon something in the forest. A good set of tracks could tell me whether the jaguar was male or female, how big it might be, and, if walking in mud, how much it might weigh, as evidenced by the depth of the tracks. I realized that anything and everything left behind by a jaguar—feces, scrapes on the ground, scent that was sprayed or rubbed on vegetation, claw marks or scratches on a tree—not only gave me information about the animal but was a specific form of communication from one jaguar to another. It was Charles Darwin, observer extraordinaire, who had first reported on such behavior many years earlier:

> One day, when hunting on the banks of the Uruguay, I was shown certain trees, to which these animals [jaguars] constantly return for the purpose, as it is said, of sharpening their claws. I saw three well-known trees; in front, the bark was worn smooth, as if by the breast of the animal; on each side there were deep scratches, or rather grooves, extending in an oblique line nearly a yard in length. The scars were of different ages. A common method of ascertaining whether a jaguar is in the neighborhood is to examine these trees.

As I would learn in far more detail in Belize, the jaguar's marking behavior was their language, akin to hieroglyphics, pieces of which I could start to decipher but never understand in its entirety. It was the voice of the animal that did not speak, a voice stating clearly who had passed this way, what they were doing, and who else could be allowed there anytime soon. Someone not understanding, not "seeing," would walk right by the silent cacophony of engagement among the big cats that might have been there days, hours, sometimes only minutes before. You had to see and listen in order to pick up the signs, these fragments of "conversation"—everything from "stay away, I'm in this area now" to "follow me, I'm ready to breed." Such signs might include:

- A large fecal deposit, sometimes in the middle of the trail, sometimes along the edge of the trail.
- Small, partial fecal deposits, spaced regularly along part of a trail.
- Scent from an anal gland sprayed or rubbed on vegetation.
- Scratches dug into a tree, perhaps older ones lower down, a fresher set higher up.
- A single scrape on the ground with the front paw, sometimes by itself, sometimes containing feces, urine, and/or anal scent.
- Double scrapes, often with the rear paws, containing feces, urine, and/or anal scent.

And besides the jaguar signs, there were the signs of many other animals that shared space with or avoided these big predators. These signs also told a story, sometimes related to the presence or absence of the jaguar itself. A piece of hair fallen along the trail, some mud rubbed on trees, the indentation of a swishing tail in the sand, broken branches, a partial track crossing the trail, partially eaten nuts and fruits—all spoke of what had passed: maned wolves, peccaries, caiman, deer, tapirs, giant anteaters, giant armadillos, and primates. The forest and swamp were alive with the energy and signs, the "language" of animals that were often close by but not easily seen.

All the time, effort, and expense for what seemed like so little data on jaguars was like unraveling the human genome, base pair by base pair. In the end, the picture that would come together from the many pieces of the puzzle—what the jaguar ate, how the jaguar hunted, how big the jaguar's territory was, how the jaguar communicated—would give us the information to better understand and protect the species. Those initial weeks with Howard and Peter in the Pantanal were crucial for me, steeling me mentally and physically for what I believed was to come in Belize. After my time in Brazil, I was chomping at the bit to get into the rain forests of Belize and be on my own with the jaguars. I was sure I was prepared for all the discovery and adventure that lay ahead.

But I was not. Success was to come at a high price for me in Belize.

Chapter 8

Meals on the Hoof

A FTER AN INITIAL SURVEY throughout the country, I selected a site in southern Belize for the jaguar study. With intact access roads, a few abandoned shacks from a small timber operation that was winding down, and a small Mayan community nearby, this wild, relatively pristine forest called the Cockscomb Basin was surrounded by mountains stretching westward into Guatemala and seemed an ideal research base. I returned to New York to talk with Schaller, get funding, and order the necessary equipment for the study. Once that was done, I drove from New York to Belize in a Ford pickup truck I'd purchased with some of my newly approved project money.

It didn't take long before I thought I was in over my head. The learning curve was steep and brutal. Going after jaguars in the dense rain forest was far different from anything I'd experienced in the Pantanal. Snares were not even an option to catch jaguars safely in this thick vegetation without the risk of a struggling jaguar getting tangled up or otherwise injuring itself. So I located a well-known jaguar hunter named Bader Hassan, who had trained dogs for hire. He was reticent at first about working with me because, while he had hunted throughout most of Belize, he had avoided the Cockscomb, which, he claimed, was a difficult and dangerous place, especially for the dogs. However, the idea of drugging jaguars and capturing them alive, instead of killing them, was an opportunity that excited him.

I understood some of Bader's concerns within minutes of starting to try to keep up with his dogs on the scent of our first jaguar in the Cockscomb Basin. Running at full speed, with only fractions of a second to look ahead where your feet are about to step, while swinging a razor-sharp machete to chop through a wall of thick, green vegetation that is trying to stab or sting you at every turn, was a disaster waiting to happen. And it did, on the first hunt and with the worst possible consequences. With a large male jaguar snarling above our heads after having been treed by the dogs, one of Bader's men was bitten by a fer-de-lance, one of the deadliest snakes in Central America, that had been coiled at the base of the tree. Despite all our best efforts—injecting him with antivenom, carrying him out of the jungle on a bamboo stretcher, and flying him to a hospital—the man eventually died.

I stopped using dogs to chase jaguars after that and, instead, learned how to design and build large box traps baited with domestic pigs that I'd purchased from the Maya. These too had problems, such as not triggering properly and letting at least one jaguar escape, but, eventually, five jaguars were collared before I shut the traps down. By then all my time and effort was required just trying to locate the collared animals and stay alive and healthy in the jungle.

For two years I lived with the Maya and tracked jaguars day and night, discovering their movement patterns, the places where they liked to sleep, when and what they hunted and ate, how they reacted to other jaguars in their range, even the parasites that infected them and likely cut their lives short in the wild. This was all new and unknown information about this species. I kept copious notes documenting all my results, my daily life with the Maya, my bouts of illness, and my personal feelings—from exhilaration to deep despair.

Initially my goal was to prove myself as a field scientist and live up to the faith that Schaller and others had shown in me, while trying to dispel my own insecurities of what I was or was not capable of. It was exciting to realize that every piece of data I collected was new for the species and was helping me unravel the mystery of these rain forest jaguars. Despite the adversity, I loved being alone, living amid the vibrancy and power of the jungle, and getting close to wild jaguars. At first, I thought little beyond just collecting the scientific data that was expected of me. Only after the first year, when I saw far too many jaguars outside my study area killed as supposed cattle killers, did I realize I had to get more involved in the issues of jaguar–cattle conflict if I was to help jaguars survive.

It was in the Pantanal that I had started realizing that jaguars were in trouble. Even in such a vast landscape, they were killed at every opportunity despite the laws in place against such killing. There was no enforcement and no place for the jaguars to take refuge. The reason given by hunters and ranchers was always that jaguars were avaricious cattle killers that needed to be controlled. But I realized first in the Pantanal and then in Belize that if jaguars truly wanted to feed primarily on cattle, then there would be a lot more dead cattle and a lot more conflict happening than what I actually saw around me. But I also realized that whether jaguars killed only one cow or many made no difference to people whose livelihoods were affected. The label of "cattle killer" or "vermin" had already stuck to the jaguar, and that meant people were going to hunt and kill the big cat. Some jaguar-range countries, in response to a small but powerful lobby of hunters, were already trying to reinstate legal hunting of jaguars, using the jaguar–cattle conflict issue as an excuse.

In Belize, killing jaguars had been illegal for eight years. But I had been there only a few months when I was shown a government report about jaguar conflict. The report listed 19 cows and 15 sheep taken by jaguars over a three-month period from seven ranches with a combined holding of 483 cows and 85 sheep. That amounted to little more than 7 percent total stock loss, a figure that might have been overlooked by the rancher had it been from "natural causes." But death by jaguar was not considered an act of nature by most ranchers. As I was to see over and over again, livestock killing by jaguars was almost a personal affront, a challenge *mano a mano* (or, more appropriately, *tigre a mano*). Even when the second-biggest cat in the region, the puma, was found to be the culprit, such killing was not taken as personally. The last two lines of the government report were the most worrisome to me:

> I recommend that controlled hunting of large cats be allowed for a specific period, say, six months, at the end of which time the situation can be reviewed. Hunters will have to report their kills to the Forest Department.
> I. Welch, Division Forest Officer,
> Southern Division, Stann Creek District, Belize.
> 18 September 1982.

From the first day I had set foot back in Belize, I was regarded by the government and others who heard of my work as "the jaguar guy," which resulted in constant requests for me to help resolve jaguar-conflict issues. Everywhere I went in Belize, people complained about jaguars killing not only cattle, but also horses, pigs, and even chickens. Any extra time I had was spent outside of Cockscomb investigating such complaints. Most ranchers wanted me to just trap and kill the problem jaguar, which I would never do. I thought it was more important to understand exactly what was happening between jaguars and cattle, and why. So I examined the dead cattle, observed how the ranchers managed their cattle, and lent a sympathetic ear to their complaints.

As it turned out, some of my best information on cattle conflict came from my own radio-collared jaguars in the Cockscomb, because of the proximity to ranches to the north and south of the basin. Early in my research it was obvious that ranchers were wrong to assume that jaguars attacked cattle whenever they encountered them. When one of my radio-collared jaguars moved to the edge of an open cattle pasture on the border of Cockscomb, I would stay awake day and night tracking the animal until the jaguar moved back into the jungle. None of my jaguars ever went into an open field to kill cattle. Instead they moved back into the jungle to feed upon wild prey.

But there were other jaguars which I never captured that did occasionally kill cattle in these pastures bordering Cockscomb. Most of the ranchers, thinking they could mitigate the conflict before it started, told their workers to shoot all jaguars on sight. Only later would I learn that it was the shooting of jaguars that helped create the conflict, making the situation far worse for the ranchers.

In the beginning, jaguars might not have known what to make of domestic cattle—animals that were never native to American soil and not part of its food repertoire. How much interaction Pleistocene jaguars might have had with such animals in Eurasia was unknown. Two species of hollow-horned ruminants, or wild cattle, existed in Europe during the Pleistocene: the bison (the European form called the *wisent* still survives in small numbers in Poland), and the auroch, now extinct. Both were likely Asiatic in origin, migrating to Europe during interglacial periods. The domestication of these wild species into the more than one billion cattle we know today has a genetic heritage dating back 10,000 years.

While most domestic cattle are descendants of the aurochs, mitochondrial DNA studies support the idea of a divergence, between 200,000 and a million years ago, of the taurine cattle, to which the aurochs belonged, from the Indian or zebu cattle (also known as Brahman). The cattle of Europe, northern Asia, and Africa have DNA closely related to the humpless taurine cattle, domesticated somewhere in the Fertile Crescent about 8,000 years ago and traded across the globe. But the humped, zebu cattle native to India belong to a genetically distinct group with origins likely in the Indus Valley of Pakistan, about 7,000 years ago.

At more than two meters (6.6 feet) high at the shoulders and weighing up to 1,000 kilograms (2,200 pounds), the auroch was considered a fierce and unpredictable animal, possibly the most dangerous animal that man ever domesticated. The desire of humans, therefore, was to tame the species, a trend that for thousands of years resulted in numerous distinct breeds of highly docile, manageable animals.

The first cattle to reach the Western Hemisphere were brought to Greenland in AD 982 by the Viking Erik Thorvaldsson, known as Erik the Red. Five centuries later, cargo manifests reveal that the first cattle arrived in the Americas, in Hispaniola, with Christopher Columbus on his second voyage in 1493. But the real founding of what was to become the North American cattle industry can be traced to the landing of Juan Ponce de León in Florida in 1521 when he brought horses and seven Andalusian cattle, the ancestors of the Texas Longhorns. Not long afterward, in 1540, Francisco Vásquez de Coronado brought cattle, sheep, and horses to the western United States.

Indigenous peoples, before ever seeing the cattle brought by the Spanish, knew about domesticating wildlife. In Mexico and Central America, some groups had domesticated deer for meat. Andean societies had domestic llamas and alpacas that they used for both meat and transport. Domesticated turkeys were common in Central America and some regions of North America. But no prior domestication had been done on anything like the scale of what was to become the cattle industry in the New World. Jaguars were soon to encounter this large, sedate, relatively sedentary meal roaming their habitat in the tens of thousands.

When the conquistadors came to the Americas in the sixteenth century, they brought not only their cattle but also their techniques of cattle management. Huge land grants by the Spanish and later the Mexican government produced the *hacienda* system, also called the *estancia* system in Argentina or the *fazenda* system in Brazil. This arrangement encouraged the practice of keeping large numbers of cattle roaming freely over vast areas, as I'd seen in the Pantanal. Ironically, the same sedateness of domestic breeds that made them safer and more manageable for cowboys also made them easy and appealing prey to big predators like jaguars.

Well into the second year of my research, with much of my effort still focused on tracking the collared jaguars in the Cockscomb Basin, one incident forced the jaguar–livestock issue to become my top priority. A valuable mare belonging to the son of a high-ranking government official had been killed by a jaguar. The official demanded that something be done immediately, and he proposed reinstating legal jaguar hunting, an idea that had not gotten much traction when it was first proposed in the report I was shown early in my work. Now, however, the Forest Department was on the spot and needed to provide some answers or take some action. The chief forest officer of Belize requested (actually insisted) that I investigate the incident and produce an official report on the situation. I was given two weeks.

Fortunately, I already had lots of data that I'd been gathering but had yet to analyze. I realized that what seemed like an inconvenience—interrupting my own research to comply with the request of the chief forest officer—was actually an incredible opportunity. Any report I might have given to the Belize Forest Department on my own would have likely been ignored. Now that the Forest Department wanted me to bail them out and placate the government official, though, I had a chance to put the facts on record officially and make management recommendations that the Forest Department might be forced to take seriously and implement.

I spent the next two weeks gathering more data and information from ranchers in parts of Belize that I hadn't yet visited. Certain jaguar behavior was clear to me now. These New World jaguars, unlike their early Pleistocene ancestors, didn't like crossing large open areas. As a stalk-and-pounce predator, the jaguar generally needed cover and was almost reticent in its movements when exposed. Coming out of the jungle to enter an open cattle pasture was not usually the jaguar's way. The common practice of letting domestic stock range freely in or at the edge of forest areas, especially during the night, was inviting problems.

It was clear to me that jaguars favored their natural wild prey, and while they would feed upon anything from an iguana to a 900-kilogram (2,000-pound) bull, they generally chose smaller animals that were easier to kill. My data showed that more cattle conflict was occurring in areas where the natural prey had been wiped out by local hunters and where jaguars were often shot at. However, when cattle roamed freely throughout the forest in Belize, these cattle, especially calves, could become an easy target for a healthy, foraging jaguar. The overwhelming number of complaints about conflict, especially repeated conflict, came from ranches with lots of hunting and poorly managed livestock that were allowed to roam freely without supervision.

As I continued to investigate more conflict situations, another fact became overwhelmingly clear, one that would be a crucial counterargument to those who wanted to reopen jaguar hunting. Many of the reported livestock losses or kills were not actually from jaguars at all. When I looked for tracks around a kill site, I would often see that when smaller domestic animals were predated upon, like chickens, small pigs, and dogs, they were taken by other predators: pumas, ocelot, tayra, fox, margay. When a large cow or horse disappeared and the carcass was nowhere to be found, there was sometimes evidence of two-legged predators at work—humans, not jaguars. And when I did have a chance to carefully examine the carcass of a large kill like a bull, sometimes it was from jaguar depredation, but sometimes it was not.

Nothing kills like the jaguar. While the jaguar can take down prey with a choke hold to the neck like other cats, the jaguar likes to use its powerful jaws to crunch bone, either on the skull or the spine, depending on the size of the prey. In Brazil, jaguars had been observed to grab the capybara, the world's largest rodent, by the head and then reposition its jaws so that it could puncture directly through the ears into the skull. For bigger prey, like cattle, puncturing or chipping of the vertebrae was common. Knowing the exact signature of a jaguar kill helped me explain to ranchers how jaguars were clearly not guilty of many of the cattle deaths that were blamed on them.

The most surprising data, it turned out, came from examination of the skeletal remains of real problem jaguars that had been killed by ranchers and cowboys. In the process of getting skull measurements to record data on the skull morphology of the species in this part of the world, I saw that virtually all of the skulls of problem jaguars that I examined showed old, semi-ossified shotgun wounds to the head; the only skull that did not was one from a young jaguar. I started to look for the same kinds of wounds on the skulls of non-conflict jaguars that I had been able to examine during the course of my work. I found no such old head wounds from the non-conflict jaguars. Surprisingly, when I told Bader Hassan, the jaguar hunter who had worked with me, what I was seeing, he reaffirmed my observations. Among the cattle-killing jaguars he'd shot, he said, all but one had old bullet wounds to the body and skull, and some had broken canines. He even suggested to me that the skull of the young cattle killer that showed no old injuries was likely an animal that had been taught to kill livestock by its cattle-killing mother.

Only shotguns were legal and readily available in Belize at the time, and most local people as well as the cowboys carried them. Over and over again I heard stories of someone walking home from their plantation or tending to livestock, then encountering a jaguar, and blasting the animal in the head to try to kill it. With its massive skull and muscularity, jaguars often survived a shotgun blast, but not without injury. Such wounds, depending on the severity, sometimes festered, caused chronic pain, and hampered the jaguar's ability to hunt and kill effectively. In short, the practice of shooting at any jaguar on sight as a way to preempt conflict was, in fact, creating more problem jaguars, which, at least in Belize, seemed to be mostly previously injured animals.

In subsequent years, data collected by other jaguar researchers would support my findings and provide even more insight. In the Llanos of Venezuela, where cattle constituted 35–56 percent of the jaguar's food, studies showed that most of the jaguars killed while preying on cattle had similar old wounds to what I'd been finding. The jaguar hunter Tony de Almeida told of a well-known cattle killer named Big Richard that, when finally killed, was found to have old wounds from being previously shot in the face with a .44 carbine rifle.

Research in Venezuela and Mexico also showed puma attacking livestock more frequently than jaguars in some circumstances, with jaguars accounting for only a small percentage of livestock killed during a five-year study period. Both puma and jaguar, the study indicated, were also often wrongly blamed for low rates of calf survival. More than 90 percent of actual confirmed cat kills in the study were associated with only three jaguars.

The senior government official's mare that was killed in Belize was a straightforward case. Upon investigation I could see that the telltale puncture wounds to the skull showed that it had definitely been killed by a jaguar. But although it was said to be a valuable animal, the mare had not been tended to properly and was left alone to wander at will, making it easy prey to a hungry jaguar. The immediate reaction by the angry owner was sadly typical. His staff immediately went out and killed four jaguars and shot at others trying to make sure they got the problem animal. In all likelihood, they had created more problem jaguars.

But as I'd hoped, the sudden urgency caused by the death of the mare turned out to be an effective springboard for a much larger comprehensive report that I submitted to the Belize Forest Department, with clear management recommendations that could mitigate if not entirely alleviate many jaguar-conflict situations in the future. Supported by data, I tried to make the report succinct and clear. There were some facts I now knew with absolute certainty: jaguars definitely did kill livestock, but not all the time and not as often as people thought; the killing of cattle by jaguars in Belize was sporadic, scattered, and relatively minor in scale compared to the abundance of jaguars in the country; numerous other factors besides jaguars, such as disease, mismanagement, and theft, were causing livestock deaths, disappearances, and/or low calf production; people killed and shot at jaguars regularly, regardless of the law, with most incidents going unreported. Major factors predisposing jaguars to kill cattle included shooting at and injuring otherwise healthy jaguars, deforestation of jaguar habitat, hunting of the jaguar's prey, and poor livestock husbandry. A ranch program that controlled illegal hunting and the use of guns, and conducted some basic animal husbandry such as vaccinations, the use of fencing, and better supervision of herds, would increase reproductive success of cattle and greatly reduce or even eliminate jaguar depredation.

I concluded the report by stating emphatically that sanctioning jaguar hunting in response to supposed depredation problems would not solve jaguar conflict. In fact, it could easily worsen the situation. But there was a very important caveat, one that harkened back to the 1982 suggestion of "controlled hunting of large cats" from the report by Division Forest Officer Welch that I was shown shortly after arriving in Belize. I recommended that if and when a particular jaguar was proven to be a habitual livestock predator, then the government should have trained officers properly assess the situation, identify the problem animal through the use of cameras or tracks, and then remove the offender.

Jim Corbett, the hunter of man-eating tiger and leopard fame in India, believed that certain circumstances might predispose a tiger to kill, attack, or even eat a human being, but that the tiger was not necessarily a menace. Corbett believed that only when a tiger attacked humans on at least three separate occasions should it be declared a problem animal that needed eradication. From everything I had been seeing, I came to believe the same things were true regarding jaguars killing livestock. Not all jaguars that killed domestic livestock were problem animals. But the continued killing of livestock by the same jaguar, despite good husbandry practices by the rancher, necessitated the removal of that animal from the wild.

Jaguar mythology and folklore aside, the jaguar–human conflict issue was at the core of how people had perceived and dealt with jaguars throughout much of their range since the time of European colonization. As I was to see repeatedly throughout my travels, people would not tolerate big predators if they felt that the animal was a threat or was being granted more protection than they were themselves. My formal report to the Belize Forest Department was used for many years as a set of government guidelines for recommended livestock management practices. But there was never any assistance to encourage ranchers to follow such guidelines. Unfortunately, although the jaguar today is legally protected over most of its range, not a single jaguar-range country has formally implemented and enforced a government protocol similar to what I recommended in the report for investigating conflict or dealing with problem jaguars.

Today, in many areas there is less jaguar conflict because ranchers have learned to better control and manage their livestock for increased productivity, and there are fewer people shooting at jaguars for sport or out of fear. On the other hand, there are still many ranchers who feel that the best policy is to kill jaguars preemptively before any problem arises. Local people continue to hunt deer and peccaries, some of the most important jaguar prey species. Thus, in many parts of their range, jaguars are still persecuted, prey is scarce, and conflict continues.

In later years, as I and other scientists learned more about jaguar behavior and searched for ways to deter jaguars from attacking livestock, we realized that slightly more aggressive domestic species, such as trained dogs, water buffalo, or donkeys, when mixed with cattle, stood a better chance of fending off jaguar attacks on the herd. This is because jaguars, in general, avoid conflict, as can be seen by the way they run from dogs chasing them. Another promising strategy could result from scientists using old auroch bone and teeth fragments to recreate the auroch's DNA and compare it to the DNA of modern European cattle. Breeds of cattle that still carried some of the auroch's genes could then be selectively bred to bring back the more aggressive characteristics of the ancient auroch. This could save thousands of lives of both cattle and jaguars.

It was July 1984, the rainy season, and I was coming to the end of my jaguar research in the jungles of Belize. While Howard Quigley and Peter Crawshaw continued to gather data in the Pantanal, I had accomplished what no one else had yet done—capture jaguars and collect extensive ecological data in the seemingly impenetrable rain forest. The cost of the study was high—one man's life, the life of at least one jaguar from injuries sustained in one of my cage traps, and a subdural hematoma that I suffered during a plane crash

Era	Period	Epoch	Time Scale
CENOZOIC	QUATERNARY (TERTIARY / NEOGENE / PALEOGENE)	HOLOCENE	Present — 10,000 years ago
		PLEISTOCENE (ICE AGE)	1.8 million years ago
		PLIOCENE	5.3 million years ago
		MIOCENE	23.8 million years ago
		OLIGOCENE	33.7 million years ago
		EOCENE	54.8 million years ago
		PALEOCENE	65 million years ago

Plate 1: Geologic time scale of the Cenozoic Era, sometimes called the Age of Mammals. *(Adapted from Geological Society of America, www.geosociety.org/science/timescale/.)*

Plate 2: The "Dancing Jaguar" at Copán, Honduras, part of the architectural and sculptural complex characteristic of the Classic Era of Maya civilization, which lasted from the fifth to the ninth centuries. *(Photo by Steve Winter, Panthera.)*

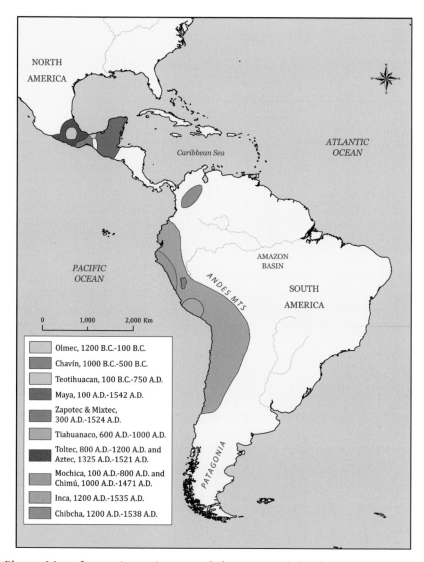

Plate 3: Map of approximate time periods, locations, and distribution of major pre-Columbian civilizations. *(Map by Lisanne Petracca, Panthera.)*

Legend:

Olmec, 1200 B.C.-100 B.C.

Chavín, 1000 B.C.-500 B.C.

Teotihuacan, 100 B.C.-750 A.D.

Maya, 100 A.D.-1542 A.D.

Zapotec & Mixtec, 300 A.D.-1524 A.D.

Tiahuanaco, 600 A.D.-1000 A.D.

Toltec, 800 A.D.-1200 A.D. and Aztec, 1325 A.D.-1521 A.D.

Mochica, 100 A.D.-800 A.D. and Chimú, 1000 A.D.-1471 A.D.

Inca, 1200 A.D.-1535 A.D.

Chibcha, 1200 A.D.-1538 A.D.

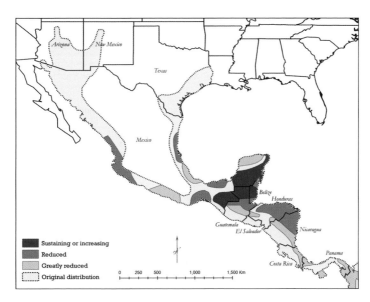

Plate 4A: Map depicting the state of our knowledge of jaguar abundance and distribution in 1987 in the United States, Mexico, and Central America. *(Adapted from Swank and Teer, 1989, fig. 1.)*

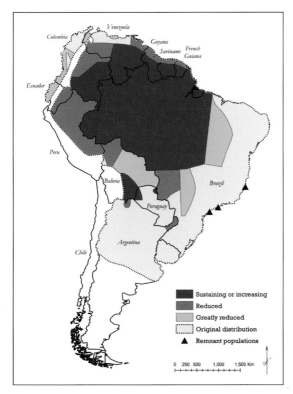

Plate 4B: Map depicting the state of our knowledge of jaguar abundance and distribution in 1987 in South America. *(Adapted from Swank and Teer, 1989, fig. 2.)*

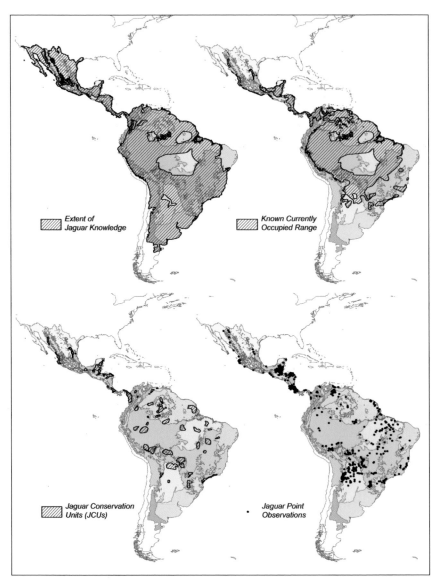

Plate 5: Maps illustrating the extent of knowledge regarding jaguar distribution, breeding populations, and point observations by experts attending the 1999 meeting in Mexico City. *(Adapted from Sanderson et al., 2002, fig. 1.)*

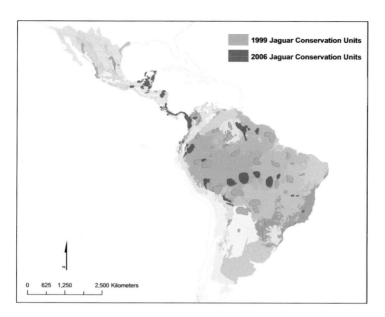

Plate 6: Known breeding populations of jaguars, called Jaguar Conservation Units (JCUs), compiled from expert data in 1999 and a second survey of experts in 2006. Background colors represent different jaguar geographic regions (JGRs). *(Map created and modified by Kathy Zeller and Lisanne Petracca, Panthera.)*

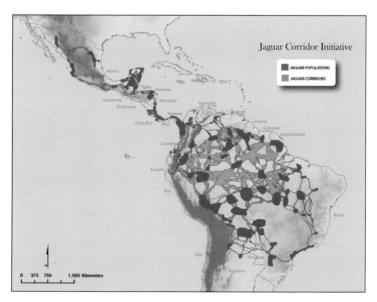

Plate 7: Early map of the potential travel pathways or corridors connecting known Jaguar Conservation Units throughout the jaguar's range. *(Map by Kathy Zeller, Panthera.)*

Plate 8: Landscape permeability for jaguar movement throughout the jaguar's existing range. Dark green represents optimal travel routes, while lighter shades indicate barriers to jaguar movement. These data indicate that nearly 80 percent of the jaguar's historic range still allows for potential jaguar movement. *(Map by Kathy Zeller, Panthera.)*

Plate 9: Jaguar traveling in daytime during the dry season at the edge of a cattle ranch along part of the jaguar corridor in the Pantanal, Brazil. *(Photo by Paul Goldstein.)*

Plate 10: Prioritization of Jaguar Conservation Units and the jaguar corridors to help direct limited manpower and financial resources to critical areas of the jaguar corridor. *(Map by Kathy Zeller, Panthera.)*

Plate 11: A jaguar crawling under a cattle fence during the night in order to move through a cattle ranch in the corridor. *(Photo by Steve Winter, Panthera.)*

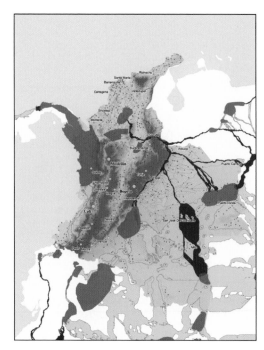

Plate 12: Country map of Colombia (2010) showing the highly threatened remaining jaguar corridors (in purple) linking the jaguar populations of Mexico and Central America to the rest of South America. *(Map by Kathy Zeller, Panthera.)*

Plate 13: Female jaguar (staring into camera) with subadult male offspring moving through an old oil palm plantation in the jaguar corridor of Colombia. *(Camera-trap photo by Esteban Payan, Panthera.)*

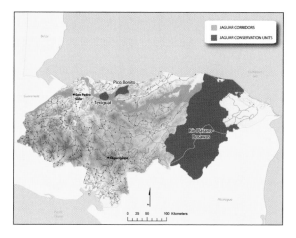

Plate 14: Early map (2007) showing a single, narrow corridor through Honduras, with a possible break north of San Pedro Sula in Honduras. *(Map by Lisanne Petracca, Panthera.)*

Plate 15: Known jaguar corridors through Honduras in 2010, after further ground-truthing, showing continuous connections and two possible corridor pathways between Guatemala and Nicaragua. *(Map by Lisanne Petracca, Panthera.)*

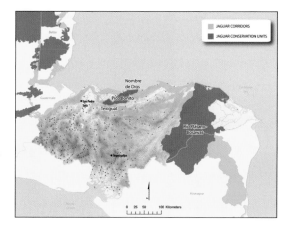

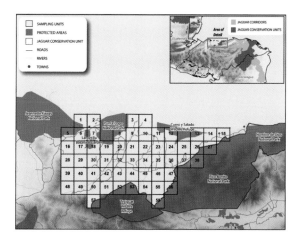

Plate 16: Representation of the grid system employed to ground-truth jaguar corridors between Jaguar Conservation Units. *(Map by Lisanne Petracca, Panthera.)*

Plate 17: Jaguar track found during ground-truthing survey along the northern coast of Honduras. *(Photo by Steve Winter, Panthera.)*

Plate 18: A jaguar chased up into a tree before being sedated, examined, and radio-collared by our research team in Brazil. *(Photo by Steve Winter, Panthera.)*

Plate 19A: Examination and measurements of paws (width: 125 mm, or 5 inches) of sedated jaguar. *(Photo by Steve Winter, Panthera.)*

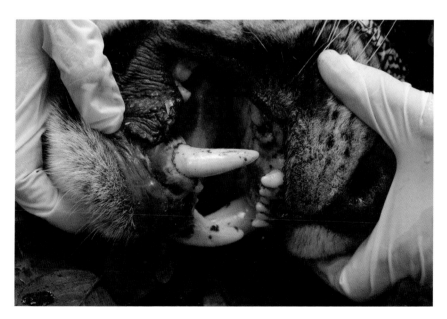

Plate 19B: Examination and measurements of dentition of sedated jaguar. Note broken upper right canine. *(Photo by Steve Winter, Panthera.)*

Plate 20: Expansive landscape mosaic of the northern Pantanal of Brazil. *(Photo by Steve Winter, Panthera.)*

Plate 21: Free-ranging cattle during the dry season on the vast open landscape of the Pantanal. Such open areas have traditionally been maintained by fire and cattle grazing. *(Photo by Steve Winter, Panthera.)*

Plate 22: Jaguar visiting an old cattle kill on a ranch in Brazil's Pantanal. *(Photo by Steve Winter, Panthera.)*

Plate 23: Jaguar swimming across a river as it moves through its range to hunt caiman and capybara along the riverbank. *(Photo by Steve Winter, Panthera.)*

Plate 24: A Tolupan woman in Honduras, the first person to open up to me about her people's beliefs regarding the Masters of Animals. *(Photo by Steve Winter, Panthera.)*

Plate 25: The author (far left) taking part in the first signing of a Memorandum of Understanding (MOU) in Colombia to officially acknowledge the jaguar corridor with former vice president Francisco Santos Calderón, along with the minister of forestry and the director of national parks. *(Photo by Panthera.)*

Plate 26: Local Maya schoolchildren being brought to the Cockscomb Jaguar Preserve in Belize to be taught about jaguars and other wildlife. *(Photo by Becci Foster, Panthera.)*

Plate 27: A jaguar along the riverbank in Brazil's Pantanal watching tourists in a small motorboat who are there to see jaguars and other wildlife. *(Photo by Paul Goldstein.)*

Plate 28: The indomitable beast leaping for a piece of food hanging from a tree in Brazil. *(Photo by Steve Winter, Panthera.)*

while tracking jaguars, which would forever afflict me with periodic debilitating headaches. But I had succeeded in the task Schaller had given me, and gone beyond. My research data and my report on livestock depredation could be the starting point for new policy initiatives not only in Belize but in other jaguar-range countries as well.

Now I was faced with a dilemma. My study was finished and I was expected to return to New York, where I hoped to get a new assignment. But the area where I had chosen to set up shop for two years, the Cockscomb Basin, had gotten under my skin. Investors in both cattle and citrus had their eyes on the lush interior valley of Cockscomb, while local Mayan communities saw an ideal land-scape for more slash-and-burn plantations. Both groups had already applied to the government for land rights in the Basin. No one was looking out for the jaguar.

I wanted Cockscomb protected, not only for the jaguars but also for all the other wildlife species living inside this rich forest. The ranchers and the Mayan communities had plenty of available land for their ventures outside of the Cockscomb. But my chances for protecting the area seemed slim in a country that still had vast for-ests, large numbers of jaguars, no real protected-area system, and no sense that anything needed saving. The challenge would be to con-vince the government to look towards the future.

With the help of a tiny group of ardent conservationists who had formed the Belize Audubon Society and who were politically well connected, I requested a meeting with then Prime Minister George Price to convince him to set up the world's first jaguar preserve. If the jaguar was to survive it needed a safe haven. I had the sci-ence to make my case, but science alone would not win the day on this issue. Belize was a poor country. People with empty bellies and politicians who needed to win these people's votes did not gener-ally have space in their lives to care much about what actions would secure a sustainable future for jaguars.

Not long after I'd put in the request, I received the message I'd been hoping for. I'd been granted an audience with the prime min-ister—but not quite the way I'd expected it. I was now requested to appear before the entire cabinet and present my case for Cocks-comb. I would be given 15 minutes and there would be no second chances.

My greatest fear, which I told no one about, was my stutter. Although it had plagued me throughout my childhood, the summer of intensive therapy when I was 19 years old had taught me how to mostly control the stuttering when I needed to. When I was very nervous or agitated, however, all bets were off. The memories of adults shaking their heads in pity as a little boy sputtered and shook, stuck on the sounds of his own name, kept playing over in my head. But it was the very determination that developed as a result of my speech impediment that got me here in the first place, I told myself. I had just finished catching and studying jaguars where no one had ever attempted it before. Now I just had to catch and hold the attention of the ministers in the cabinet, focusing them on the jaguars, not on me. I had to be the voice for jaguars.

I structured my opening words carefully, practicing them over and over again, making sure they were sounds I would not get stuck on. But when I entered the room and was introduced to the cabinet, Prime Minister Price immediately chimed in and made a surprising request that, inadvertently, broke the tension and put me at ease. "Could you show me how a jaguar sounds?" he asked. "People talk about hearing them in the night, but I have never heard one."

I laughed. It was not his request that I found funny but the fact that making the kind of noises I was about to make was one of the basic therapy techniques I'd learned at the stuttering clinic in order to get air flow going and to relax my throat muscles. I remember thinking at the time how silly this would look and sound to people outside the privacy of this room. Several cabinet members were still taking their seats as I stood at the head of the table and started making deep guttural grunts and coughs like a jaguar. The prime minister started laughing while other ministers just stared. I had no more worries about stuttering.

I looked into the face of each minister in turn as I talked about the rain forest as an economic asset to the country and about the importance of protecting the watersheds and the other natural resources of Belize for the future. I explained about the 200- to

400-year-old granite bedrock of the basin with its shallow siliceous soils that were highly erodible and largely inadequate for long-term agriculture. Though the concept of ecotourism was only in its infancy, I discussed the possibility of people visiting Belize for its pristine nature and abundance of animals like jaguars. My scheduled time of 15 minutes came and went, but no one stopped me. Finally, after more than an hour, I ended the presentation by urging them to look into the future and see Belize not as it was now but as it would be—a developed, thriving country that would need clean water, good air, and healthy forests. "Protect the Cockscomb for Belize," I asked of the cabinet before leaving the room. *Give the jaguars a safe home*, I pleaded silently.

Was I the human voice of the jaguar, that day? I would like to think so. Later I was told that the ensuing discussion about the pros and cons of protecting the Cockscomb was lively, with the minister of natural resources opposing my request. In the end, the cabinet was split in their decision, forcing the prime minister to cast the tie-breaking vote.

On December 2, 1984, the minister of natural resources, under instruction from the prime minister, declared the Cockscomb Basin a National Forest Reserve with a no-hunting provision for protection of the jaguar. Belize was to become the first country in the world to give the jaguar its own official home.

In 1986 my first book, *Jaguar: One Man's Struggle to Establish the World's First Jaguar Preserve*, was published, recounting all my travails in Belize. The book was cathartic for me, revealing not only what I had learned about this mysterious big cat but what I had learned about myself. That same year the Cockscomb Basin Jaguar Preserve was declared "the major achievement in cat conservation for the triennium" by the Cat Specialist Group of the International Union for the Conservation of Nature (IUCN), the world's oldest and largest global environmental network. Shortly afterward, Prince Philip of the United Kingdom, then chair of the World Wildlife Fund International, visited Cockscomb and presented an award to one of my former field assistants, the first guard hired to protect the reserve, Ignacio Pop.

I was elated. I had made good on the promise I'd made so long ago as a child to an old caged jaguar at the Bronx Zoo. I said I'd be their voice and would find a place for them. Now I had. I thought Chan K'in would be proud of me. I also knew that Cockscomb was just a baby step. There was so much more still to do. But I was certain that others would soon follow in the footsteps of George Schaller, Howard Quigley, Peter Crawshaw, and myself to study and protect the jaguar amidst all the wild areas it needed for survival.

Sadly, I was far too optimistic.

Chapter 9

Thinking to Scale

AFTER MY TIME IN BELIZE, the Wildlife Conservation Society hired me as a staff research scientist for their international conservation program. George Schaller and others were pleased with what I had accomplished in Belize with so few resources, so they left the door open for me to choose my next project. George invited me to his home in Connecticut and we bounced around ideas about species that needed more research and attention. In the end, George pointed me across the ocean, to Asia, where we were losing forests with species that the world didn't even know existed yet. I didn't need any further encouragement.

Over the next two decades, during prolonged stints in Thailand, Laos, Malaysian Borneo, and Myanmar, I conducted some of the first studies on Indochinese tigers, clouded leopards, Asiatic leopards, leopard cats, civets, and Sumatran rhinos. I discovered a species new to science, the leaf deer, documented new range occurrences of blue sheep, the newly discovered saola (*Pseudoryx nghetinhensis*), and the rare striped-back weasel, and helped create six new protected areas. By 1990, six years after completing the jaguar research in Belize, I felt at the top of my game. I was doing important field science, using my voice on behalf of animals, and working in some of the most remote places on the planet.

But despite my accomplishments, I felt I was fighting a rear-guard action, going to sleep at night to the sounds of gunshots, and seeing countless body parts of animals in the marketplaces through-out Southeast Asia. In Belize, all the problems and conflict I'd expe-rienced with jaguars, cattle, and people seemed fixable. Now, among some of the planet's most populated countries with some of its old-est civilizations, I was confronted with something I was not prepared for—Asian medicinal practices, dating back some 5,000 years, that highly valued the parts of almost any animal that flew, swam, walked, or crawled the earth, especially if it was big and strong. Tigers topped the list, with everything from tiger blood to eyeballs to dried feces being used to promote vitality or to cure a wide variety of ailments, such as malaria, laziness, ulcers, toothache, and hemorrhoids. Some of the most remote, wildest jungles I explored were already empty of their tigers. The plight of tigers and the threats that confronted this cat haunted me. The biggest and best-known cat in the world, a modern-day cultural and corporate icon, was slipping away as the world sat by and decried its loss. This was a species I could not easily walk away from.

I made several trips back to the jaguar reserve in Belize during the time I was working in Asia, hoping for more-positive news than what I was learning about tigers. I was not disappointed. The idea of wildlife conservation as a part of a nation's development strat-egy had become entrenched not only in Belize but regionwide, as people better understood the interconnectedness of nature and the importance of intact wild areas to their own well-being. The con-cept and practice of ecotourism had firmly taken hold, and the dol-lars generated from this new kind of travel were highly valued and sought after. In 1996, the Belize government enacted a $3.75 "con-servation fee" to be paid at the airport upon departure. Revenues

isolated an island becomes, the greater the likelihood of extinction for many of its species. As a result of MacArthur and Wilson's work, and that of others, by the 1980s the idea of landscape matrices, allowing for natural corridors to link increasingly fragmented wild areas that might otherwise become "islands," was introduced as an important part of conservation planning and species management.

All of this was leading up to the new conservation paradigm being heralded by the end of the twentieth century and summed up in two words: preserving biodiversity. The term *biodiversity*, a shortened form of *biological diversity*, had all but replaced terms such as *species diversity* or *species richness* as a means of depicting all the variant life forms of a region, the totality of the gene pool for species and ecosystems. This now became the flag bearer for embodying the highest ideals of conservation, de-emphasizing species as units of conservation and promoting strategies that conserved ecosystem functions and diversity writ large.

Large conservation organizations went to work developing new talking points for fund-raising appeals: biodiversity "hotspots," globally significant ecoregions, continental networks, and "last frontier" forests. The concepts were not without merit. In fact, such ideas helped broaden conservation thinking and actions to a more appropriate scale. The problem was that they sought to protect the whole without watching over the parts, often creating beautiful boxes lacking key components, big impressive machines that didn't run properly. Many were losing sight of that fact that species are the gears that drive the system: birds, bats, and insects pollinating a variety of plant species; rodents, raccoons, and civets dispersing the seeds from trees in their fecal droppings; tapirs, peccaries, and chimpanzees dispersing large seeds of particular trees that had few other seed dispersers; and carnivores such as the tigers, jaguars, wild dogs, and foxes helping keep the populations of rodents, deer, pigs, and other prey species in check so that the system stays in balance. Losing individual species is like pulling the building blocks from a stack, one by one, until the whole stack collapses. The "empty forest syndrome," in which a seemingly intact forest is devoid of much of its wildlife or at least its top predators, was fast becoming a reality, particularly in many parts of Asia.

As scientists hovered over maps using coarse-filter approaches to get a measure of biodiversity and ecosystem functions, individual species like the jaguar and the tiger and their ecological and functional roles in the system were all but forgotten. Coarse-filter approaches were based on the idea that a region's biodiversity could be preserved if certain broad categories of classification, such as standing vegetation and human densities, were used to identify intact ecosystems. A fine-filter approach, seen by some scientists as too narrow a focus, used the habitat needs of particular species or groups of species to represent intact natural systems.

While conservationists were debating which of these approaches best represented biodiversity, perhaps the greatest incipient conservation failure of our time—the extinction of the tiger—stood out like a flashing neon sign for all to see. Although the tiger was one of the most iconic and recognizable animal species on the planet, many organizations and media stories were already hammering the nails into the tiger's coffin. No other large mammal had such a clear need for intervention to stem its rapid slide towards extinction. Yet despite years of conservation efforts seemingly focused on this species, it was still in rapid decline.

Until the late 1990s, the traditional approach to conserving tigers was site-specific, with different conservation NGOs focusing on the threats to a few high-profile protected areas that contained known, viable populations of tigers. But with scientists and government agencies hampered by political and linguistic differences, there appeared to be no consensus on how best to examine priorities for conservation of the species as a whole, and no cooperative, overarching strategy for tiger conservation across the species' entire remaining range. With new genetic tools allowing us to consider the genetic distinctiveness of tigers along with the behavioral, demographic, and ecological differences of the species, it was time to create a better game plan that prioritized tiger sites irrespective of political boundaries, and that moved tiger conservation forward in a sensible, strategic manner.

By 1997, I was director of the Big Cat Program that I had started at the Wildlife Conservation Society, and I helped organize a small group of experts to come together in Washington, D.C., to address the tiger dilemma. Working in cooperation, the World Wildlife Fund and WCS raised funds to produce a new map of the tiger landscape by employing a hierarchical framework that divided existing tiger range into five bioregions, each thought to have distinct subspecies of tigers: the Indian subcontinent, Indochina, the rest of Southeast Asia, South China, and the Russian Far East. Within each of these bioregions, different tiger habitats were listed and, within each habitat type, areas that, based on existing tiger data and remaining natural vegetation, appeared to have the greatest potential for large, sustainable tiger populations, called Tiger Conservation Units (TCUs), were identified and ranked. Potential corridors connecting these TCUs were also delineated. We now had the first rangewide, ecologically based strategy for tiger conservation.

The exercise with tigers opened my eyes to how badly we needed such conservation blueprints for all the big cats, particularly jaguars. Given the rates of population and economic growth in the Americas by the end of the twentieth century, jaguar habitats were becoming increasingly small and fragmented, and jaguars were now viewed more as an obstacle to economic development than as a mythological icon. The threats to jaguars were increasing even as the species was being all but ignored by the international conservation world. Classified by IUCN only as "near threatened" and not "endangered" like the tiger and lion, the jaguar appeared to inspire far less urgency for protecting this species.

While there were indeed greater immediate threats to tigers and lions, whose numbers were already dangerously low, I was troubled that we still knew less about jaguar numbers, ecology, and distribution than we did about any of the other biggest cat species—tigers, lions, and leopards. If you inquired in the 1990s where exactly jaguars still lived and roamed, you would likely be referred to Wendell Swank and James Teer's 1987 distribution map closely resembling a Rorschach test—a black-and-white line drawing delineating the North and South American continents with a large gray blotch in the middle indicating jaguar presence from southern Mexico to northern Argentina. But people in the field knew how misleading this was: jaguar numbers were lower and their distribution more fragmented than this map indicated.

CITES had made a noticeable dent in curtailing the trade in jaguar skins. From 1976 to 1989, 2,000 jaguar skins had been reported in trade; from 1990 to 1994, only 16 skins were reported. In reality, though, far more jaguars than that had been killed illegally during those years. Even with strong laws protecting jaguars, countries were putting few resources into enforcing those laws. Venezuela didn't ban jaguar hunting until 1992, and then, with promises of big money from international trophy hunters, they turned around in 1997 and petitioned CITES to allow limited sport hunting of jaguars. Still, the spotted-cat skin trade was in decline.

While I would never abandon the fight for the tiger, whose condition I considered akin to a body on life support in the intensive care unit of a hospital, I also couldn't turn my back on the jaguar, which had perhaps the best chance of any of the world's big cats to survive long into the future in a truly wild state. This powerful cat was still the animal closest to my heart. I would never forget the boy whispering to the jaguar through the bars of the Bronx Zoo, or the youthful exhilaration I had felt with my new PhD degree, chasing and capturing a wild sedated jaguar, and even rubbing my hands through its fur. But I was far more seasoned now and, after two decades in the field, I realized that if I and others were ever to make a real difference in saving any of these big cats, it was time to break from the failed paradigms and small-scale thinking of traditional wildlife conservation. No truer words were spoken than when Albert Einstein said "we can't solve problems by using the same kind of thinking we used when we created them."

I felt I now understood why conservation was always playing catch-up, lurching from crisis to crisis, often failing to focus on the most critical issues, which are—inevitably—difficult and controversial. Scientists were not trained to deal with poachers or law-enforcement issues, and few conservation organizations were willing to submit a grant proposal requesting funds for guns and bullets to better outfit forest guards. Yet the illegal killing of wildlife remained the most pervasive and important issue that needed to be addressed if conservation efforts were to be successful. And most conservation efforts were focused at too small a scale, usually only at particular protected sites that were already well established. Success at such sites did not necessarily translate into action at other sites unless the efforts were part of a larger rangewide framework for the entire species.

We saw the importance of such a strategy with the tiger, prioritizing remaining tiger populations by using ecological, demographic, and genetic criteria. Now I wanted to use that kind of strategy to help the jaguar before we reached a crisis. The jaguar, despite its range contraction since the Pleistocene, still had populations spread throughout large areas of the neotropics. And as the top predator in the food chain, the jaguar required areas with many other layers of plants and animals to support stable, reproducing jaguar populations. This meant that jaguar conservation could be a good candidate for large-scale conservation planning throughout much of Central and South America.

The jaguar would not be saved by the relatively few dedicated individuals who were concerned about them, nor by governments and local people who had other priorities. Small-scale, ad hoc conservation efforts focused over narrowly defined areas, such as the Cockscomb Basin Wildlife Sanctuary and Jaguar Preserve, would not by themselves stem the tide of jaguar extirpation. We needed to develop and implement a conservation plan and conservation priorities at a scale commensurate with the functionality of the species over the full extent of the jaguars' geographic range.

The strategy for doing this was simple—or so it seemed to me at the time. From Mexico to Argentina we needed to identify the most important and viable jaguar populations while considering the genetic, behavioral, demographic, and ecological distinctiveness of the animals throughout their range. With at least an order of magnitude more jaguars than there were wild tigers in the world, we nevertheless knew too little about jaguar numbers and distribution to conduct a proper assessment that included all this information. So initially we had to figure out exactly what we knew and didn't know about the state of jaguars—their distribution, ecology, status, and threats. If we didn't have the necessary data or knowledge at hand, getting it would have to be a top priority.

In March 1999, I brought together staff from the Wildlife Conservation Society and the Institute of Ecology at the National Autonomous University of Mexico to carry out a geographically based, rangewide assessment and priority-setting exercise for the jaguar. Over the course of several days, 35 of the world's jaguar experts who had been involved with the species in the lab and in the field presented their own research, broke into discussion groups, and hovered over maps and charts to compile both data and expert opinion. The point of all this activity was to assess our knowledge of jaguars, clarify the known range of the species, and to delineate areas throughout their range with potentially viable jaguar populations, labeled Jaguar Conservation Units (JCUs). Since we had so many more populations of jaguars to assess than we had had with tigers, we could develop a much more sophisticated model in order to prioritize sites and consider how aggregate populations contribute to the survival of the species across its entire geographic range. Nothing like this had been done before for any other big cat.

After we reached consensus on where potential JCUs would be located on a map of the Americas, along with a subjective determination of the long-term survival prospects of jaguars at these sites, an algorithm was developed for prioritizing JCUs within regional habitat categories, called Jaguar Geographic Regions. The highest-priority research sites were those where we lacked good data on jaguar numbers, distribution, or viability.

Combining records of nearly 6,000 jaguar observations over 535 different localities, we saw that jaguars still occupied at least 46 percent of their historic range, but that jaguar status and distribution was uncertain in nearly 20 percent of their range, including large areas of Brazil, Mexico, Colombia, Ecuador, and Guatemala. In the end, an initial 51 JCUs representing 30 Jaguar Geographic Regions were defined as having substantial jaguar populations, adequate habitat, and a stable and diverse prey base. But only 3 percent of the total area of the JCUs was considered effectively protected, with the killing of jaguars, the hunting of jaguar prey, and the loss of jaguar habitat as the major threats to survival. The excitement at the meeting was palpable. We were short on data and long on conjecture, with huge gaps in our knowledge about everything jaguar. But none of us had ever worked with such an extensive data set for the species. A bigger picture was finally emerging.

In addition to the work of extracting and collating the knowledge of the participants, the workshop featured 35 research papers that had been submitted for publication in a book, *The Jaguar in the New Millennium*. But just producing another book to take up space and gather dust on the shelf was not my objective. Workshops such as these were worthless unless there was a clear statement of the actions required to achieve the stated priorities, and the costs of implementing them. And most important was identifying the funding to meet those required costs.

Before arriving in Mexico, I had worked hard to get approval from the Wildlife Conservation Society to use this meeting as an opportunity to launch a new jaguar conservation program within the organization. From my good friends Liz Claiborne and Art Ortenberg, who were to be lifelong supporters of my work, I obtained funding both for the workshop and for implementing some of the highest-priority activities necessary to save the jaguar, as agreed upon by the participants. But even with additional funds that might be raised, we would still be dispersing limited resources over such a large area that we needed to apply a form of triage, choosing JCUs whose populations had the greatest chance of survival and the best-preserved species diversity and resiliency.

I wasn't comfortable with the idea of "triage" in wildlife conservation. It meant choosing which jaguar populations to save, and which to ignore. Originally a term from battlefield medicine, where quick life-and-death decisions had to be made with incomplete information, the process of triage implied a finality that was dangerous in a world where nature was in a constant state of dynamic disequilibrium and our understanding of the natural world was constantly evolving. Yet there seemed no other logical choice at the time. In areas where the chance of saving jaguars was low, or if there was another, seemingly better jaguar population nearby, some jaguars would have to be left to fare for themselves, as they had done for millions of years.

It was nearly a year after the meeting before I had a chance to read through all 35 papers that had been submitted to the workshop. I read them selectively, choosing first those I believed might better help to clarify how to immediately implement some of our priorities. Twice I skipped over a particular paper titled "Evolution and Genetics of Jaguar Populations: Implications for Future Conservation Efforts," by Warren Johnson, Eduardo Eizirik, and Stephen O'Brien. Saving it almost until the last, when I finally got to it, I started reading almost grudgingly. I never made it past the abstract, which I read three times to make sure I was understanding it correctly. As my geneticist wife is quick to affirm, genetics is not my forte. But I understood enough. Suddenly my world turned topsy-turvy.

> . . . We sequenced 715 bp of the mitochondrial DNA (mDNA) control region and determined the size variation in 29 microsatellite loci in 37 and 42 individuals, respectively, from throughout the jaguar's distribution. Measures of genetic diversity for jaguars were low. . . . Two weakly supported phylogeographic groups were identified with mtDNA although there was evidence of continued gene flow between both groups. . . .

This was a jaw-dropping, lightbulb-over-the-head moment.

As a graduate student memorizing the taxonomic nomenclature of mammal families, genera, and species, I was told by my instructors not to worry about subspecies classifications because they were not definitive. But I was intrigued by the number of subspecies names that scientists assigned to every large carnivore species when they all looked essentially the same to me. While some subspecies divisions were based on clear anatomical differences between populations that had been separated for long periods of time, others used less substantive criteria such as size, weight, and coloration. Among the cats alone there were supposedly 6 subspecies of tigers, 7 subspecies of lions, 8 subspecies of jaguars, 11 subspecies of leopards, and potentially as many as 32 subspecies of puma. Then there were 39 subspecies of wolves, 19 subspecies of coyote, 45 subspecies of red fox, and 16 subspecies of the American black bear. The take-away message for me as a graduate student was that the proliferation of subspecies was the norm for large, wide-ranging carnivores. Paradoxically, it also implied geographic separation of populations and limited genetic exchange—a possible fast track to extinction.

The first comprehensive summary of jaguar taxonomy, published in 1933 by biologists Edward Nelson and Edward Goldman, listed 16 subspecies of jaguars (5 in North America and 11 in South America) based on measurements of 92 jaguar skulls. Acknowledging small sample sizes and "imperfect" classifications, the authors described two subspecies of jaguars in the northern extremity of the species' range alone: the larger Arizona jaguar and the slightly smaller Northeastern jaguar, differentiated only by a single skin and a few skull measurements. This taxonomic classification was revised in 1939 by British zoologist Reginald Pocock using characteristics from 59 jaguar skulls but more accurately considering the range of individual variation that could occur in skull measurements. Pocock divided jaguars into eight subspecies, as follows:

- *Panthera onca onca* (topotype—lower Amazon basin)
- *P. o. peruviana* (coastal Peru)
- *P. o. centralis* (El Salvador, Nicaragua, Honduras, Costa Rica, Panama, Colombia)
- *P. o. hernandesii* (Mexico west of Central Plateau)
- *P. o. arizonensis* (Arizona, Sonora, and New Mexico)
- *P. o. veraecrucis* (eastern and southeastern Mexico to Texas)
- *P. o. goldmani* (Yucatán Peninsula, Mexico, to Belize)
- *P. o. paraguensis* (Mato Grosso, Brazil, to northern Argentina and Paraguay)

Pocock's classification of jaguars held for nearly six decades. In 1997, a paper published by Shawn Larson in a journal little read outside the zoo world, *Zoo Biology*, examined data from 170 jaguar skulls. Using sophisticated statistical analysis of 11 morphometric variables that are definitive for skull formation, Larson found some variation between extreme northern and southern jaguar populations but no significant taxonomic differences between jaguars throughout their range. She went so far as to recommend that jaguar populations should be managed as a single taxon (one species with no subspecies). Despite these findings, which I read shortly after the paper was published, I and other jaguar biologists continued to assume that the relatively diminutive 45-kilogram (100-pound) jaguars of Mexico had to be a different subspecies from the 115-kilogram (254-pound) jaguars of southern Brazil. It was poor analytical thinking on my part—and a missed opportunity for the revelation that would not come for almost three more years, when I finally read the genetics paper from our Mexico jaguar workshop.

As soon as I read the first few lines of the abstract to the Johnson, Eizirik, and O'Brien genetics paper, I knew immediately that we had had it all wrong. I remembered Larson's paper and I knew that this genetic research would put any doubt to rest. There were not eight subspecies of jaguar. There were no subspecies of jaguars.

There was only one jaguar!

The implications were enormous. Not only did this make the jaguar the only large, wide-ranging carnivore with no clearly defined subspecies, but it also meant that, at least until recently, individual jaguars were finding their way through the human-dominated landscape, jaguar population to jaguar population, from Mexico to Argentina. While the genetic analysis showed that certain natural geographic features, such as the Amazon River and Darien Straits, were causing difficulty for jaguar movement with some restriction in gene flow, more recent man-made barriers, such as highways, towns, agricultural fields, and even the Panama Canal, were clearly not completely restricting jaguar movements. So a male jaguar cub I had seen in Belize might, in fact, have made its way to Guatemala or Honduras before settling and finding a mate. At least one of its offspring, in turn, might end up in Nicaragua and so on—such that the jaguars in Belize had essentially the same DNA as those I'd seen in the Pantanal of Brazil.

In a second paper put out shortly afterward by Eizirik and several new co-authors, they went further in their abstract than they did in their previous paper, stating:

> ... Operational conservation units for this species can be defined on a biome or ecosystem scale. . . . Conservation strategies for jaguars should aim to maintain high levels of gene flow over broad geographical areas, possibly through active management of disconnected populations on a regional scale.

While a species technically became extinct only when the last existing member died, a species may start to become functionally extinct when so few individuals are interbreeding that reproduction stops, or if there is limited genetic exchange. Interbreeding among many individuals of a species creates a larger gene pool (that is, more-extensive genetic diversity) that is associated with greater "fitness," or the ability to better survive threats and catastrophic events. Low genetic diversity in small populations, on the other hand, can reduce the range of adaptions possible and thus decrease survivability. What Eizirik and his co-authors were now recommending in their paper was a conservation strategy that allowed individual jaguars to move and breed with others throughout the geographic range of the species. Enabling such a process would be the greatest hedge against extinction.

It was clear what had to be done. We had to look at the entire jaguar population, from north to south, as a single ecological unit instead of as the discrete, isolated populations we had assumed they were, some of which had been prioritized over others. *The entire interconnected jaguar range was a priority.* I was furious at myself for not seeing or understanding this sooner. Looking back, there were times, such as while I was in the Russian Far East, when I had hovered at the edge of this realization without grasping it. Larson's paper had definitely made me wonder, but I was too entrenched in the status-quo thinking to understand the earthshaking truth staring me in the face. The seemingly paradigm-shifting rangewide priority-setting exercise that we had conducted in Mexico was no longer the endpoint: it was the springboard to go further. The allocation of limited resources would be even more of an issue to be reckoned with now, because triage was out of the question.

Had I carried out our original plan for jaguar conservation, all funding and efforts would have been focused on no more than 10–20 percent of the delineated JCUs, many of which would have been chosen according to an incorrect assumption about preserving subspecies variation. Most of the world's top jaguar experts had agreed on that approach. We had all come to a consensus that put jaguar conservation in a nice, neat box that fitted all our preconceived notions of what jaguars did and didn't do. We had not only underestimated the jaguar's resiliency, but we were creating a plan that would have helped some jaguar populations while removing any focus or aid from other sites that were still contributing to the genetic continuity of the species. Perhaps the jaguars at some of the discarded sites might have survived on their own. But over time we would likely have lost important populations and genetic linkages without ever even knowing about them. It was a mistake I promised myself I wouldn't make again.

The new paradigm was that everything within jaguar range was potentially important—big populations; small populations; small, fragmented patches of forest that had no resident jaguars; and the vast human landscape through which these jaguars were apparently moving. The jaguar's world would no longer be viewed as isolated populations surrounded by the black abyss of humanity. The protected areas, where the jaguars made their homes, were still the most important sites to focus on. But people living near protected areas or within the jaguar corridor were the modern-day people of the jaguar. It was the behavioral and land-use patterns of local communities—cattle ranches, citrus groves, community gardens, oil palm plantations—that created and maintained the pathways that jaguars used to move through the landscape. Even conflicts involving instances of livestock and/or jaguar deaths in areas where jaguars lived or traveled were now a necessary part of the conservation equation if we were to maintain connectivity between populations. People were part of the solution, not the problem.

I was stunned by the realization that, in many respects, the Pleistocene Jaguar Corridor, or at least the behavior that had created it, had never really gone away. The species resiliency that forged that ancient prehistoric pathway had continued forward, morphing into the modern-day jaguar corridor. If we were to truly help save the jaguar, and maintain the genetic connectivity that remained, we had to figure out and understand the complexity of what these jaguars were doing when they left or were forced out of the safety of their "clans."

Thus was born the Jaguar Corridor Initiative.

Chapter 10

The Underground Railway
of the Jaguar

IN THE 1990s, a psychology professor at Harvard University asked students to watch a one-minute video of a basketball game and to count how many passes were made only by the team wearing white, ignoring the team in black. Halfway through the video a student wearing a full-body gorilla suit walks into the scene, looks at the camera, and pounds his chest. Only half the students who watched the film reported seeing the seven-second appearance of the gorilla. Some of those who had not reported seeing the gorilla insisted that the gorilla had definitely not been there, or that the tapes were switched. The experiment was cited as pervasive proof that we experience far less of our visual world than we think we do. The designers of the experiment, Christopher Chabris and

Daniel Simons, later published a book, *The Invisible Gorilla: How Our Intuitions Deceive Us*, in which they show how people, and experts in particular, are primed to see patterns that fit their well-established expectations, and that the unexpected often goes unnoticed. The jaguar corridor was my invisible gorilla.

The idea of identifying and protecting wildlife travel routes, or corridors, between viable breeding populations of animals, also called source populations, was a well-established concept as early as the 1980s. With the recognition that the risk of extinction decreases when more individuals can breed with each other, the idea of corridors linking relative small areas was a valid way to increase the effective size of one or more small populations or small protected areas. Theoretically, if all the populations of a species could be linked, then the entire species would be a single breeding unit with a greatly reduced chance of extinction. But in the real world, with natural habitats becoming increasingly fragmented, this theory was easier to conceptualize than to put into practice, particularly for large, wide-ranging carnivores.

The most commonly known wildlife corridor is that of a narrow tract of forest that forms a passageway linking at least two protected areas and thus allowing for movement of species between those areas. Usually, such corridors are private or public lands with no special protected status, and thus the movements of animals through these lands is cut short when human settlements or development interests destroy or degrade the area. But with some species, such as jaguars, we were learning that undetected movements between breeding populations could occur in already-degraded human landscapes. Such pathways comprised corridors that were often overlooked when conservation actions for a species were being considered.

After the workshop in Mexico, we had a much better idea of where jaguars still lived and where there were gaping holes in our knowledge of jaguar presence and distribution. But one thing was clear: the best remaining populations (or Jaguar Conservation Units—JCUs) were scattered among the two continents of Central and South America like islands floating in a sea of human-altered landscapes. More than 50 percent of intact jaguar habitat was already lost to human settlement and development and there appeared to be little if any connectivity between most of the jaguar populations. In the conservation community, the common assumption until now was that any jaguar leaving a source population would certainly be killed before it traveled very far in the human-dominated landscape. I was convinced of that as well.

But now, with the newly published jaguar DNA data, I was confronted with a scenario that completely contradicted my assumptions and shattered existing jaguar taxonomy. The "invisible gorilla," the probability of linkages or movement pathways between jaguar populations, had just been revealed, forcing me to completely rethink my approach to jaguar conservation. At the same time, the relatively new field of landscape genetics was taking hold, combining landscape ecology's study of the relationships among environmental patterns, processes, and scales, with the field of population genetics' study of the spread of genes among populations. This combined approach examined genetic data on a broad spatial scale, providing an understanding of how landscape characteristics, such as mountains and rivers, influence the structure of populations. Given what we had just learned with the jaguar genetic data, this new approach greatly aided our ability to both conceptualize and design the potential jaguar corridor.

In 1987, a summit of the Central American presidents in Guatemala resulted in the Esquipulas II Declaration, affirming that peace, democracy, and development were inseparable in the region. In 1989 these heads of state created the Central American Commission on Environment and Development (CCAD) to evaluate and protect the region's rich biological diversity, including a commitment to stop the illegal trade in wildlife. It was on this stage, with the prospect of lasting peace and regional cooperation appearing to take hold, that an initiative called Paseo Pantera emerged in 1990, proposing to unite protected areas throughout the length of the Central American isthmus in order to ensure wildlife movements through biological corridors. Comprised of a consortium of international conservation organizations, the larger goal of preserving biodiversity in these corridors was linked with proposed sustainable development activities such as ecotourism and agroforestry. By all accounts, it was a grand and innovative plan.

The Paseo Pantera project, aimed at designing a formally recognized regional network of wildlife corridors in Central America, was in some respects the progenitor of the Jaguar Corridor Initiative, although they were conceived independently. Paseo Pantera ("The Path of the Panther") was the brainchild of Dr. Archie Carr III, a passionate wildlife conservationist and my close friend from the Wildlife Conservation Society. The panther, or puma, whose movements often overlapped with those of the jaguar, is the widest-ranging cat in the Americas, and so this species, Archie believed, symbolized the need for continuity of the natural environments throughout Central America and could serve as a unifying theme for the region's collective conservation efforts. To Archie, this was the best conceptual model of regional wildlife conservation based on ecology, not politics.

But Paseo Pantera turned out to be the victim of its own political success. After a suitability and feasibility analysis led to a proposed route for corridor establishment, the concept of prioritizing wildlife conservation over human needs was immediately met with resistance by indigenous groups and advocates for the poor, who felt excluded or were worried about land-use restrictions. By the mid 1990s, the primary focus on wildlife had been diluted as Paseo Pantera morphed from a strict environmental agenda into a bureaucratic framework meant to address not only conservation but also sustainable development and poverty alleviation. In 1997 an agreement was signed by the governments of Central America renaming the regional initiative as the Mesoamerican Biological Corridor (MBC), now specifically defined as:

a system of land-use planning comprised of natural areas under special administrative regimes, nucleus zones, buffer zones of multiple uses and areas of interconnectivity, organized and consolidated, that offers various environmental goods and services to the Central American society and the rest of the world, providing social harmonization opportunities to promote investment in the conservation and sustainable use of the resources.

The Mesoamerican Biological Corridor, placed under the management and coordination of CCAD, was to become the largest conservation project in Central American history. An initial pledge by the World Bank of at least $90 million dollars attracted additional donations; within three years, pledges reached over $280 million, and over $500 million a decade later. In 2000, the MBC formally commenced operations under the auspices of the Ministries of the Environment and Natural Resources in each of the participating countries. But the new map of proposed corridors seemed almost ad hoc, shifting from a strict ecological basis and trying to include everything from wildlife pathways to impoverished villages.

At the first Mesoamerican Parks Congress in 2003, which highlighted the MBC, there was a clear shift to a donor-driven agenda focusing on economic integration and poverty reduction. The ambitious goals of the MBC to balance human needs, sustainable development, and biodiversity conservation did not give wildlife conservation the focus and priority that was originally intended. Still, despite its failings, this was perhaps the largest and most comprehensive plan to move beyond simply the management of individual protected areas to more-complex regional programs that crossed national political boundaries. And it was the first attempt on such a scale to create a framework that defined and legally recognized core zones, buffer zones, corridors, and multi-use zones in a systematic manner. All of this was good for wildlife and the jaguar.

In 2000, as the MBC got under way, the Jaguar Corridor Initiative became the top priority of the Big Cat Program that I was heading at the Wildlife Conservation Society. Initially operating independently of other corridor initiatives such as the MBC, our early efforts centered on determining where the corridor was and how the jaguar was maneuvering through the human landscape. We were not creating a corridor; rather, we were looking for one that had already been created by the jaguar. In 2004, I hired a bright young geographic information systems (GIS) expert, Kathy Zeller, to map the possible jaguar corridors between the known source sites, or JCUs, that we had identified in the 1999 jaguar workshop in Mexico. To update and widen the scope of that data, we carried out a second prioritization of JCUs using information from 110 jaguar experts from the United States to Argentina. This new consensus allowed us to increase our number of JCUs while better refining the boundaries of the original ones.

Since we were searching for an already-existing corridor, our efforts were divided into two distinct phases. First, there was the almost two years of collaboration with other jaguar experts and the collating of all their data and information into a computer database that allowed us to design the most likely jaguar travel routes between known jaguar populations from northern Mexico to northern Argentina. Once this was completed for a particular country, the more difficult and painstaking task of verifying the corridor on the ground (called "ground-truthing") could begin. With whatever additional funds we could muster, teams of scientists in each country had to be hired and trained to use the tools we gave them to ground-truth the corridor and help us make adjustments where needed. I anticipated years of effort before the entire corridor would be complete.

For the first phase, given the scale of the range we were considering, we decided to assess potential linkages or corridors between JCUs by using an analytical tool called the least-cost corridor model. The first step was to create a matrix of grids over the entire landscape, and within each grid to assign a resistance value that represented the level of difficulty a jaguar might have moving through that particular area. In order to assess such a value, six landscape characteristics or layers were chosen that most affected jaguar movement and survival: land-cover type, percent tree and shrub cover, elevation, distance from roads, distance from human settlements, and human population density. Lacking much empirical data, we asked jaguar experts to assign values to the different components of each landscape layer, based on their knowledge of jaguar behavior, regarding how difficult or "costly" a particular attribute (such as a road or a village) would be in terms of jaguar movement. Cost values ranged from zero, if there was no cost or difficulty to jaguar movement, to 10, if there was a lot of resistance to jaguars moving through the landscape. Models from the emerging field of landscape genetics, mentioned earlier in the chapter, would help us use such data with genetic information from jaguar feces, hair, blood, or other possible sources to further elucidate the degree to which the jaguars were behaving as we thought they would.

The first analysis of jaguar movement based on such a model coming out of the 1999 workshop in Mexico was much less a picture of clear corridors than a complex weblike matrix that looked strikingly similar to the 1987 jaguar distribution map drawn by Swank and Teer when little was known of the species. While our 1999 map never accurately depicted where jaguar populations lived, it was an important depiction of the permeability of the landscape to possible jaguar movement between such populations. What our analysis now indicated was that, despite all the intensive human activity outside of protected areas and the consequent loss of more than 50 percent of the optimal habitat where viable populations might still live and breed, nearly 80 percent of the jaguar's historic range still allowed for potential jaguar movement. This important revelation helped explain the genetic findings which, at first, seemed impossible. The black abyss of humanity was not so black after all.

The JCUs, the places where jaguars lived and bred, were the backbone of our proposed conservation network, and these sites had to be carefully assessed and delineated. Our survey provided data to characterize 90 JCUs ranging in size from 211 square kilometers (81.5 square miles) in northwestern Ecuador to 99,574 square kilometers (38,224 square miles) in central Brazil. All the JCUs together covered 1.9 million square kilometers (0.73 million square miles), approximately 16 percent of current known jaguar range. Although the initial boundaries of the JCUs drawn during the workshop in Mexico were often subjective, we also asked our jaguar experts to assess habitat quality, threats to the habitat and wildlife, and land-tenure issues in the JCUs. From these data we created two general categories: Type I JCUs, with a supposed population of at least 50 breeding jaguars and a stable prey community, and Type II JCUs, with fewer jaguars, adequate habitat and prey, but with ongoing human threats that had to be addressed. Most of the JCUs (N=46) were Type I, with the remainder either Type II (N=38) or areas that were not yet classified due to lack of information.

Next we had to fine-tune the data and take a close look at the most likely pathways within the larger permeability matrix that jaguars used when moving between the JCUs. Using the same least-cost dispersal model, we delineated 182 specific corridors, outside of protected areas, that connected virtually all 90 JCUs and covered an area of 2.6 million square kilometers (1 million square miles). The average corridor length in Mexico and Central America was 174 kilometers (108 miles) (range: 3–1,102 kilometers, 1.9–685 miles), while in South America the average corridor was 489 kilometers (304 miles) (range: 12–1,607 kilometers, 7.5–999 miles).

When the genetic connectivity of the jaguar throughout its entire range was first revealed, the most pervasive question was: How could any jaguar survive outside protected areas over such large distances of human-modified landscape, where prey was sparse to nonexistent and where most jaguars were shot on sight? One of the answers involves an evolutionary mandate known as natal dispersal, found in almost all mammals and birds, whereby young animals that have not yet reproduced, suddenly leave the area of their birth and disperse over large distances, with the intent of reaching a new area and another population with individuals with whom they can successfully breed. In mammals, it is the males that disperse widely, while in birds, it is the females. There is also a phenomenon called breeding dispersal, whereby adults that have already been reproductively active disperse over relatively large distances to new breeding areas.

Natal-dispersal-distance data of large, wide-ranging carnivores are sparse and often underestimate real distances traveled, because of the difficulties scientists have of finding and following individuals over extensive distances. Also, once outside of protected areas, many dispersers are killed before reaching a new home. Data on jaguar dispersal is particularly lacking. In the 1950s, Aldo Leopold speculated on one particular jaguar dispersing more than 800 kilometers (500 miles). In the 1980s, Howard Quigley and Peter Crawshaw collected incomplete data on two male jaguars in the Pantanal dispersing 30 kilometers (19 miles) and 64 kilometers (40 miles) before they were killed. A young male of the next-largest cat of the Americas, the puma, has been documented to disperse as far as 1,250 kilometers (777 miles), while a young male leopard in South

Africa covered a minimum distance of 353 kilometers (219 miles) until it was killed. Clearly, it's not out of the question that a young dispersing jaguar could follow the evolutionary clarion call and move to a new breeding population that could be anywhere from 3 to 1,600 kilometers (1.9 to 994 miles) away, the range of corridor lengths between JCUs through Central and South America.

Extensive travel by jaguars through the human landscape seemed even more possible once we examined our maps more closely and realized that within the corridors there were often small patches of forests that we had overlooked or never considered previously because of their size. In fact, small forested areas that lack large resident predators often create refuges for prey species to flourish. Such forest patches, too small to support resident jaguar populations, could serve as temporary refuges or "stepping-stones" for a dispersing jaguar intent on reaching the next adequate site to occupy. These stepping-stones, which would have been overlooked in our original plan to save jaguars in only the highest-priority breeding populations, were clearly important components of jaguar travel routes, needing investigation and perhaps protection as part of the jaguar corridor.

As I discussed in chapter 9, interbreeding between individuals, either within one large population or between fragmented, separate populations, helps maintain a larger gene pool with more genetic diversity, thus ensuring that populations survive—and ultimately that the species survives. But how much interbreeding is needed? Many dispersing jaguars are killed once they set foot outside of protected areas, and very few individuals are likely to succeed in their trek to breed among other populations. Luckily, only a few individuals need to succeed. Research suggests that a population needs at least one migrant but not more than 10 migrants per generation to preserve genetic vigor. Computer models further show that small, fragmented populations with occasional migrants actually preserve more genetic diversity than a single large population with the same number of total individuals. This is because the social dynamics of a single large population of jaguars often prevents or regulates random breeding among individuals. On the other hand, while two or more small protected areas connected by viable corridors might in fact have greater genetic vigor than one very large protected area of the same total size, the smaller protected areas are harder to defend from human encroachment and degradation. The ideal, therefore, would be to strive for both large protected areas and the maintenance of genetic corridors between such areas.

Considering both the JCUs and the corridors, our jaguar conservation program was dealing with a combined area of 4.5 million square kilometers (1.7 million square miles). In order to best focus limited manpower and other resources across such a vast region covering 18 countries, we decided on three criteria to prioritize JCUs and corridors: ecological importance (large areas of intact, highly diverse ecosystems), network importance (areas that were crucial to the continuity of the corridor), and corridor vulnerability (areas that might be in imminent danger of being lost). Eight JCUs stood out as important ecologically and necessary for the integrity of the network, and nine corridors were both vulnerable to fragmentation and also necessary for the network's integrity. As expected, jaguar populations were most vulnerable at the northernmost and southernmost extremes of their range, where environmental and anthropogenic factors limited their further expansion. But many crucial areas of linkage lay along the already narrow and restricted Central American isthmus. One particular corridor in Colombia was both a crucial and a highly vulnerable link between Central and South American jaguar populations.

Our efforts to identify and implement functional corridors throughout the entire range of a large carnivore species were unprecedented. But the jaguar situation was unique, just like the species itself. Because jaguar populations were still linked genetically in a way no one had previously contemplated, we now had the opportunity to figure out how landscape features and human use of the land was allowing, rather than preventing, jaguar dispersal and movements between seemingly disparate populations.

We knew that the jaguar's movements through the human landscape of the Americas did not depend on an unbroken stretch of intact forest. So unlike the biological corridors of the Paseo Panthera, which were designed as an attempt to meet the needs of numerous critically endangered species at once, the jaguar corridors could comprise a mosaic of forest along with areas of human settlement and development. And since the jaguar corridor was not of our own making or design, but rather of the jaguar's own choice, there was little about it that could be contentious. The genetic analysis could not be clearer: some jaguars had found their way throughout Latin America, creating a corridor through citrus groves, oil palm plantations, cattle ranches, and backyard gardens—areas where no one had thought they could survive. Many traditional land-use practices of local communities, while degrading good forest, were actually helping to sustain the jaguar corridor. It was our job now to keep possible pathways open for the jaguar and let the species do what it had done for so long—survive.

After 2000, while continuing our mapping efforts and publishing some of our initial findings, the second phase of our corridor activities were accelerated as we hired and trained more staff to work on the ground. Now the Jaguar Corridor Initiative was starting to create a buzz in the Latin American conservation community. In 2006, I was invited to speak to more than 600 people from nine countries at the Second Mesoamerican Congress of Protected Areas, organized in Panama City by CCAD and the National Authority of the Environment from Panama. By this time, despite a myriad of conservation achievements, the MBC initiative was losing some of its regional support and collapsing under the burden of donor-driven agendas and a loss of clear vision. To support that program, the theme of the congress was that of strengthening protected areas through an agenda of sustainable development throughout Central America.

For me, this invitation was the ideal opportunity to publically promote the jaguar corridor among the Central American jaguar-range countries. As some participatory groups were eager to show that the essence of Paseo Pantera still survived, I was asked to speak on the uniqueness of the jaguar corridor and how it fit into the ongoing framework of the MBC. Then another significant opportunity presented itself. In tandem with the triennial Mesoamerican Congress of Protected Areas, there was to be a meeting of all of the ministers of environment from Central America, Mexico, and the Dominican Republic. The chairman of the meeting, Costa Rica's

Minister of Environment and Energy Carlos Manuel Rodriguez, extended an invitation to me to present the Jaguar Corridor Initiative to the private meeting of ministers before presenting it to the entire congress. Unbeknownst to me, the minister, an avid outdoorsman and one of the most dynamic and influential figures in conservation at the time, not only had an inordinate fondness for jaguars but was an ardent follower of my work since reading my book *Jaguar* while he was in graduate school.

Kathy Zeller and her team put together an impressive array of maps as part of a slide show that I could present to both the ministers and the attendees at the congress. The meeting with the ministers, which had the potential to affect many of our planned corridor activities, came first. I explained the current plight of the jaguar, the cat that had survived the Pleistocene extinctions to become one of the most revered and iconic wildlife species of the Americas. I presented the early depictions of jaguar range, created by the experts at the Mexico meeting, showing discrete populations that we assumed at the time to be fragmented, disjunct, and needing to be prioritized and triaged. Then I revealed the shocking genetic research, and, in layman's terms, I explained how it showed that genetic continuity still existed throughout much, if not all, of the jaguar's entire current range. I showed the newer maps, projecting where these movement corridors might exist, some of them overlapping with biologically intact corridors of the MBC while others went directly through the human occupied landscape.

This was a network of corridors unlike any other, I explained to the ministers, trying not to be intimidated by the single largest gathering of politicians who could make or break our efforts moving forward. We were making unprecedented progress in our understanding of the natural behavior and movements of an apex predator as it lived, moved, and survived among us. Our task now, I said, was to immerse ourselves in the field in order to find the jaguars and verify the corridors, site by site, country by country. The genetic data showed us that the corridors were out there, at least in the very recent past. Some of them might be degraded or perhaps even broken by new development. But this was not a theoretical model. It was the jaguar that dictated where these corridors lay.

My speech was passionate and, for the most part, fluent. More than once I thought back to my meeting more than a decade earlier with the prime minister of Belize and his cabinet as I pleaded my case for the world's first jaguar preserve. That was a defining moment in my life. This was another. Only now I wasn't afraid of speaking. I was afraid of failing.

As had happened in Belize, no one interrupted me as my allotted time came and went. I closed with a plea to the ministers that they formally acknowledge the jaguar corridor, and I asked them to grant me access to the necessary government agencies in each of their countries for permission to get on the ground and verify the corridors. When I finished speaking, Minister Carlos Manuel Rodriguez stood and supported my request, speaking to the gathering with the passion of someone who had more than once been accosted by the deafening silence of a forest without jaguars. Then I was escorted out of the room as the ministers concluded their other business and took votes on various issues that had been raised, including mine.

Less than 30 minutes later, Carlos Manuel came out smiling, waving his hand as if it had been a slam dunk all along. My request was unanimously approved, he said (unlike the 50–50 split of the Belize cabinet), and in the final signed document promoting multilateral cooperation on environmental and social initiatives, the ministers resolved to support and implement the jaguar corridor project. CCAD would help coordinate our activities in each of the countries. This decision was now part of the Declaration of Panama signed by all the ministers at the meeting.

All the hard work lay ahead. If I had learned anything from my travels and research since the early days in Belize, it was to anticipate adversity. Verifying the jaguar corridors would present a unique challenge: searching for likely sparse sign—scat, a kill, paw prints— of the occasional jaguar traversing mostly private lands that were sometimes heavily degraded with varying degrees of human activity. On top of that, I knew that the attitudes of some landowners as well as the unpredictable field conditions could make access into certain areas difficult and dangerous.

We had to somehow prove the existence of jaguars moving through areas where they had developed the ability to be "invisible" because being seen could mean getting killed. These corridors were reminiscent of the network of secret routes and safe houses formed by Harriet Tubman during the Civil War, saving human lives by moving them discreetly through hostile human environments. Now it was the jaguar's life that needed to be saved—the jaguar corridor was the "underground railway" for the species. Because of this, conventional techniques for jaguar detection, such as motion-sensor cameras or pugmark surveys, were not always feasible in these landscapes, nor did we have the staff or funding to sufficiently cover all the corridor area.

But the same year as the Panama signing, we formed a partnership with the American Museum of Natural History's Sackler Institute of Genomics in New York City to create a new felid genetics program that would soon become the largest of its kind in the world. Using the kind of knowledge and genetic tools that led to the discovery of the jaguar corridor in the first place, better protocols for the lab and field were developed to identify and use jaguar feces to monitor activity along the corridor, making the "invisible" clearly visible (without jeopardizing the big cat's safety).

In other areas, interviewing local people along the potential corridor about jaguars or jaguar sign was one of our best options for data gathering, since certain individuals, particularly hunters, were credible sources of information about wildlife presence. But questions had to be designed and asked carefully. People unfamiliar with jaguars often misread the tracks of other species, such as dogs and pumas, thinking it could be jaguar. I knew from my time in Belize that livestock losses attributed to jaguars were often from other causes such as disease, theft, or other predators. And sometimes people wanted to simply provide the answer that they felt researchers wanted to hear. So Kathy Zeller and her team once again jumped on the challenge of designing and publishing a rigorous protocol for collecting jaguar detection data through interviews with local people.

Despite the clear delineation of the corridors as depicted on our maps, I fully expected that, in the field, the jaguar corridor would be fragmented and difficult to verify. I was terribly worried that in areas where the jaguar corridor contained extensive human landscape it would be difficult, perhaps impossible, to verify a jaguar moving along a particular route. As it happened, though, that wasn't the case. Data from feces, tracks, camera traps, and local community interviews not only gave us the definitive evidence we needed to prove and properly scale the corridor, but showed that jaguars were using these corridors more frequently than we had anticipated. I was also surprised at how often the residents in the jaguar corridors knew of the occasional jaguar passing by their homes or in the nearby forest. Just the track of a jaguar was enough to generate excitement and bring up stories of the past. There was still a connection to this mysterious animal of the night.

Time was our biggest enemy. At 4.5 million square kilometers (1.7 million square miles), we were working with the largest conservation model in the world. On the positive side, 67 percent (1.3 million square kilometers, or 0.5 million square miles) of the JCUs and 46 percent (1.2 million square kilometers or 0.46 million square miles) of the corridors were already under some form of protection. While protected status did not always guarantee safety for the jaguars and their habitats, a sudden loss or degradation of such areas was unlikely. On the other hand, parts of the nearly 2 million square kilometers (0.8 million square miles) of human-dominated landscape that was potentially used by jaguars and remained unprotected could be lost at any time and without our knowledge. So it was in the highest-priority areas of these 2 million square kilometers that we started our work.

With limited resources and manpower in the field, I focused our initial efforts on Central America, where the political support, as pledged in the Panama Declaration, would be of great help in getting the permission we needed to work in remote areas. Also, this region had many vulnerable corridor connections. While there were additional areas of concern for connectivity in South America, particularly in the southern part of the jaguar's range in Brazil and Argentina, the vast remaining forests of that continent still appeared to have large strongholds of jaguars, extensive connections between populations, and perhaps the strongest remaining cultural beliefs regarding the jaguar's special status, particularly in the vast Amazon Basin.

Even with the help of the Panama Declaration of 2006, the Central American corridors took more than five years to verify in the field. While the exact location, size, and shape of some corridors needed adjusting, our least-cost dispersal analyses, with few exceptions, had resulted in corridor maps that proved highly accurate. Only after we had verified the corridors and assessed current threat levels to high-priority sections of the jaguar corridor did I start requesting meetings with ministerial officials. At that point, we needed to initiate the process of formal government recognition of the jaguar corridor for each country, as an entity to be considered in any future land-use planning or for any environmental-impact assessment on impending development projects. Ultimately, my objective was to sign agreements, country by country, that created government partnerships and allowed us to help officials develop national jaguar action plans that set clear guidelines for protecting jaguars, monitoring the jaguar corridor, training personnel, and addressing jaguar conflict issues.

On the ground, inside the corridors, we sought out site-based partnerships with everyone who had a stake in the region—local officials, landowners, protected area managers, local businesses or developers, and indigenous groups. If there was no political framework in place already, we helped form local corridor councils or rancher outreach groups that took on the responsibility for monitoring the corridors or addressing threats. In indigenous areas, we encouraged and funded education initiatives and community programs that preserved oral histories to keep any remnants of the Jaguar Cultural Corridor alive.

The Jaguar Corridor Initiative turned out to be more than just a new model of species conservation but also a modus operandi for working cooperatively and productively with governments, private landowners, and developers. The idea of engaging with people at all levels before, rather than after, the commencement of projects that might degrade the environment and alter livelihoods was a welcome change for most people. Developers seemed more amenable to compromise and mitigation measures when discussions occurred before capital expenditures were carried out. And the designation of jaguar travel routes as part of land-use zoning guidelines that allowed for a multitude of land-use practices was viewed as a win for the land rights of local communities. The jaguar corridor, if handled properly, demonstrated how people and predators, development and conservation, could for the most part coexist. Most importantly, it guaranteed a future for the jaguar.

Chapter 11

Borderland Jaguars

S AVING JAGUARS—saving any wildlife—means dealing with the political and social realities of the time and place in which you are working. This was never truer than with the jaguar corridor, which used public and private lands, had to be backed by national governments and local communities, and needed multinational cooperation among 18 countries spread over two continents. Since conservation is a complex mix of science, policy, social issues, and politics, the strategy for moving any such initiative forward must benefit both wildlife and the people who live with that wildlife in a particular region. Implementing the right kind of strategies would determine the success or failure of the jaguar corridor.

In chapter 9, I stated my belief that conservationists are not trained in addressing critical nonscientific issues such as law enforcement. While the most effective conservation policies are rooted in good science, their implementation often takes place in a sociopolitical context that has little to do with science. There were no courses in graduate school to teach me how to address the prime minister of Belize and his cabinet, how to deal with the dictators in Myanmar, how to navigate the struggling socialist government of the Lao People's Democratic Republic, or how to get every environmental minister from every jaguar-range country to officially sign off on the jaguar corridor. I might have benefited from a better understanding of forensics, psychology, economics, and business. But in the end, it was about passion, and the unwavering belief that animals needed a voice in the human world.

It was that passion, and what I had accomplished in Belize, that landed me in the kitchen of a ranch house in Douglas, Arizona, on the Mexican border in June 1997 at the request of the conservation NGO, The Nature Conservancy. Sipping a mug of steaming black coffee, I listened carefully to the soft-spoken voice of the two-meter-tall (six-and-a-half-foot), 60-year-old rancher and professional puma hunter, Warner Glenn, as he recounted the details of the nearly year-old incident that had thrust this remote backwater region into the national news, and would eventually be memorialized in his book *Eyes of Fire*. The result of this incident, and the reason for my trip from New York, was the first photograph ever taken of a living wild jaguar in the United States.

At the break of dawn, we rode mules up into the stark, remote Peloncillo Mountains and topped the bluff where Warner had faced the jaguar. I sat there on the horse and took from my pocket the picture that Warner had given me. Poised majestically atop the rocky outcrop now facing us, the jaguar stared directly into the camera. There was no indication of the surprise and confusion likely felt by this animal that, having made its way across the nearby Mexican border, was now being chased by a pack of howling hound dogs like an illegal immigrant trying to flee a sudden confrontation with the border patrol. Only in this case the pursuer was Warner Glenn. Thinking that his dogs were after a puma, Warner was perhaps more surprised than the jaguar when, upon sighting what he later described as the most beautiful creature he had ever seen, he rushed back to his mule to get the camera he kept in a saddle pouch, never considering going for the gun he had close by.

We followed the jaguar's route down from the bluff to the spot where it was cornered by Warner's hounds again. Only this time, with the jaguar desperate, Warner moved in too close for another photograph. The jaguar lunged towards him, but only enough to create an opportunity to make its escape again. Warner's last view of the jaguar was, as he described it, "heading south at a long trot."

I stayed back while the others rode ahead, looking over the expanse of dry, open, empty lands where Warner said the jaguar had last been seen. I imagined the jaguar stalking the steep, rocky terrain of this area in its search for food, water, another jaguar—a home. There were not supposed to be any jaguars still living and breeding in the United States since the early to mid-1900s . . . but were there? Warner's jaguar was never again seen north of the border. But it had already made history. And this lone cat was about to ignite a controversy between ranchers, conservationists, and the United States federal government that no one, least of all Warner, could have foreseen at the time.

I was traveling repeatedly to Asia during the 1990s, immersed in the struggle to save tigers, when I received the request that I make this trip to Arizona. Jaguars were believed long extirpated from this border area, and The Nature Conservancy, interested in protecting the unique flora and fauna of the region, wanted my assessment on the jaguar situation here. My dismay at the paucity of new information and conservation efforts on jaguars since I left Belize years earlier had been gnawing at me for a while now, particularly in light of the rapid destruction of forests and wildlife that I was seeing in Asia. This latest occurrence of a jaguar where it was not supposed to be helped steel my resolve to push forward with an idea that had slowly been taking shape for some time—a large-scale attempt to learn more about jaguars and prevent them from following the downward spiral of the tiger. These feelings manifested themselves in the decision to convene the 1999 jaguar workshop in Mexico that, ultimately, would change everything for jaguar conservation.

As was discussed earlier in the book, jaguars still roamed the hinterlands of the southwestern United States into the twentieth century, though by that time they were considered rare. Possibly one of the first records of a jaguar in the Southwest was that of trapper James Ohio Pattie, who, in 1826 while with a party of beaver trappers in the lower Colorado River valley, described a "leopard" that was killed when it walked into their camp. In 1841 the United States–Mexico Boundary Survey reported "leopards" seen along what is now the New Mexico–Arizona border, and during the second 1855–1856 boundary survey, they noted claims that "*el tigre*" was common along the Santa Cruz River valley in southern Arizona. But already by the mid-1800s, the jaguar population in the United States was thought to be declining rapidly as a result of shooting, trapping, and poisoning of the animal itself and its prey. Elliott Coues, assigned to study the natural history of Arizona in the 1860s after it entered the Union as a territory, never mentions jaguars in his investigations.

Warner's incredible once-in-a-lifetime jaguar encounter might in fact have been a short-lived piece of news, relegated to the kind of campfire lore appreciated by naturalist Aldo Leopold on his outings into this region, had the story ended there. But less than six months after Warner's encounter, a second male jaguar was photographed and videoed by rancher Jack Childs and his friend Matt Colvin while they were hunting in the Baboquivari Mountains of south-central Arizona. Now there were two verified sightings, occurring within a very short time period and with impressive photographs that got a lot of media exposure. The national attention garnered by these sightings prompted the Arizona Game and Fish Department to initiate a jaguar management plan and create the Arizona–New Mexico Jaguar Conservation Team.

After visiting with Warner, I continued farther into the borderlands and met up with Jack Childs and Matt Colvin for an excursion, again on mules, into the Baboquivari Mountains where they had seen their jaguar. Before making this trip to the Southwest, I had researched reports on previous evidence or sightings of jaguars in this area, and I was surprised at what I found. Since 1900 there had been at least 60 reports of jaguars killed in Arizona and New

Mexico, at least one every decade. Nearly a third of these reports were from 1900 to 1910, a time when jaguars were still considered regular occupants of this region. Another 24 percent of the reports were from 1911 to 1920, 12 percent from 1921 to 1930, and 12 percent from 1931 to 1940. After that there were no more than three jaguar reports in any decade up until 1970, and only one report for each of the subsequent decades until 1991. But the reports of occasional sightings continued up to the present.

The number of jaguars that might actually have still been resident in the United States or simply traversing the border from Mexico, we will never know. There were few people like Warner and Jack running around this remote area sending back reports, or reporting kills, particularly since the 1970s, when bounties on predators were rescinded and it became illegal to kill jaguars. While the data were sparse, the information in the reports, which spanned almost a century, provided insight into what I believed was happening. Of the 26 times that the sex of the jaguar was reported, only six were listed as females. Two females had been seen with cubs, in 1906 and 1910. David Brown, a professor at Arizona State University who collated much of the data on jaguars, believed that regular sightings of jaguars in the Southwest until 1950 were indicative of a thinly scattered population of resident jaguars. But the last verified female was reported in 1963, and the last sighting of cubs in 1910. Any breeding or resident population of jaguars, he purported, was gone from the United States by the 1960s.

After seeing the areas where Glenn and Childs had had their jaguar encounters, and considering the sex and age data from available reports, I was convinced that recent jaguar sightings in the United States were young dispersing males or occasional adult breeding dispersers coming up from Mexico. There was no evidence to suggest any resident population of jaguars inhabiting the United States, nor any recent breeding of jaguars in the United States. This supposition seemed even more likely when, several years later, David Brown and Mexican biologist Carlos Lopez-Gonzalez verified the existence of jaguar populations, with breeding females, in the northern Mexican state of Sonora. The most northerly of these populations was only 140 miles south of where Warner Glenn had photographed

his first jaguar in the Peloncillo Mountains, and 200 miles from
where Jack Childs had treed his jaguar in the Baboquivari Mountains. Yet the 1987 jaguar surveys and the distribution map of Swank
and Teer showed the jaguar's range occurring from central Mexico
to northern Argentina, having contracted more than 1,000 kilometers (621 miles) from its former northernmost extent, along the
United States–Mexico border, and a similar distance from its original southernmost distribution in central Argentina. Swank and Teer
had assumed that in the face of rampant hunting pressures and habitat loss, the most recent northern jaguar populations in Mexico had
been totally extirpated. But that assumption had clearly not been
verified in the field—because it was wrong.

I was not going to underestimate the jaguar again. The species'
repeated forays into the United States borderland region spoke of
its capacity to move over large distances, trying to settle new areas
or find new jaguar populations, as it was doing throughout the rest
of the jaguar corridor to the south. For that reason alone, though
much of the existing landscape seemed less than optimal for jaguars, this area needed to monitored. My initial concern that perhaps
there was a small remaining resident population of jaguars in the
United States, somehow overlooked, was now alleviated. Still, the
available data did show that the southwestern United States was still
a part of jaguar range. This, in turn, revealed an important oversight on the part of the federal government: the jaguar had no legal
standing in the United States. Wildlife advocates were demanding
an answer to the question of why jaguars were not granted protection under the Endangered Species Act if, by all accounts, they have
regularly occurred on United States territory, whether resident or as
transients.

As mentioned in chapter 7, the predecessor of the 1973 Endangered Species Act was the Endangered Species Preservation Act of
1966, authorizing the secretary of the interior to list native endangered domestic fish and wildlife, to direct federal land agencies to
preserve habitat, and to authorize funds in order to purchase habitat
for listed species. In 1969, the Endangered Species Conservation
Act (ESCA) amended the original law to provide additional protection to species in danger of worldwide extinction. It also called for

an international meeting to adopt a convention or treaty to conserve endangered species, resulting in the multilateral CITES treaty in 1973. Under the ESCA, two separate lists of endangered wildlife were maintained, one for foreign species and one for species native to the United States. The jaguar appeared on the list of endangered foreign wildlife.

In 1973, President Richard Nixon declared species conservation efforts to be inadequate and called for more comprehensive legislation, which resulted in the Endangered Species Act (ESA). Under this new law, the two lists maintained in the ESCA were now replaced by the single "List of Endangered and Threatened Wildlife." The jaguar was not on this list—and thus was not protected by the new ESA. Realizing their mistake, the United States Fish and Wildlife Service (USFWS) published a notice in 1979 acknowledging their oversight in failing to list the jaguar (along with six other endangered species). They asserted that it was always their intent to list all populations of jaguars as endangered, whether they occurred within the United States or outside the borders. Still, believing the species had been virtually extirpated from the United States, they did nothing further.

In 1997, the USFWS, partly in response to litigation by the Center for Biological Diversity (CBD), a nonprofit organization, as well as to the tide of public opinion after the press regarding the Glenn and Child encounters and photographs, finally listed the jaguar on the Federal Endangered Species List. I fully endorsed this action by the USFWS, because the data were clear: jaguars were still making their way across the border into the United States with some, albeit declining, regularity. Whether resident or not, these jaguars deserved protection. Once a species was listed, the ESA prohibited any person within the jurisdiction of the United States from "taking" an individual of that species, whether by killing or capturing.

However, there was a caveat to my endorsement. Typically, the ESA not only protected species legally but also called for a species recovery plan and, with certain exceptions, mandated the designation of critical habitat for the species. But *critical habitat* was defined as "the specific areas within the geographical area occupied by the species, at the time it is listed ... on which are found those physical or biological features essential to the conservation of the species." These guidelines made sense, unless there was no population to recover in the first place.

With no evidence of a resident population of jaguars in the United States since the early to mid-1900s, there was no reason to declare "critical habitat" for the species north of the border with Mexico, particularly since such designation could negatively affect the activities and livelihoods of people living in that region. The USFWS appeared to concur with this thinking when they deferred any listing of critical habitat for the jaguar.

I found myself in a strange and unlikely position: fighting against critical-habitat designation for a species that I had spent most of my professional career trying to save seemed an odd turn of events. But the designation of critical habitat was perhaps the strongest mandate of the Endangered Species Act when trying to save and protect an endangered species or a distinct population from extinction. And the link between official "endangered" status and the designation of critical habitat was logical in almost every case—except this one. Jaguars deserved protection when they set foot in the United States, to be sure, but they seemed unable or unwilling to re-establish themselves in this region. And even if the habitat in the southwestern United States could be restored to some semblance of its former state when jaguars occupied the region, the area could not be called "critical" to the survival of the species.

I was no stranger to controversy surrounding the Endangered Species Act. Ironically, many years earlier I had been a minor participant in the first and most famous landmark case testing the full power of the ESA and the mandate for critical habitat. The case involved the Tellico Dam project in Tennessee, which had been started in 1967, long before the passage of the ESA. In 1973, my ichthyology professor, Dr. David Etnier at the University of Tennessee, discovered the snail darter, a tiny fish the size of a paper clip thought to be relatively few in number and limited in distribution. In 1975, the snail darter was listed as an endangered species, and the area of the Tellico Dam was listed as the species' critical habitat. With millions of dollars already spent on the project, and the promise of jobs, water, and electricity hanging in the balance, massive public protests ensued on both sides. Congress went forward with approving funds for completion of the dam and passed legislation stating that the ESA did not prohibit construction already in progress. The environmental community sued for an injunction against further construction. The 1978 ruling by the United States Supreme Court reaffirmed an injunction stopping the Tennessee Valley Authority from completing the Tellico Dam project because the dam's impoundment area would destroy the only known spawning grounds of the snail darter. On the surface, this was a landmark victory for conservation.

As a young, passionate graduate student in zoology at the University of Tennessee, I followed the case avidly, appearing at protest rallies and even writing an op-ed piece for the local newspaper laying out the argument of why convenience and economics should not be allowed to extinguish an entire species. Even the government, I stated, recognized that we should avoid the possible future ramifications of pushing a species to extinction through human actions. The few pieces of hate mail, including one actual threat to my life, that I received as a result of that simple act marked my first foray into the tension-filled, often nasty world of environmental activism, where logic does not always win out. Filled with moral outrage at human stupidity, I was convinced I was on the side of Right.

Long after the case was over, more extensive scientific investigation showed that there were many different types of snail darters and that they were abundant enough, and found in enough places, to actually be taken off the endangered species list altogether. "The best available data" that the ESA called for in declaring critical habitat had not, in this case, been the result of thorough scientific investigation. Scores of family farms were inundated, people had their land condemned for real estate speculation, a pristine river and its natural habitat was ruined, and a lot of taxpayer money was wasted.

In retrospect, I still had no regrets for the stand I had taken back then. In the face of uncertainty, human actions should always favor life over extinction. However, I now realized, after setting up the Jaguar Preserve in Belize and numerous protected areas throughout

Asia, that actions taken even with the best of intentions have far-reaching consequences that are not always positive for everyone. Decisions that affect animal and human lives should not be taken lightly. Scientists and conservationists should not jump to conclusions too readily or accept uncertainty if additional information and data still need to be obtained.

After 2000, as we worked to delineate the jaguar corridor throughout their range, I continued to follow the United States jaguar situation closely. In response to constant litigation by the Center for Biological Diversity, now partnered with Defenders of Wildlife, a conservation NGO, the USFWS reviewed their consideration of what actions should or should not be taken with respect to the endangered status of the jaguar in the United States. In 2006, under the administration of President George W. Bush, the USFWS published the following in the *Federal Register*:

> We, the U.S. Fish and Wildlife Service (Service), under the Endangered Species Act of 1973, as amended (Act), have determined that it is not prudent to designate critical habitat for the jaguar (*Panthera onca*). This determination is based on a thorough review of the best available data, which indicate that there are no areas in the United States that meet the definition of critical habitat as defined in the Act. As such, designation of critical habitat would not be beneficial to the species and therefore is not prudent.

That same year, 2006, I appeared before the ministers of environment from Central America and Mexico to plead our case for official recognition of the jaguar corridor. Our corridor maps did not include any area in the United States, because there was no evidence of a resident jaguar population north of the Mexican border that a corridor could link to. If jaguars were to re-establish themselves in the United States and maintain a viable breeding population, our corridor would be extended.

But the litigation by CBC and Defenders of Wildlife continued and, again under pressure to prepare a recovery plan for the jaguar in the United States, the USFWS issued a press release in January 2008:

> The U.S. Fish and Wildlife Service has formalized its determination that a U.S. recovery plan for the endangered jaguar would not advance the conservation of the big cat. The vast majority of jaguars and jaguar habitat lay south of the United States. . . . The United States contains one percent of jaguar habitat. . . . Too few jaguars and too little habitat in the United States signify that a recovery plan would have little influence on protecting the jaguar population.

Then, in January 2010, with further litigation hanging over their heads, and under the new presidency of Barack Obama, the USFWS reversed itself, as published in the *Federal Register* with the following summary:

> We, the U.S. Fish and Wildlife Service (Service), under the Endangered Species Act of 1973, as amended (Act), have reconsidered our prudency determination concerning the designation of critical habitat for the jaguar (*Panthera onca*) and now find that designation of critical habitat is prudent. We are preparing a proposed designation of critical habitat for the jaguar in accordance with the Act this fiscal year and anticipate we will publish a proposed designation in January 2011.

This was a shocking turn of events. The full statement in the *Federal Register* claimed that the reversal was due, in part, to "new data" that had become available. But the new data showed nothing to warrant a change of policy. Three years of research, supported by the Arizona Fish and Game Department, had resulted in more than 30,000 camera-trap nights in the region of the United States–Mexico border and at sites in the mountains extending up into Arizona and New Mexico. This extensive use of camera traps produced a plethora of wildlife pictures, including 69 photos of two adult male jaguars, and a possible third unidentified jaguar. One of the adult males was different from any recorded previously, while the second, called Macho B, was the same jaguar photographed by Jack Childs in 1996.

Now more than 10 years old since first being photographed, Macho B was photographed 65 times during the study, indicating that he had traveled throughout a minimum area of 1,359 square kilometers (525 square miles), including supposed forays across the Mexico border. The principal investigator of the study concluded that Macho B was, until his death in 2010, a United States resident. He speculated further that Macho B and the few other jaguars photographed in Arizona and New Mexico during the course of the study were neither dispersing transients from Sonora nor members of a distinct United States population, but part of a widely distributed low-density population at the northern extreme of the species range. Nevertheless, such speculation was not supported by the data.

The extensive camera trapping over three years had shown only, at most, two or three individual jaguars—a clear indication of the rarity of jaguars traveling north over the United States border. Macho B might indeed have become a United States resident, but his extensive ranging pattern, much larger than that normally shown by jaguars, indicated range instability brought about, perhaps, by poor habitat and food conditions, or the search for a female that did not exist. The fact that so few jaguars, other than Macho B, were ever caught again by the cameras indicated that they had either returned to Mexico or had been killed. Given the government assessment that hunting pressures were low in the region, and with no reports of people killing jaguars, it was more likely that the jaguars had returned to Mexico. There were no new data to indicate that the United States was part of the normal ranging pattern for any jaguar other than Macho B. Hence, there were no new data to substantiate any claim for critical habitat for jaguars in the United States.

The presence of Macho B in the United States, followed closely by the media, was part of the rationale used by the USFWS to reverse their previous assessments and re-open the issue of jaguar critical habitat in the United States. Privately I was told by government officials that their stand on the issue had not really changed; it was the burdensome litigation and shifting political winds that had contributed to the new statements.

So the battle continued. I agreed to several interviews with the media to clearly state my assessment of the situation, which remained unchanged since my initial visit to the area more than 10 years earlier. I said simply that this situation needed to be watched. Jaguars that set foot in the United States had to have legal protection. If jaguars started to live and breed in the United States, then their habitat should be protected. But with no resident population in the United States, and with tens of thousands of jaguars still struggling to survive in Latin America, the focus on jaguars should be south of the border.

Regardless of the data, in March 2014 the USFWS officially declared a little more than 3,000 square kilometers (nearly 1,200 square miles) in the southern borderlands of the United States as "critical habitat" for the jaguar. With most of the land in Arizona and a small piece in New Mexico, the federal designation was hailed as a victory by the Center for Biological Diversity, which believed this would lead to "a thriving population of these beautiful big cats to this country." The declared region was now off-limits to any kind of development that might make the land unsuitable for possible jaguar habitation. Larry Voyles, director of the Arizona Game and Fish Department, was not so pleased, stating that "designating critical habitat for the jaguar simply fails in both logic and biological foundation. . . . All conservation efforts and use of precious limited resources need to be focused where most jaguars actually exist."

The reversal by the USFWS in response to litigation and politics was, interestingly, the opposite of what had happened with the snail darter and the Tellico Dam so many years earlier. With the snail darter, the survival of an entire species was believed to be at risk. Unfortunately, our knowledge was insufficient and there should have been better research before actions were taken that affected people's lives. Still, no risk is worth the eradication of a species. In this case, the species was not at risk at all. But human emotions and politics, not data and logic, gained the high ground and forced what I believe to have been a damaging reversal of policy by the government agency tasked to protect United States wildlife and wild lands. Sadly, after hearing that many local people in the region felt betrayed by both the state and the federal agencies involved in this issue, I believed that the occasional intrepid jaguar making its way into that isolated area in the future might be more at risk of being killed than ever before.

As we push forward with the Jaguar Corridor Initiative, we have our eye on this region now, mostly through our work with the breeding population of jaguars in Sonora, the area of known jaguar habitat closest to the United States border. At my urging, Howard Quigley became co-chair of the USFWS Recovery Team, tasked with looking into habitat suitability and the feasibility of the recovery of the jaguar on both sides of the border. I was definitely on the side of the jaguar in its efforts to survive in this challenging region of its northernmost range. But its resettlement into the United States any time in the foreseeable future seemed unlikely.

Chapter 12

In Search of Jaguarness

A T FIRST LOOK, the third-largest cat in the world after the tiger and the lion seems to closely resemble the spotted leopard, which follows it in the big cat hierarchy. But with its massive head, stocky build, and relatively short tail, the jaguar is strikingly different and much more imposing than the leopard—structurally more akin to the tiger. But when describing any of the larger cats, humans tend to distinguish between them in descriptive rather than functional terms: the awesome power of the tiger, the majestic complacency of the lion, the astute cunning of the leopard, the elegant grace of the puma, the lithe agility of the snow leopard, and the sleek beauty of the cheetah. There is a sense that, beyond physical appearance, there is more to these big predators than meets the eye. As a child visiting the zoo, I intuitively sensed something more to the jaguar than what

I could see through the bars of its cage. Now, so many years later, this species was still a focus of my life.

I had captured jaguars, I had tracked them for countless days and weeks, I had watched them for fleeting moments in the wild, I had touched them when they were sedated, and on a few occasions, I had even come face to face with them with no bars between us. Everything about what I saw in the field gave me a picture of a powerful brutish force—big in structure, moderate in size, massive but short and low to the ground. For years, I described the jaguar as the sumo wrestler of the animal world, or as a "fireplug." Finally I realized it was the jaguar's differences from the other cats, not the similarities, that enabled it to survive, dominate, and become the animal that it is.

But I always felt I was missing something. Strength, power, dexterity—these were only a hint of the important elements that enabled this cat's survival. The "something" I was missing is what drove the jaguar thousands of miles from the Old World to the New, why it survived the massive Pleistocene extinctions not only to survive but, beyond that, to thrive, re-adapt, and become the apex predator throughout much of the Americas. The Olmec, the Maya, the Aztec, the Inca—early cultures who lived with this cat had felt its power and had tried to emulate or harness jaguarness by recreating its image, wearing its parts or, in some cases, by becoming the jaguar itself. Carvings and sculptures often depicted the nature of the jaguar as somehow tied to man's world but not entirely of this earth. Having a jaguar totem meant the ability to successfully take on multiple situations, whether in battle or in everyday existence. Only the most special or elite might have a jaguar "co-essence," sharing in the power and nature of the animal. The Desana Indians in the Brazilian Amazon believed that a true jaguar shaman must not only see himself, but be perceived by others, as acting "like a jaguar." The more "jaguar essence" a shaman possessed, the more powerful and successful he would be. Possession of true jaguarness was revealed through one's actions as a person. If I was going to help save the jaguar, I needed to understand it in its entirety. At least as much as any human being could.

In the earliest days of my fieldwork, when George Schaller first sent me to Belize to survey the country for jaguars, I was in the north, an area called Gallon Jug near the border with Guatemala. It was a remote, wild place, uninhabited except for a few *chicleros*—hardened jungle men who collected the thick, milky chicle sap from sapodilla trees that was once used exclusively to make chewing gum. After World War II, the use of synthetics in gum slowly strangled the trade in wild chicle. But these men hung on as long as they could, knowing no other life and having nowhere else to go.

I was following the fresh tracks of an adult male jaguar, when I came upon the two- to three-day-old remains of a peccary kill. The skeleton was picked clean and disarticulated but, after finding the skull a few meters away, I had no doubt as to the cause of death. The top of the cranium was gone, like a missing piece of a jigsaw puzzle. Tracks and matted vegetation in the area indicated that the jaguar had been following a herd of peccaries, when perhaps this unlucky individual started to lag behind.

In my mind's eye, I envisioned the jaguar crouching low to the ground, inching its way through the bush, head lifted, eyes never leaving its prey. Suddenly a leap with the powerful hind limbs and, like the bullet from a gun, the jaguar bursts through the vegetation and closes the distance between itself and the peccary. In an instant, the jaguar's canines clamp down on the peccary's skull, and the large front paws grab and twist the neck at an impossible angle while the jaguar's powerful neck muscles snap the head back. The peccary is dead before it hits the ground.

I knew well the killing power of the jaguar by now, having examined many cow skulls and skeletons with the telltale puncture holes in the skull or the spinal vertebrae. I had seen perfectly paired canine bite wounds through the braincase of capybara along the banks of the Cuiba River in the Brazilian Pantanal. And I had seen the shells of 90- to 135-kilogram (200- to 300-pound) green turtles, crunched and ripped open along the beaches of Tortuguero in Costa Rica. No other animal in the world killed in quite this way.

Still kneeling with the peccary skull in my hand, I felt exposed, and glanced behind me at the wall of jungle. It was hard to contemplate the ferocity of an animal that could rip apart a skull. This kind of killing required not only an incredibly powerful musculature but also very specialized skull and dental characteristics. All big cats killed savagely. But now I understood that the unique killing ability of the jaguar was one of the secrets to its survival.

Some of the earliest writings describing the power of a jaguar's bite came from Dr. William Hornaday, a zoologist and conservationist who, as the first director of the New York Zoological Park (now the Bronx Zoo), speculated that the strength of a jaguar's jaws was greater in proportion to its size than the jaw strength of any other member of the cat family. His reasoning was influenced by an incident involving a large male jaguar named Señor Lopez that had been brought from the interior of Paraguay to become the first inhabitant of the zoo's Lion House, which opened in 1906. A 54-kilogram (120-pound) adult female jaguar was purchased as a cage-mate for Señor Lopez and placed in an adjacent cage for two days so that the two jaguars could become familiar with each other. When the jaguars were put together, Señor Lopez immediately rushed the female, seized her neck between his jaws, and crushed two of the neck vertebrae, killing her "as quickly as if her head had been cut off with an axe." Hornaday's immediate reaction was to describe the jaguar as "a bad citizen" and "a born murderer."

It took a hundred years before Hornaday's speculation about the jaguar's jaw strength was quantified through accurate calculation of the species' average bite force. Using the relationship between skull dimensions and jaw muscle area, while accounting for differences in species' body mass, a bite force quotient (BFQ) could be determined for different species. The BFQ of jaguars, indicating the potential prey size that could be taken down, was 7 percent, 18 percent, and

31 percent greater than that of tigers, lions, and leopards, respectively, despite tigers and lions having significantly larger skulls and out-weighing jaguars by at least 45 kilograms (100 pounds). The only other cat of the 11 species examined that had as large a BFQ was the clouded leopard, *Neofelis nebulosa*.

While all felids are built to be strictly carnivorous, different mor-phological adaptations determine how they hunt and kill. Among *Panthera* species, tigers and lions have the largest skulls, followed by jaguars, then leopards, then snow leopards. However, in terms of musculature, bite strength, and skull characteristics, the tiger, lion, and jaguar are generally lumped together as the largest of the "snouted, massive-headed cats." Considering bite force alone, jaguars have the most robust canine teeth relative to size of all cats measured, allow-ing them to use their canines more forcibly and in different ways than other cats. One study showed that a jaguar's maximum canine bite force is just short of 682 Newtons, sufficiently high to cause fracture of a rigid structure such as the cranium of a peccary. To understand this better, consider that one Newton is the force capa-ble of accelerating a one-kilogram (2.2-pound) object one meter (3.3 feet) per second every second. The jaguar's bite is almost 700 times that force, and with canines that are structurally reinforced to reduce the chance of fracture when biting into hard material.

But effective predation does not rely on the bite alone. Animals that take large prey, such as jaguars, lions, and tigers, need robust forelimbs for subduing large animals and positioning themselves for the killing bite. The anatomical structure and musculature of the forelimbs of jaguars in particular allow for a wide range of motion for positioning and grappling. And with relatively short limbs, the jaguar has a low center of gravity for more efficient use of its body weight and for climbing trees. The large paws of jaguars facilitate stronger, more stable grips during an attack and also aid in swim-ming. All of these traits are optimal for a slow, stalking predator that is after large, slow-moving prey wherever it finds it.

While tigers and lions are strictly terrestrial, the jaguar, along with the leopard, is scansorial (adapted for climbing). But the jaguar is also an excellent swimmer, easily crossing rivers and even hunting in the water. This allows the jaguar to exploit virtually every dimension of its surroundings. With an average weight about half that of lions and tigers but nearly twice that of the leopard, the jaguar, in almost every way, is built to be able to act like a big small cat—or a small big cat, as circumstances dictate.

In John Bonner's book *Why Size Matters*, he explains how size is the extreme regulator of all things biological, a prime mover in evolution and a major determinant in the survival of a species. Size influences strength, complexity, physiology, longevity, metabolism, generation time, and abundance of a species. The natural selection for size, either up or down, is what guides the development of what Bonner calls "novelties" in the structure of the organism. Ultimately, whether a species succeeds or fails in the face of changing environmental circumstances or human threats will, in a large part, be due to its size. That might explain why the New World jaguar needed to be significantly smaller than its conspecific Eurasian counterpart. Size matters! How much it matters for the jaguar will be made clearer throughout this chapter.

While a part of jaguarness involves the body and structure (i.e., the size) designed and honed by evolution and natural selection, there is much more to the animal than that. The animal's behavior in reaction to threats, stress, prey availability, and all the changes occurring constantly around it goes well beyond the mechanical functionality enabled by structural characteristics alone. How the animal thinks and how it reacts are parts of complex behavioral patterns developed by the species in tandem with its physical abilities. But trying to realistically understand the jaguar's cognitive process is challenging. In her book *Beyond the Brain*, Louise Barrett warns that animal thinking and behavior might be far different from anything we might imagine because of animals' differing evolutionary trajectories. But clearly either human or animal behavior, she contends, is an interaction involving physical structure, cognitive processes, and the environment.

While the jaguars in Central America, generally weighing between 41 and 68 kilograms (90–150 pounds), were half the weight of their

South American relatives, they were still physically capable of taking down bulls 10 times their size. Yet in my Cockscomb study area, the jaguars I studied were subsisting on mostly smaller prey, primarily the 4- to 5-kilogram (9- to 11-pound) nine-banded armadillo. I was concerned about this, thinking that such large, muscular animals could not possibly stay healthy on such small prey items. But research that followed my work at Cockscomb and elsewhere showed that I needn't have worried.

Due partly to their size, jaguars are capable of being the ultimate opportunists among the big cats. Feeding on dozens of different food items in tropical forests, from birds and lizards to monkeys, peccaries, tapir, caiman, and domestic animals, jaguars are built to kill very large prey when they need to, or survive on very small prey. Jaguars will jump on the back of a 400-kilogram (880-pound) tapir and try to bring it down even while being dragged through the thick forest, they will swim along the bank of a river and pounce on a 2.5-meter-long (8.2-foot-long) caiman while still in the water, they will climb a tree and go after a troop of monkeys, or they will quietly wait along rivers or small animal trails grabbing up unsuspecting armadillo, paca, or lizards.

Food habitat studies throughout the jaguar's range indicate the species' ability to optimize its foraging, taking whatever is most available. Jaguars specialize on peccaries in Calakmul Reserve in southern Mexico but focus on white-tailed deer in Jalisco, Mexico. In the Maya Biosphere Reserve of Guatemala, jaguar feed mostly on armadillos and coatis. In Manu National Park in Peru, turtle and crocodile are a major part of jaguar diets, while in parts of the Pantanal in Brazil, jaguars feed primarily on cattle, with caiman and peccaries of secondary importance. In areas of the Chaco in Paraguay, brocket deer and rabbits are the major food sources for jaguars. During nesting season for the green turtles in Tortuguero, Costa Rica, jaguars will come down out of the forest and feast primarily on these behemoths. And if a jaguar happens to encounter a fresh carcass of another jaguar, even that potential meal is not wasted.

As noted in chapter 2 of this book, at least five genera of large felids lived in North America during the Pleistocene. With the extinction of the large herbivores, all but two, the puma and the jaguar, disappeared. One scientist, Louise Emmons, speculated that the jaguar's massive head and stout canine teeth gave jaguars the ability to break open the carapaces of the once-abundant turtles of the neotropics, thus allowing it to survive and dominate in this difficult habitat, far removed from its place of origin.

But when large prey were not available, how did a big cat like the jaguar survive on smaller prey? In the Cockscomb, the jaguars were active almost 60 percent of the time, presumably looking for food while traveling within relatively small areas. When peccaries moved through the area, jaguars would pursue that favored prey for large distances. But usually the jaguar moved within an area of approximately 30 square kilometers (12 square miles), similar to that found for the much smaller ocelot, and half of the home-range size found for jaguars in the Pantanal, where they had larger prey to regularly feed upon. Research showed that compared with other cats, jaguars consume approximately the same amount per day, per kilogram of body weight, as pumas, but less than larger cats like tigers and lions, and less than much smaller cats like jaguarundi and lynx. This part of jaguarness would be greatly advantageous to a dispersing young male making its way over large distances of human landscape through the Jaguar Corridor.

Although I now better understood how the structure and outward behavior of the jaguar gave it advantages that other bigger and smaller cats did not have, the cognition of the jaguar, what I considered the essence of jaguarness, continued to elude me. During my early years in the field, I thought I knew a lot about jaguars. I had more data than almost anyone else in the world, but mostly through indirect evidence. I rarely saw the jaguars I was following, and was never able to watch one for any length of time. After trapping and observing Ah Puch, the young wild jaguar that had never seen a human before, I knew I wasn't even close to understanding this animal. And on the few occasions when I was in the jungle alone at night and the jaguar's gruff cough pierced the darkness, raising the hairs on the nape of my neck, I wondered if any human could ever truly know this beast.

Strangely, at least some of the answers I was seeking were revealed in a most unlikely place—the zoo world. Having spent more than 20 years working for the Wildlife Conservation Society based at the Bronx Zoo in New York City, I never considered animals in cages to be anything more than mere shadows of their wild counterparts. Most of the big mammals, like the cats, were born in captivity and seemed broken and defeated. But one day, I'd found the clue I'd been looking for, pointing me right back in the direction of the captive animals I had so wrongly categorized as irrelevant to my efforts.

In the small private library of the Bronx Zoo, while catching up on the most recent scientific journals, I came across a copy of William Hornaday's *American Natural History* from 1904. Flipping through the yellowed pages, I read how the seasoned naturalist believed jaguars to be fierce, powerful, and dangerous beasts. This led me to the book *Wild Animals in Captivity* by a former general curator of the Bronx Zoo, Dr. Lee Crandall, who described jaguars as "morose," inclined towards occasional savagery, especially when compared with the leopards he had worked with. This was the first time I saw men of science using adjectives to try and characterize the nature of the jaguar. A realization dawned on me. If the ancient Maya in Copán truly did keep or raise jaguars in captivity, as the famed felid burial site there suggested, than perhaps their knowledge and observations of the captive animals were what allowed the Maya to empathize with the species in the way they did. Perhaps there were others like Hornaday and Crandall, but alive today, who had spent time with jaguars in captivity.

Finding people who had worked with captive jaguars for long periods of time was more difficult than I'd anticipated. Unlike tigers and lions, jaguars were not a common zoo animal. I was told that they were not a good exhibit species because they were "unreliable" and "untamable," terms not usually used with the other large cats. But the people I found who had spent time with captive jaguars all had stories to tell, with far more convergence in thought about the behavior of the species than I would have imagined. Here are some excerpts from my notes:

- Alan Woodward, carnivore keeper at the Chester Zoo in England for 39 years, said jaguars were more *secretive* than lions and tigers. They were always looking for something to do, something to find. He considered them *less sociable* than other big cats, preferring to stay in their dens much of the time rather than out in the enclosure.

- Martin Krug, director of Zoo Hodonin in the Czech Republic had worked with big cats at Zoo Bratislava in Slovakia for many years. While individuals had distinct personalities, he said, they all were *constantly looking, searching*, trying to find errors a keeper might have made.

- Gregory Breton, curator at Le Parc des Félins in France, said that the jaguars always followed you with their eyes, while tigers, leopards, and lions quickly shifted back to their normal behavior if you behaved normally. Not jaguars, he reiterated. They stayed *curious* their whole life. In French zoos, he told me, the jaguar is taken "more seriously," even feared by zoo staff more than other big cats. They are considered *more* "*brutal*" than tigers, and slower, "less explosive" than leopards.

- At the Woodland Park Zoo in Seattle, researchers reported significant effects of both visitor density and visitor intensity on the behavior of two captive jaguars. With increased exposure to people, the jaguars spent more time *non-visible* and more time pacing. The male also showed increased aggression.

And there were some rare, unfortunate incidents in zoos, when captive jaguars reacted aggressively when presented with particular opportunities:

- In 1985 at the John Ball Park Zoo in Michigan, a six-year-old male jaguar opened an automatic door in a holding area, attacking and killing a pregnant zookeeper.

- In 2002, three jaguars at the Schoenbrunn Zoo in Austria got through an improperly closed gate and killed an employee while she was in the enclosure preparing their food.

- In 2007 at the Denver Zoo, a male jaguar got through a door left open in its enclosure and mauled a zookeeper, who later died of his wounds.

- In 2009 at the Catoctin Wildlife Preserve and Zoo in Maryland, a 10-year-old male jaguar got through a poorly secured gate and mauled a keeper who was cleaning out a den area.

- In 2010, a three-year-old male jaguar escaped from the Belize Zoo after a hurricane destroyed its enclosure, and killed a man living nearby. It was thought that, just prior to the attack, the man's pet dog might have gone after the jaguar.

These incidents were all the more telling because wild jaguars, unlike tigers, lions, and leopards, are not considered a significant threat to human life and are generally not feared by the local people with whom they live. But a cornered or trapped jaguar is a different beast, as Warner Glenn had experienced and I had seen when they were in my box traps.

During my inquiries, one big cat keeper stood out from all the rest. Matthew Hennessy, senior keeper at the London Zoo, had worked with big cats for more than 50 years and was still at work in his sixties when I learned of him. He loved big cats and often spoke of jaguars, I was told; he considered jaguars to be the most magnificent, smart, and challenging cats to keep in captivity.

My first attempt to contact Mr. Hennessy by phone was not successful. When I was told that he might be reluctant to speak to me because of a stuttering problem, I remembered how I too hated to speak on the phone when I was a child. I felt an immediate affinity for this stranger and wondered if he had found solace, as I had, with the big cats. Finally I made contact with Mr. Hennessy through an intermediary and in July 2012 I hopped a plane to London.

We met in a small utility room off the back of the London Zoo's Lion House, a place where Matthew clearly felt at home. Standing about 1.7 meters (5 feet, 9 inches) tall with thick silver hair, rounded shoulders, and a slight stoop, this man was no stranger to a life of hard physical work. Yet like the cats he cared for, he radiated strength. I was clearly more nervous than he was about our meeting. Truth be told, I was uncomfortable speaking to another stutterer, a fact that I have never admitted to anyone. Hearing someone else stutter brought knots to my stomach and reminded me of the terrible pain and fear I lived with as a child and into adulthood—difficult memories.

But all discomfort disappeared quickly as I watched Matthew's face light up and he started speaking passionately, almost lovingly of the cats that had defined his life for more than half a century. He confirmed many of the observations about jaguars I'd been told by others: jaguars liked to stay up high and remain hidden; they were always looking for something, whether it was food, a way out, or some "weakness" of their environment; they were always watching; when their food was hidden, even under water, they found it faster than any of the other cat species. Then, as he warmed to the topic, he told me some of his more subjective feelings about jaguars' behavior: they seemed more alert, more clever, and more cautious than the other cats. If a routine was changed, jaguars quickly ascertained how to adjust to the change, but then it took them longer than other cats to settle down into the routine and act "normal" again.

I related the story told so long ago by William Hornaday about the big male jaguar, Señor Lopez, crushing the skull of the female at the Bronx Zoo. Matthew smiled and told me a similar, more recent story. The London Zoo had designed a seemingly indestructible ball that was to be used for the enrichment of the big cats. Tigers, lions, even the gorillas played with it and put the ball through its paces. But the first time it was given to a jaguar, the jaguar grabbed it and crushed it without hesitation. Everything I heard from Matthew made the picture clearer for me. His stories all spoke of a beast that was powerfully self-contained, always trying to take control of its environment and of its own survival.

Matthew said that he never saw a jaguar run out of its holding pen when it was released from a smaller cage into a larger enclosure. Jaguars were incredibly careful, he said, mindful of open areas and everything that was happening around them, always checking their way first. If a mother was moving with her cubs, Matthew would watch the adult place the first cubs only a short distance away before going back for the other cubs. Only when they were all together, he explained, did the mother start the process of moving them again until reaching the place where she wanted to be. Other big cats, Matthew said, carried their cubs farther, even out of sight, before leaving them and going back for the others.

The jaguar hunter I'd worked with in Belize, Bader Hassan, told me stories about raising jaguar and puma cubs that he used to train his hunting dogs. When they were still young enough to be kept in his house, he said, the puma walked straight across a room towards where it wanted to go. The jaguar however, would cross rooms by moving under the couch and behind chairs, using whatever cover it could.

When my collared cats in Belize were moving at the edges of a cattle ranch, I rarely saw them come out in the open. They used trees, shrubs, grass—whatever cover was available—as they skirted the edges of the pastures, often taking a circuitous route to get where they wanted to go. If they did come out into the open, they minimized the time spent exposed. I used this behavior, in fact, to instruct ranchers how to better control their cattle from depredation. Fencing, lights, even other animals that made noise in response to a jaguar—anything that kept cattle in the open or exposed a jaguar's presence—made the cattle safer.

Matthew believed that his most interesting observations, the ones that perhaps held the key to explaining adult jaguar behavior, came from his experiences raising jaguar cubs. The cubs got stronger, more aggressive, and smarter, more rapidly, he said, than the cubs of other big cats. Other zoo keepers also told me that jaguar cubs became independent more quickly and were more difficult to handle than cubs of other big cats. At the Marwell Zoo in England, a three-month-old black jaguar was so difficult to control that keepers needed a broom to keep distance with the animal. At four to five months old, the cub was considered dangerous. Although Hennessey had never seen jaguars in the wild, he was convinced that, from birth, jaguar cubs were better equipped than leopard or tiger cubs to survive.

I spent much of the afternoon with Matthew, listening to this man whom I felt was in some ways better qualified than myself to write a book about life with the big cats. Though I had started taking copious notes when we met, I quickly realized I was missing important nuances and facial expressions of Matthew as he spoke. After a while I chose instead to watch his face, hold eye contact as stutterers are taught to do, and feel his passion. Cats touched a deep place in him that had nothing to do with the job itself. I wanted to revel in his world as long as I could. My life was filled with too few jaguars and too few Matthew Hennessys.

As the afternoon drew to a close, I asked Matthew what individual words he would use to describe jaguars, especially in comparison with the other big cats.

He didn't hesitate. "Alert, confident, persistent, efficient," he said.

"What do you mean by efficient?" I asked.

"Like a long-distance athlete," he replied. "If a jaguar moves, something is going on and he is going to get what he wants."

I read my notes from my conversations with Matthew and others over and over again. I replayed numerous discussions in my mind, and I thought back on all my own experiences. I would never believe that we could fully understand the thinking, the cognition, of another animal species. But I believed that I now understood more of the essence of jaguarness.

Words often used to describe jaguar behavior, like *brutal, fierce,* and *aggressive,* were being filtered through the psychological mechanisms of the human brain. We were trying to understand and label the animal's strength and power. Adjectives like *morose, sneaky, scary,* and *dangerous* were describing behaviors that were cautious, measured, and efficient. I had my own label for the jaguar now, one I had never used nor heard used by others—*audacious.*

The jaguar had the audacity to survive, despite what was put in its way. Evolution and hardship gave the jaguar the tools for such audacity. But there was a touch of luck as well. The North American jaguar, unlike its African and Asian big cat relatives, did not have to deal with humans for a very long time. When *Homo sapiens* traversed Beringia and appeared on the North American scene some 30,000 years ago, the jaguar had already been there for as much as a million years. This allowed the jaguar to fully develop its biological and behavioral survival skills. By the time man was a factor in the jaguar's life, the species had developed and honed the cunning to know how, when, and whether to use those skills.

The term *fudoshin* is used to describe the state of mind of only the most advanced practitioners of Japanese martial arts. It denotes a determined, immovable spirit, a state of imperturbability. This immovable spirit is part of what has made up the audacity of this species, the jaguarness. This is why, I believe, the jaguar survived all the trials and tribulations of the Pleistocene, and all that confronted it afterward—parasites, hunters, habitat loss, prey depletion, range contraction. Perhaps this was what was recognized so clearly by disparate Native American groups like the Maya in Mexico and the Desana in the Amazon. This is also, I believe, what made that little stuttering boy rush to the cage of the jaguar at the Bronx Zoo.

Chapter 13

The Reluctant Warrior

SINCE FIRST APPEARING ON THE SCENE some 2 million years ago, *Panthera onca* has remained, in outward appearance, essentially unchanged. But changes were indeed occurring. The jaguar's smaller size allowed for the evolution of new or modified behavioral responses in the face of changing environments. The American jaguar was a more flexible predator now, well-honed by the Pleistocene jaguar's genetics and with new selective forces fine-tuning the species' epigenetics to retain memories and behaviors that would help meet the challenges of the New World tropics. The American jaguar's morphology, physiology, and emerging behavioral patterns, all working together, became what I termed *jaguarness*, creating an audacious predator, a truly indomitable beast.

Humans (of the genus *Homo*) were latecomers to the jaguar's world, emerging 2 million years or more after the jaguar's Eurasian origins. While all the earlier species of hominids blinked out, *Homo sapiens*, appearing only about 250,000 years ago, was the only human species to survive. They followed the jaguar across Beringia to become the only large, social, tool-using biped in the New World, whose development of unique killing and foraging abilities allowed them to successfully dominate new environments. From that point onward, the jaguar's greatest challenge would be surviving the growing human dominance of the jaguar's world.

For many years, early man's numbers and activities had little impact on the jaguar's life. But that eventually changed. The Anthropocene is an informal chronological term (proposed to the Geological Society of London in 2008 as a formal geological division) that denotes a period when humans had begun to significantly alter the earth's ecosystems and all life that depends on those systems. Some put the Anthropocene's beginnings as early as 8,000 years ago, when farmers cleared forests to grow crops, while others point to the Industrial Revolution, in the late eighteenth century, when major impacts on the atmosphere became evident. However, there is some agreement that a plausible starting date for the Anthropocene would be about 2,000 years ago, at the end of the Holocene. At this time in the world there already existed the Roman Empire, the Chinese dynasties, the Middle kingdoms of India, and the Napata/Meroitic kingdom of Sudan and Ethiopia. In jaguar world, the Olmecs were fading while the great civilizations of the Maya were ascending.

Whatever adaptive abilities evolution and natural selective pressures had bestowed upon the jaguar, its ability to survive in an increasingly degraded, overpopulated world of humans with abundant weapons eventually came to hinge on how feared, valued, and tolerated it was by humans occupying what had been the jaguar's world. Perhaps this is why the most important and most distinctive element of jaguarness, the characteristic that has allowed the jaguar, one of the planet's most powerful living beasts, to coexist with humans in a way that other large mammals or apex predators could not, is that of nonaggression.

I call the jaguar "the reluctant warrior" because of the choices it makes, how it uses its jaguarness. Humans who have lived or worked with jaguars all acknowledge the power, fierceness, and savagery of the animal and, at the same time, its nonaggressive nature towards humans. Since the early nineteenth century, tens of thousands of people have been killed by tigers, lions, and leopards. In some cases, individuals from each of these species have become serial man-eaters. From 1900 until recent times, at least 25 kills of humans by puma were confirmed in the United States and Canada. But in the wild, there are very few recorded instances of jaguars killing people and *no* instances of jaguars becoming a hunter of men, a true man-eater. One attempt to explain this phenomenon points to the fact that jaguars did not evolve alongside hominids, with the first real evidence of jaguar–human interactions found only in the New World.

Rafael Hoogesteijn, a respected veterinarian and jaguar biologist whose 1992 book *The Jaguar* is still one of the classic natural-history books on the species, now works with Panthera in the Brazilian Pantanal. As of this writing, he has had 79 jaguar encounters with up to four jaguars seen together at once. Twenty-two of the encounters occurred while he was walking alone and unarmed or when he approached a jaguar from a car, bicycle, motorcycle, or horse (other encounters involved boats, helicopters, and captures). During these encounters, each of which lasted up to 20 minutes, he followed jaguars traveling and watched them mating. Only once did Rafael feel threatened.

While following approximately 30 meters (99 feet) behind a male jaguar that was following a female in heat, the animal suddenly turned, roared, and charged straight at him, teeth barred, ears back, and nape hairs erect. Rafael stood his ground and the jaguar stopped 10 to 15 meters (33 to 38 feet) away, then turned and disappeared into the nearby river. Perhaps this was a bluff, or what Rafael called "a mock attack." Perhaps, had Rafael turned and run, the outcome might have been different. Clearly the jaguar must have felt threatened and reacted explosively, but then it reassessed the situation and made the decision to stand down. Killing or hurting Rafael would have accomplished nothing for the animal, except perhaps injury to itself.

I had a similar experience to that of Rafael while watching a big male jaguar recover from sedative after I had captured and radio-collared it during my work in Belize. I had laid the jaguar back in an open trap to recover, waiting nearby to ensure that no other jaguar came and injured the immobilized animal. Worried that the jaguar was taking too long to wake up, I walked to the side of the trap and poked him in his hindquarters with a stick. Suddenly, a clear-eyed jaguar looked directly into my face, leapt up, and was out of the trap in seconds. As I sprinted for the safety of my truck a short distance away, the jaguar chased after me. Realizing I could not outrun the jaguar, I turned and screamed "*NO!*" with all the energy I could muster and with no reason to think that this would stop the charging predator. Yet, the jaguar did stop, the anger of the moment dissipated, and he turned calmly towards the jungle. Clearly, this drugged and newly collared jaguar had cause for dismay, even retribution. Still, he walked away.

When animals are faced with conflict, they react with a discharge of the sympathetic nervous system priming the animal for either fighting or fleeing—the classic "fight or flight response." Sometimes the response initiates a period of heightened awareness, during which the animal rapidly processes behavioral signals from the adversary before choosing to react. In this complex behavioral arena of conflict or stress situations, jaguars, more often than not, ultimately choose non-engagement.

Some have misinterpreted the wariness, secretiveness, and non-aggression of jaguars as cowardice. During his explorations of Honduras in the 1800s, William Vincent Wells stated that "the jaguar is naturally a coward, and is seldom seen except in unfrequented places." Hunters who have run jaguars with dogs have been surprised by what they suppose to be the "fear" exhibited by a predator that could easily overpower or kill the much smaller dogs chasing it. But the jaguar's flight from danger through dense forest with lots of possible hiding places and escape routes is likely a better evolutionary strategy than a direct encounter with anything capable of inflicting injury. Injury is best avoided in the disease- and parasite-filled tropical jungles. And anyone who has witnessed the power and ferocity of a jaguar that is cornered or on the attack would never describe this species as "cowardly." I will never forget the feelings I had looking into the face of the first jaguar we had chased for hours through the jungle until it was treed with our dogs. One line from my field notes, as detailed in chapter 7, said it all: "Those eyes were watching me with no trace of fear or anger, but with thoughts I'd never know, and listening to voices I'd never hear."

Only the foolish do not respect a jaguar's space when they encounter the animal. The feeling of being cornered or trapped might have been the reason for the zoo attacks listed in the last chapter. As people like William Hornaday and Matthew Hennessey can attest, though jaguars usually spend their time watching, waiting, and maintaining a state of readiness, when the jaguar takes action, its movements are quick, brutal, and highly aggressive. One needs only to examine the remains of jaguar kills—holes in the skull and crushed vertebrae—to see the big cat's potential ferocity. Jaguars are warriors. And like all great warriors, their success and longevity comes not from the number of fights fought, but the number of fights avoided. When a fight does occur, it is to accomplish a necessary end result. Ideally, the fight is finished quickly and decisively with an expedient return to calm equanimity. As with the symbolic loosening of the jaguar helmet cord after a boxing bout between two contestants during the annual ceremony in Chiapas, Mexico, as described in chapter 4, the violence, once completed, does not leave the battlefield.

But most of the confrontations in a jaguar's life, whether avoided or initiated, have nothing to do with humans. With a strictly carnivorous diet, these top predators are always on the hunt for other animals. While large, meaty prey are preferred by a jaguar, these are also usually the species that can be difficult to kill or can cause serious injury to a jaguar. I'd heard numerous anecdotes from local hunters of jaguars being chased up trees by a herd of peccaries clanking their long, dangerous tusks, or of tapirs charging through dense brush and rivers to shake off the jaguar on its back, or of caimans trying to drag a jaguar underwater.

On the other hand, smaller, less aggressive prey, such as armadillos, turtles, pacas, capybaras, and brocket deer may be easier for a jaguar to kill, but the constant crushing and chewing of bone also extracts a price. At best, older jaguars show worn carnassial teeth (fourth upper premolar and first lower molar used for shearing flesh in a scissor-like way), and worn or chipped canine teeth. At worst, older jaguars may have lost or broken one or both of their canines. In domestic animals, worn or chipped carnassials or canines often cause infection and abscesses and can potentially lead to death. This, along with parasites, is likely another reason why jaguars live half as long in the wild as in captivity (apart from human threats).

When it comes to confrontation, whether with humans or animals, jaguars are constantly making choices to survive, choices that sometimes seem surprising, given their physical structure and abilities. These are the choices of the reluctant warrior. It is the variations of engagement with humans and other wildlife species—whether prey, co-competitors, or co-inhabitants—that makes the jaguar not only a species that humans can live with, but an important and necessary part of our natural world.

Whether feeding on armadillos in Belize or Guatemala, peccaries and white-tailed deer in Mexico, turtles in Costa Rica and Peru, or rabbits in Paraguay, or facing off with the pumas or ocelots they happen to encounter, a healthy population of jaguars helps to structure and stabilize the ecological system in which they live. On the one hand, jaguar behavior creates a dampening effect on the abundance and distribution of other sympatric carnivores as well as on prey species. On the other hand, some plant and animal species thrive as an indirect result of the jaguar's presence.

When jaguars are removed from the picture, however, a process that biologists John Terborgh and James Estes call "trophic downgrading" occurs—that is, a top-down trophic cascade of ecological disruptions that go through a natural system when a key species from the top of the food chain is eliminated. These disruptions, involving both plants and animals, cause some species to thrive while other species decline or are wiped out. As a result, the forest is changed. I would soon see that for myself.

In 2013, I traveled for the first time to Barro Colorado Island (BCI) in Gatun Lake, in the middle of the Panama Canal. While I had agreed to lecture on the Jaguar Corridor at the Smithsonian Tropical Research Institute (STRI) on BCI, my purpose was to see this tiny 15.6-square-kilometer (6-square-mile) island for myself. Until the construction of the canal, BCI has just been another hill-top forest within a large expanse of forest occupied by both jaguars and pumas. When the impoundment of the Chagres River flooded the region and created BCI, the island was far too small to support any resident big cats. BCI did, however, become a potential stepping-stone island for occasional jaguars swimming across the canal. In 2009, a camera trap captured the first photograph of a jaguar on the island. According to the island's scientists, the jaguar was there only briefly, possibly picking up a meal or two, and then it was gone.

Now the island looked and felt like a Hollywood setting for a tropical forest paradise, except for one thing—there were no more jaguars here. In the absence of any resident big cat predators (jaguars or pumas), BCI's ecosystem had changed over the decades since the impoundment of Gatun Lake, an oft-cited example of the effects of a top-down trophic cascade in a terrestrial system. Medium-sized predators became more abundant, nesting and ground-foraging bird populations disappeared, and certain tree species were replaced by others. The natural biodiversity of the seemingly picture-perfect jungle on BCI, 4.5 billion years in the making, had been disrupted and degraded. Extinction was now part of the scenario. And it was due, at least in part, to the disappearance of the jaguar.

But why should the loss of jaguars and other species on BCI matter if the forest was still vibrant and beautiful, despite whatever extinctions or disruptions man's activities had caused? The best answer to such a question was penned years before I first set foot in Belize to study jaguars, in a 1974 article by Daniel Janzen, "The Deflowering of Central America," discussing the effects of trophic cascades:

> What escapes the eye . . . is a much more insidious kind of extinction: the extinction of ecological interactions. . . . All that is green and trees is not a forest. Forests are not random collections of animal and plant species. For a plant or animal to be something other than what it is in a zoo, all of the elements of the ecosystem must be present.

Aldo Leopold, decades earlier, had expressed it in a different but equally important way, referring specifically to the loss of the jaguar from the American Southwest: "Freedom from fear has arrived, but a glory has departed from the green lagoons."

The human species, the last of our genus, is itself by no means exempt from the risk of extinction. We breed too fast, consume too much, engage in battle too readily, and have a strong propensity to destroy the natural world. And usually we capture, kill, and consume the biggest, the strongest, and the fiercest species that share the planet with us. We now know that there are deleterious and unanticipated impacts of eliminating apex predators like jaguars from a natural landscape. Creating a vacuum that causes trophic cascades can affect processes as diverse as fire, carbon sequestration, the dynamics of disease, the introduction of invasive species, and even biogeochemical cycles (the pathways by which substances such as water, carbon, and oxygen cycle through the earth's systems). Imbalance, disequilibria, and disruption of the ecological systems on which we depend are not good building blocks for a healthy future.

A 2014 paper in *Science* by William J. Ripple and his associates states that tolerance and coexistence with large carnivores is a societal challenge that will ultimately determine not only the fate of those carnivore species but of humans as well. We already know that humans and jaguars can coexist. We should better understand why we need to.

Chapter 14

Survival in a Changing World

IN 2008, AFTER ALMOST THREE DECADES with the Wildlife Conservation Society, I left my position as executive director of the
Science and Exploration and Big Cat Program to take over as president and CEO of a new organization, Panthera, focusing specifically
on the plight of wild cat species, particularly the largest and most
iconic of the species: tigers, lions, jaguars, and leopards. Panthera was
the brainchild of Dr. Thomas Kaplan, one of the most passionate,
committed people I had ever met, and soon to become the kind of
close friend I had always hoped for, but never had, as a child. Yet our
lives could not have been more different.

While I was a young teen still struggling on the streets of New
York City with my stuttering and self-confidence, Tom was spending his eleventh birthday on an expedition with his mother, seeking
jaguars in the Amazon. It would take four decades for our paths,

our passions, to cross when, already a highly successful entrepreneur with a PhD in history from Oxford, he sought to fulfill his dream to help the animals he had so loved throughout his own life. He contacted me at the Bronx Zoo and, within minutes of our meeting, the world shifted for us both. Panthera was born not out of Tom's or my desire to form yet another charitable organization, but instead out of a mutual and growing frustration with the increasing bureaucracies of large international conservation organizations that had become inefficient and were cumbersome to deal with. We both knew that the conservation world was losing the fight against the sweeping tide of extinctions of the earth's most iconic and important species. And we both knew that the extinction of the big cats was by no means a forgone conclusion. It was a fight that could be won!

With most of my staff from the Big Cat Program at the Wildlife Conservation Society, a handful of key donors who believed in our efforts, and a generous startup donation from Tom, Panthera immediately became the world's largest wild cat conservation organization, right out of the gate. We hired, or put on our advisory board, many of the world's wild cat experts. In 2009, my old friend Howard Quigley, with whom I had chased jaguars in the Pantanal, left his position as president of a small conservation NGO in Wyoming to take over the Jaguar Corridor Initiative for me. In 2010, Dr. George Schaller, my mentor and one of the greatest living icons in field conservation, retired from the Wildlife Conservation Society in order to become a vice president of Panthera. With all its passion and expertise, Panthera was now the powerful voice for cats that I had always dreamed of having. By this time, we had several teams in the field and the Jaguar Corridor Initiative was gaining traction throughout jaguar range. Now, with the wind at our backs, we could focus more energy and resources on the jaguar corridor, as well as the other wild cat species that needed our help.

I had confidence that the Jaguar Corridor Initiative, with fresh life and energy in Panthera, was the boost we needed to help guarantee the survival of the species. But there was still an important piece of the picture that I had yet to fully understand. From the beginning, my overwhelming focus had been on the jaguar—not its environment, not the villages it roamed through, not the political leaders of the countries it still inhabited. In Belize, where I first worked closely with the jaguar, I viewed the people who lived among the jaguars mostly as antagonists to the animal's survival and to my own conservation efforts. At best, I thought, humans took away the jaguar's land and consumed its needed prey. At worst, they hunted the jaguar for trophies, for sport, or out of fear that the animal threatened them or their livelihoods.

But as I tried to better understand the people of the jaguar, I came to appreciate the historical importance of what I called, in chapter 3, the Jaguar Cultural Corridor, which began perhaps with the Olmecs more than 3,500 years ago. The people of this early civilization held cultural beliefs that were rooted in the idea that humans and nature were intertwined, and that both humans and the jaguar were important parts of species' psyche, helping each other to survive. This system of beliefs and practices related to the jaguar existed both spatially and temporally throughout jaguar range, at least in pre-Columbian times. After European colonization, jaguar culture was devastated along with the indigenous communities. Now many of the old beliefs and practices, the connections to nature, appeared to be all but gone.

Some practices of the past still existed in the Amazon Basin right up into the 1970s and '80s, far longer than in any other place throughout jaguar range. In eastern Bolivia, the Mojo Indians had a "jaguar cult" whose shamans would supposedly talk to jaguar spirits in the forest before entering villages to demand payment of food and drink for their protective services. Among the Xingu in Brazil, the Guahibo of Venezuela, and the Desana of Colombia, only the fiercest warrior could kill a jaguar, and doing so garnered one great prestige. The Rikbatsa of Brazil avoided killing jaguars and snakes because they might be the reincarnation of evil people who could still transmit bad luck. The Bororo in Brazil and Bolivia viewed jaguars as a source of strength and a link to the spirit world. At death a person's soul could move into the body of a jaguar. Members of the Matses tribe in Peru and Brazil used jaguar-like facial adornments: nose piercings to resemble whiskers, sticks in the lips to resemble canine teeth, and tattoos of spots on the face.

It all seemed part of a dying past that no longer had a place in the modern world. More important, it didn't seem relevant to my efforts to secure the jaguar corridor.

I was wrong.

In 1994, a decade after the establishment of the Cockscomb Basin Jaguar Preserve, I returned to Belize to find a far different world than the one I'd left behind. My study area had become a major tourist destination in Belize, and the Maya people with whom I'd lived and worked now lived on the perimeter of the preserve at a town called Maya Center. They had been granted legal ownership of their land, along with a new school, health clinic, and community center. The swollen bellies from parasites, festering open wounds, and high infant mortality that had been everywhere in 1984 were gone.

The Maya women, who had been confined to their daily chores of cooking and cleaning, were now operating a small craft center for tourists visiting the preserve. At first they made only simple clay-bead necklaces and little clay turtles, but it was not long before the women were using local stone to carve images of jaguars and other animals of the region. Now contributing to the family coffers, the women carried themselves proudly and with greater self-assurance.

But the biggest change I saw was a new respect for the jaguar. Foreigners came from far and wide to visit the Cockscomb Jaguar Preserve and hike into the forest, thrilled at the possibility of just encountering jaguar paw prints or feces. As the local Maya men became guides for the tourists and the Maya women carved and sold crafts, the animal that they had so long feared now provided substantive benefits to their families. The men no longer felt a need to carry guns into the forest for hunting or protection, and the children started telling stories and myths of the jaguar to the tourists as if such knowledge had been handed down since ancient times, though I knew that this was not true.

With new protected areas like Cockscomb supporting a burgeoning ecotourism industry, a new relationship with the jaguar was taking hold in Belize. The jaguar was no longer just a killer of live-stock to be eliminated whenever possible—it now had economic benefit for the people, and jaguars were worth more to the community alive than dead. A jungle with jaguars was a place people wanted to visit, to experience. Jaguar stories and myths from the mouths of the people who lived among them had value as well. This phenomenon not only occurred in Belize, but spread throughout Central and South America, penetrating even into the deep tribal regions of the Amazon, with some communities setting up their own eco-lodges. This relationship of indigenous communities to nature was different from what had existed among their ancestors in the distant past, but the commonality was the re-emerging symbiosis between jaguars and people.

From the almost serendipitous discovery of the jaguar corridor that came about after the 1999 workshop in Mexico, through the rangewide mapping and the initiation of the ground-truthing of the corridor by Kathy Zeller and her team, it took almost 10 years until we had the data and confidence to initiate national agreements with governments throughout jaguar range. These non-binding agreements, now initiated through Panthera, were memorandums of understanding (MOUs) signed by the relevant ministers or representatives of the heads of state that formally recognized the existence of the jaguar corridor in each country. This allowed the corridor data to be incorporated into national databases that would be used for development planning and land-use zoning, a crucial step in a country managing and taking "ownership" over its piece of the jaguar corridor.

Official recognition of the jaguar corridor also, by necessity, acknowledged that the beliefs and activities of the people living inside these areas were important to the maintenance and integrity of the corridor. Not only did the land-use practices of the local people have to remain suitable for jaguar movements, but the people had to refrain from killing the jaguar or even its prey species on which the jaguar depended for survival. I had seen that people's attitudes about jaguars could be changed if there were clear economic benefits related to the species or, at least, if jaguars posed no perceived threats to their lives or livelihoods. Now I also knew that any still-existing myths, stories, or ceremonies relating to jaguars were important for the corridor and could be revitalized within local communities.

As I had witnessed firsthand during my initial trips to both Brazil and Belize, jaguar land and the people of the jaguar had changed radically from what had existed in pre-Columbian times. And while jaguar numbers and jaguar habitat had declined for centuries as human populations and exploitation of the land had steadily increased, the jaguar was not history—it was real. It was not just historical memories that were present in the jaguar corridor, but real memories or recent experiences with an animal that, while no longer seen as supernatural, was part of the life of the people among whom it lived. The new reality of man's relationship to jaguars, whether it was beneficial through ecotourism or contentious due to livestock conflict, had to be recognized and dealt with in a way that enhanced the lives of both. Oral histories of ancient times, where they still existed, needed to be identified and preserved. We had to visit local communities along the jaguar's travel routes to learn more about people's needs, perceptions, and knowledge of the past. This was now part of our mandate to ensure the success of the jaguar corridor.

The forging of government agreements and the interactions with local communities followed our ground-truthing efforts, initially occurring in countries with the most threatened and integral corridors along the jaguar's rangewide travel pathways. But the actual signing of agreements with ministers or heads of state was not as easily scheduled as our other activities. Fortunately, after the Panama Declaration most of the ministers of environment for Central America were already prepared for what we were now asking them to do.

Our first signing of an MOU, however, was not in Central America but in Colombia, one of the most biologically diverse countries in the world, where, ironically, the possibility of losing just a few remaining tendrils of the corridor threatened to split all the Mexican and Central American jaguars from all those in South America. In February 2010, I flew to Bogotá and met with then Vice-President Francisco Santos along with his minister of environment and the director-general of national parks, who signed the agreement to recognize the corridor and secure the tenuous remaining pathway for the jaguar from northwest Colombia into the Colombian Amazon. This was a milestone in our efforts to protect the jaguar corridor, and Colombia, as the founder of the Organization of American States, would help bring other Latin American governments to the table.

Still, it was two years before we could arrange our next government signing. In March 2012, I was on my way to Honduras, the archetypal "banana republic" (a term coined by the writer O. Henry after living in Honduras from 1896 to 1897) and a country of huge concern to our jaguar corridor team. With one of the highest rates of forest loss of any country in Latin America, Honduras now contained relatively little intact forest, few protected areas, and few jaguars. Our maps showed only a very narrow strip of corridor along the Caribbean coast of Honduras, and a blank spot with no clear linkage in the northeast corner of the country near the border with Guatemala. Before signing any agreement with the government, I had to convince myself that the corridor still existed there.

My destination was not Tegucigalpa, the capital, but San Pedro de Sula, whose more than 2 million people make it the country's second largest city and whose industries generated two-thirds of the country's gross domestic product (GDP). This bustling metropolis, the murder capital of the world at the time due to illicit drug and arms trafficking, sat smack in the middle of what we hoped to show was still part of a viable jaguar corridor. After meeting up with Howard Quigley and Honduran biologist and Panthera country coordinator Franklin Castañeda, we drove up into the Merendón Mountains, a degraded, forested watershed overlooking San Pedro

de Sula. Franklin had already learned of the occasional jaguar sightings in these mountains, but no one was bothered by them. People
moved through these mountains carefully, Franklin said, not because
of jaguars but because of the drug activity and murders.

As we crested the main ridge and looked down upon the city, I
could see what our maps and corridor model had not seen. Despite
the proximity to dense human habitation, roads, and industrial development that had caused our model to discard this area as unsuitable,
the forest came right up to both sides of the roads and the rug-
ged topography had lots of suitable water sources. This unlikely area
had all a jaguar needed in order to sneak by. In many ways, this
was an ideal piece of the corridor, probably safer for jaguars than
humans. After two years of intensive fieldwork, Franklin had collected enough track data, camera-trap photos, and actual sightings
to show that jaguars were indeed still present and finding their way
along mountains and forest patches from the northern border with
Guatemala, along the coast of Honduras, to the southern border
with Nicaragua. We continued onward to the Caribbean coast and
spent the next two weeks traversing what was left of the jaguar corridor in Honduras. A few days into the trip we detoured into a small
airport in the city of La Ceiba.

My palms were sweaty as I sat in the co-pilot's seat of a Cessna
206, a slightly larger version of the plane I had crashed in while
working on jaguars in Belize almost three decades earlier. Howard,
Franklin, and I were flying inland to a private airstrip owned by
the Standard Fruit Company. From there, a car would take us to a
relatively remote area of central Honduras, an active piece of the
jaguar corridor occupied by the indigenous Tolupan people. During
my trips to meet with government officials and secure the jaguar
corridor, I took advantage of any opportunity to visit or learn more
about the current beliefs and practices of indigenous communities
that still lived among jaguars.

In the 1950s, anthropologist Anne Chapman studied the Tolupan
and documented their close relationship with wild animals and their
belief in "Masters of Animals" that watched over individual wildlife species. According to Chapman, the Tolupan believed that the
Masters allowed them to hunt what they needed in exchange for

allowing these same species to occasionally feed upon their crops. But if a Tolupan hunted excessively or wounded an animal without killing it, the Master could take vengeance by killing the hunter in an accident. Baptized Indians, they believed, could no longer hunt the Master's animals because they were no longer true Tolupan. Each Master had a real-world assistant, usually either a feline or a bird of prey, which could feed upon the animals but also carry out the Master's wishes. The assistant to the Master of the peccary was the jaguar, and the assistant to the Master of the deer was the puma.

We sent word ahead to alert the Tolupan community of our arrival, requesting a meeting with the elders. A sizeable crowd was on hand to greet us and I was escorted over to where four men were sitting, ranging in age from the 54-year-old headman, Jorge, to Alonzo, who believed he was 98 years old. At first, none of them acknowledged that they knew anything about the Masters of Animals. Eventually, though, one old woman sitting to the side of our group started telling stories about her parents, bragging about her father's hunting prowess. He had spoken about the Masters of Animals, she said. Then, waving her hand towards the men almost dismissively, she said that such things were no longer talked about. They were all Christians now, and most of the wildlife was gone anyway.

Not to be outdone, one of the elders, 85-year-old Timoteo, chimed in to affirm that he too was no longer afraid of the Masters because he believed in God.

"So God controls the animals now?" I asked Timoteo.

"No," he answered immediately. "The Masters still control the animals, but God is more powerful than the Masters so I am not afraid of offending them."

I was to hear this kind of response often during my inquiries with indigenous groups throughout jaguar range. Traditional beliefs and practices, if not forgotten, had often been transformed into some form of Christian animism. Later that year, when Franklin journeyed into the remote 5,000-square-kilometer (1,930-square-mile) Río Plátano Biosphere Reserve, he spoke with two elders of the Pech indigenous community who remembered the rituals their fathers had performed for the Masters of the animals before they went out to hunt. But the Masters were quiet now, the elders said, because they had no power. The power was in the hands of God.

In July 2012, I flew to San José, Costa Rica, to meet with the minister of environment and energy, Dr. Renee Castro Salazar, who had a PhD from Harvard University in natural resource economics. Considered a bastion of environmental foresight with 30 percent of its land in protected areas, Costa Rica was one of the first countries where we put boots on the ground in 2007 to ground-truth the Jaguar Corridor. Five years later the corridor was to become an officially recognized entity. As in Colombia, there was an extensive protected-area system and high biodiversity, but the two important corridors in Costa Rica linking the protected areas were highly vulnerable, which threatened the movements of jaguars and other species. These two corridors contained indigenous reserves of the Cabécar people, a mountain tribe that still maintained some of their traditional practices. I had stayed with the Cabécar as part of the initial survey team in 2007 looking for jaguars in these areas.

After the signing ceremony with the minister, the Costa Rica program director for Panthera, Roberto Salom, drove me to a prearranged meeting with several young Cabécar men at an outdoor café in Limón, part of the same community I had stayed with six years earlier when these men had been in their teens. Unlike the elder Tolupan, these young Cabécar were eager to talk, almost competing with one another to tell stories about how many times they had seen a jaguar around their homes and the problems they had with jaguars occasionally killing their free-roaming pigs. They were dismayed, they said, that jaguars were not as abundant as in their father's time, but at least they had little fear of being attacked by one.

I asked if they thought there was anything more to the jaguar than simply a big cat that killed their pigs, whether they had heard any old stories about jaguars.

No one answered at first. Then the youngest of the three, a man named Arnoldo, spoke up. "Very few of our people follow the old ways anymore," he said. "The elders no longer tell stories from the past because young people don't care. It doesn't help us live. The old stories are like fairy tales."

"Would your life be better off if there were no more jaguars at all?" I asked.

A second man, Énoc, leaned over the table towards me. "Our life is not better now," he said. "When the world was made, jaguars could become humans. They married with humans and lived with humans. Then there was a battle between humans and jaguars and humans won because they had a more powerful bow and arrow and jaguars had only their claws. From then on jaguars respected the people but were not strong anymore and did not change into humans anymore."

Énoc seemed to catch himself and paused, looking almost with embarrassment towards his two friends for their reaction. But they were both nodding their heads in agreement.

"Jaguars are weaker now," Énoc continued. "All the animals are weaker. So the world is weaker. People are much weaker, too."

Énoc leaned back, reached for the Coke I bought him, and was silent. I tried to get more out of him, out of any of them, but the atmosphere of our friendly lunch had turned somewhat somber; perhaps they were pondering both the reality of their words and the conflicts among their beliefs. Strangely, I was heartened. This reinforced my hopes for the continuity of the Jaguar Cultural Corridor, just not in the way I had originally envisioned it. It had become all the more clear to me that, whether masked in Christian animistic beliefs or pushed deep into the recesses of memory to resurface when the need arose, throughout most of jaguar land young and old understood that their survival was linked to the natural world, and that the jaguar was still a force in that world.

My next trip for the jaguar corridor was unexpected. In early 2013, I traveled to Guyana on the invitation of the minister of natural resources, Robert Persaud, who had learned of our work through the media, and wanted Panthera's help in protecting their national animal, the jaguar. With an area of approximately 215,000 square kilometers (83,000 square miles), this former British colony reminded me of the untamed wilderness I'd experienced in Belize when I first arrived there in the early 1980s. The third-smallest nation in South America, Guyana still retained more than 80 percent of its forest intact, one of the largest unbroken stretches on the continent, with most of the fewer than 1 million inhabitants living in the capital of Georgetown or elsewhere along the coast.

Guyana presented opportunities for our corridor work that I had not considered previously. There we might have the ability to examine from the onset the effects of development and fragmentation from mining and roads on large areas of pristine jaguar habitat. Also, as one of nine nations encompassing the 7 million square kilometers (2.7 million square miles) of the Amazon Basin, with nine indigenous tribes still living in remote areas, we could gain insight into cultural effects where the traditional practices of indigenous peoples in this part of the Amazon might still be intact. Panthera's regional coordinator, Dr. Esteban Payan, and one of our biologists, Dr. Evi Paramelee, who were with me on the trip, started to plan our work in a country where we had little data but seemingly lots of jaguars.

With insufficient time to travel into the vast jungle interior in order to visit with some of the most remote tribal groups, I arranged a meeting in Georgetown with Sydney Allicock, an Amerindian and a member of Parliament representing the indigenous communities of the country. Mr. Allicock confirmed to me that practices like shamanism, obeah (folk magic and sorcery mentioned earlier in the book with regard to Belize), and *canaima* (a form of ritual killing called "dark shamanism") were still present in Guyana, but just barely.

The situation was much the same as elsewhere in Latin America, even in a country whose wilderness had remained mostly intact. Most traditional practices were gone from all but the most remote indigenous groups, primarily due to the incursion of the modern world and conversion to Christian beliefs. In 2011, UNESCO declared the Jaguar shamans of the Amazonian rain forest one of 19 cultural traditions around the world in danger of extinction. Mr. Allicock himself knew of only one true shaman still living in Guyana, a man in his late eighties, as well as an apprentice shaman in his thirties. Both said that there would be no one to follow them. But one of Mr. Allicock's last statements to me before we parted reinforced my new perception of the Jaguar Cultural Corridor. "We still have lots of jaguars," he said. "They are not only our national animal, they are part of the strength of the nation."

By 2014, we had ground-truthed the jaguar corridor throughout all of Central America and a few select places in South America. We had signed government agreements to develop national jaguar action plans and to implement jaguar corridor management with the countries of Colombia, Honduras, Costa Rica, Guyana, Panama, Belize, and Nicaragua. High-priority sections of the corridor had been investigated in Brazil and Bolivia. Two new protected areas, needed to ensure connectivity along the corridor route, had been established through our efforts: the Laboring Creek Jaguar Corridor Wildlife Sanctuary of 28 square kilometers (10 square miles), an important stepping-stone for jaguars traversing the corridor in Belize, and San Lucas Park of 3,000 square kilometers (1,158 square miles) in Colombia, preserving the link between the Darien Gap and the eastern plains, and beyond that the Amazon region of Colombia. While most of the corridor that we investigated was still intact, even if tenuous and contracting in places, one important site was not so lucky. The Atlantic Forest in southeastern Brazil, an area of over 4,000 square kilometers (1,500 square miles) and likely where jaguars were first encountered by Portuguese colonists more than 500 years earlier, was now cut off from all other jaguar populations, due to large-scale land conversion for agricultural endeavors. It would be difficult to remedy. The future of this jaguar population was in grave doubt.

There was much work to be done in the years ahead. We wanted no more cases like the Atlantic Forest. Many things—politics, lack of cooperation, funding—would continue to hinder our efforts. But now the Jaguar Corridor was a known, recognized entity, and, as more countries worked with us to secure the corridor, it would become more and more difficult for any single government to allow unfettered development that threatened the integrity of the rest of the corridor. If we continued our efforts, the jaguar corridor would succeed—of that I was convinced.

At the same time, I understood that the ancient folklore and the cultural antecedents of the jaguar's world were changing, probably forever. Still, I was no longer terribly bothered by that fact. The Jaguar Cultural Corridor was not gone, I realized—it was different. Having originated with pre-Columbian indigenous groups, it was now a part of the lives of all those who lived with jaguars. Past beliefs were still valuable and would never be entirely eradicated. Ancient myths might be changed or modernized, but they were rarely lost completely when the subject of the myth, the jaguar, was still manifest in the real world, and when stories could be shown to have as much relevance to the present as to the past. Among the Runa people of Ecuador's Upper Amazon, shamans claim to receive messages from Christian gods, and the were-jaguars that wander the forest are thought to be white. The Nahua people of Mexico describe myth as an ever-present truth, helping people understand who they are and how to live. I heard both the past and the present in the words of Timoteo of the Tolupan, Énoc of the Cabécar, and Sydney Allicock in Guyana.

The original Jaguar Cultural Corridor was created by people living in an environment that was dangerous and challenging—not entirely within their control. Part of that world was dominated by the jaguar, which became a key figure in better understanding and controlling their environment. Diseases brought by European colonization ravaged indigenous communities, replacing their beliefs and practices with Western culture and Western religious beliefs. But while Western culture promoted a stark separation between nature and people, an idea contrary to traditional indigenous views, it didn't deny the role of nature in people's lives.

As people felt more in control of the natural world around them, there was no longer a need to believe in the mystical nature of the jaguar, but there was still a need to understand the natural world in which they lived and which they depended upon. And where the jaguar still walked, respect and awe for the power, potential savagery, and the mystery of the living animal remained. Cultural beliefs and practices often resurfaced in different forms when more modern beliefs proved inadequate. The desire to kill a jaguar and gain power through wearing or displaying its body parts still exists today among many ranchers and hunters. In certain cities and towns, at certain times of year, faces are painted, masks are donned, and stories are told, still linking the people to the jaguars that once lived among them.

What was clear to me, after watching the changes among the Maya in Belize, and after speaking to a multitude of indigenous peoples wherever I traveled through the jaguar corridor, was that the presence of jaguars, whether through economic benefits or spiritual and religious uplift, helped invigorate and strengthen whatever community it was a part of. Where the jaguar roamed, people felt they were a part of something larger and stronger than themselves. Where jaguars were gone or in decline, people felt the loss. The Jaguar Cultural Corridor, having adapted to new people, new beliefs, and the practicalities of the modern world, was still alive.

The human species, with its unregulated population growth, hunting practices, and spread of disease, as well as the pollution, conversion, and destruction of natural habitat, has not always been kind to its own home nor to the other species that live with us. A 2012 book called *The Fate of the Species* by Fred Guterl, executive editor of the journal *Scientific American*, details the unintended consequences of the success of *Homo sapiens* and the real dangers that we, as a species, are now faced with. As he explores a series of very frightening scenarios of our planet in the near future, one of which is continued extinctions of plant and animal species, he explains his view of how ingenuity and technology, which got us into this mess in the first place, could also be the answer to our survival. In the book's final chapter, Guterl concludes that to ensure our own survival, humans will have to take a more active and enlightened role in maintaining the planet's wildlife, and that this task must be informed by good science. His example of how we have already begun to do this? The Jaguar Corridor.

The Jaguar Corridor exists today because the jaguar shaped it and owned it, overcoming all obstacles that stood in its way. Although human beings are relative latecomers to the story of the jaguar, they are the crucial determinant in what comes next for the species. Jaguars and people can live together, but the jaguar needs the help of humans to survive. That help will likely not come easily. But the human race now better understands how jaguars, and other apex predators, help strengthen and maintain the ecological balance of the world they share with us. If we utilize some of the wisdom of the original people of the jaguar, we will not only protect this species but we will learn from it. The jaguar is not simply a part of our natural world, it is part of the answer to our own survival.

As for the jaguar, if it is to survive the activities of the human race in the future—it will need the full measure of its jaguarness— all the audacity, strength, and nonaggression characteristic of the species. I am convinced that the jaguar will prevail. Millions of years of evolution and survival will not easily be snuffed out.

Glossary

Beringia A region extending from western Siberia into North America that includes the Bering land bridge, roughly 1,600 kilometers (1,000 miles) wide at its greatest extent, which connected Asia with North America at various times during the Pleistocene ice age.

breeding dispersal When an individual (often an adult) moves away from one breeding location to breed elsewhere. Usually involves gene flow between populations.

butterfly effect The idea that a very small difference to the initial state of a physical system can make a significant difference to the state of that system at some later time.

Caucasus A mountain range in southwest Russia, running along the northern borders of Georgia and Azerbaijan, between the Black Sea and the Caspian Sea; mostly over 2,700 meters (9,000 feet).

coarse-filter conservation Originally the concept of conserving entire plant and animal communities in reserves, now the coarse-filter approach has evolved to conserving species diversity by providing adequate representation (distribution and abundance) of ecological land units. This approach does not necessarily prescribe reserves, but recognizes ecological processes and provides for a dynamic distribution of ecological units across the landscape over time.

epigenetic Denoting processes by which heritable modifications in gene function occur without a change in the sequence of the DNA.

Felidae The biological family of the cats; a member of this family is called a *felid*. Extant felids belong to one of two subfamilies: Pantherinae (which includes the tiger, the lion, the jaguar, the leopard, the snow leopard, and the clouded leopard), and Felinae (which includes the cougar, the cheetah, the lynxes, the ocelot, and the domestic cat).

fine-filter conservation An approach focused on conserving individual rare or specialized species that might slip through the coarse-filter model and are not necessarily protected in designated reserves.

genetic connectivity Gene flow or exchange between populations of plants and animals, necessary for increasing genetic diversity, maintaining healthy populations, and decreasing the risk of extinction.

genetic memory Memory present at birth that exists in the absence of sensory experience.

ground-truthing A term used in remote sensing, referring to information collected on location. Ground-truthing allows image data to be related to real features and materials on the ground and thus aids in the interpretation and analysis of what is being sensed.

GIS Geographic Information System, describing any information system that integrates, stores, edits, analyzes, shares, and displays geographic information for informing decision making. GIS applications are tools that allow users to analyze spatial information, edit data in maps, and present the results of all these operations.

hominids Used in this book in the more restricted sense as hominins or humans and relatives of humans closer than chimpanzees. All hominid species other than *Homo sapiens* are extinct.

Ice Age The most recent glacial period, which occurred during the Pleistocene Epoch, approximately 2 million to 10,000 years ago.

Latin America The countries of the Western Hemisphere south of the United States, especially those speaking Spanish, Portuguese, or French.

least-cost corridor model A method for predicting most likely movements leading to functional connectivity between designated sites, based on parameters relating to dispersal and movement behavior of the species in question, and accounting for landscape structure.

megafauna The component of the fauna of a region or period that comprises the larger terrestrial animals.

Mesoamerica A region extending south and east from central Mexico to include parts of Guatemala, Belize, Honduras, and Nicaragua.

natal dispersal The movement of an individual (often a juvenile) away from the place it was born to breed and settle in a new location.

obeah A form of religious belief involving sorcery, of African origin and practiced in some parts of the West Indies, Jamaica, and nearby tropical America.

Panthera A genus within the Felidae family comprising the tiger, lion, jaguar, and leopard on the basis of cranial features. Results of genetic analysis indicate that the snow leopard also belongs to the Panthera. Only the tiger, lion, leopard, and jaguar have the anatomical structure that enables them to roar. Panthera is also the name of the charitable organization that the author helped to found and now leads as CEO (www.panthera.org).

pantherine Term used to describe the early Panthera-like cats that diverged from the subfamily Felinae.

permeability Capable of being penetrated or passed through. In the case of the jaguar corridor, the level of ease with which a jaguar can move through an area.

phylogency The evolutionary history of a group of organisms.

Pleistocene Pertaining to the epoch forming the earlier half of the Quaternary Period, beginning about 2 million years ago and ending 10,000 years ago, characterized by widespread glacial ice and the advent of modern humans.

race An interbreeding, usually geographically isolated, population of organisms differing from other populations of the same species in the frequency of hereditary traits. A race that has been given formal taxonomic recognition is known as a subspecies.

refugia Geographical regions that remained unaltered by climatic changes that have affected surrounding regions, forming a haven for relict fauna and flora.

source population A reproducing group of organisms that produces enough offspring to be self-sustaining and provide excess young that must disperse to other areas.

subspecies See definition of *race*.

shaman A member of certain tribal societies who acts as a medium between the visible world and an invisible spirit world and who practices magic or sorcery for purposes of healing, divination, and control over natural events.

tigre (**or** *el tigre*) Spanish term for jaguar.

topotype A specimen of an organism taken from the type locality (the place where the individual was taken, as used for the naming of the species).

totem An animal, plant, or natural object serving among certain tribal or traditional peoples as the emblem of a clan or family and sometimes revered as its founder, ancestor, or guardian.

Bibliography

Note to the reader: All of the quotations, facts, and figures in this book are drawn from the sources listed below, chapter by chapter.

Chapter 2: The Pleistocene Jaguar Corridor

Barnett, R., I. Barnes, M. J. Phillips, L. D. Martin, C. R. Harington, J. A. Leonard, and A. Cooper. "Evolution of the Extinct Sabretooths and the American Cheetah-like Cat." *Current Biology* 15, no. 15 (2005): 589–90. DOI:10.1016/j.cub.2005.07.052.

Christiansen, P. "Phylogeny of the Great Cats (Felidae: Pantherinae) and the Influence of Fossil Taxa and Missing Characters." *Cladistics* 24, no. 6 (2008): 977–92.

Christiansen, P. "Craniomandibular Morphology and Phylogenetic Affinities of *Panthera atrox*: Implications for the Evolution and Paleobiology of the Lion Lineage." *Journal of Vertebrate Paleontology* 29, no. 3 (2009): 934–45.

Eizirik, E., J. H. Kim, M. Menotti-Raymond, P. G. Crawshaw, S. J. O'Brien, and W. Johnson. "Phylogeography, Populations, History, and Conservation Genetics of Jaguars (*Panthera onca*, Mammalia, Felidae)." *Molecular Ecology* 10 (2001): 65–79.

Fagundes, N. J. R., et al. "Mitochondrial Population Genomics Supports a Single Pre-Clovis Origin with a Coastal Route for the Peopling of the Americas." *Genetics* 82, no. 3 (2008): 583–92.

Harpending, H. C., M. A. Batzer, M. Gurven, L. B. Jorde, A. R. Rogers, and S. T. Sherry. "Genetic Traces of Ancient Demography." *Proceedings of the National Academy of Science* 95 (1998): 1–7.

Haury, E. W. *The Stratigraphy and Archaeology of Ventana Cave, Arizona.* Tucson, AZ: University of Arizona Press, 1975.

Hemmer, H., R.-D. Kahlke, and A. K. Vekua. "The Jaguar—*Panthera onca gombaszoegensis* (Kretzoi, 1938) (Carnivora: Felidae) in the Late Lower Pleistocene of Akhalkalaki (South Georgia, Transcaucasia) and Its Evolutionary and Ecological Significance." *Geobios* 34 (2001): 475–86.

Hemmer, H., R.-D. Kahlke, and A. K. Vekua. "*Panthera onca georgica* ssp. nov. from the Early Pleistocene of Dmanisi (Republic of Georgia) and the Phylogeography of Jaguars (Mammalia, Carnivora, Felidae)." *Neues Jahrbuch für Geologie und Paläontologie, Abhandlungen* 257 7/1 (2010): 115–27.

Hemmer, H., R.-D. Kahlke, and A. K. Vekua. "The Cheetah *Acinonyx pardinensis* (Croizet et Jobert, 1828) s.l. at the Hominin Site of Dmanisi (Georgia)—A Potential Prime Meat Supplier in Early Pleistocene Ecosystems." *Quaternary Science Reviews* 30 (2011): 2703–14.

Johnson, W. E., E. Eizirik, J. Pecon-Slattery, W. J. Murphy, A. Antunes, E. Telling, and S. O'Brien. "The Late Miocene Radiation of Modern Felidae: A Genetic Assessment." *Science* 311 (2006): 73–77.

Koch, P. L., and A. D. Barnosky. "Late Quaternary Extinctions: State of the Debate." *Annual Review of Ecology, Evolution, and Systematics* 37 (2006): 215–50.

Kurten, B. *Pleistocene Mammals of Europe.* London: Transaction Publishers, 2007.

Kurten, B., and E. Anderson. *Pleistocene Mammals of North America.* New York: Columbia University Press, 1980.

MacPhee, R. D., and P. A. Marx. "The 40,000-Year-Plague: Humans, Hyperdisease, and First-Contact Extinctions." In *Natural Change and Human Impact in Madagascar*, edited by S. M. Goodman and B. D. Patterson, 169–217. Washington, DC: Smithsonian Institute Press, 1997.

Martin, P. S., and H. E. Wright. *Pleistocene Extinctions: The Search for a Cause.* New Haven: Yale University Press, 1967.

Mattern, M. Y., and D. A. McLennan. "Phylogeny and Speciation of Felids." *Cladistics* 16 (2000): 232–53.

Mazak, J. H., P. Christiansen, A. C. Kitchener. "Oldest Known Pantherine Skull and Evolution of the Tiger." *PloS ONE* 6, no. 10 (2011): 1–23.

O'Regan, H. J., A. Turner, and D. M. Wilkinson. "European Quaternary Refugia: A Factor in Large Carnivore Extinction?" *Journal of Quaternary Science* 17, no 8 (2002): 789–95.

Prescott, G. W., D. R. Williams, A. Balmford, R. E. Green, and A. Manica. "Quantitative Global Analysis of the Role of Climate and People in Explaining Late Quaternary Megafaunal Extinctions." *Proceedings of the National Academy of Science* 109, no 12 (2012): 4527–31.

Sawyer, G. J., and V. Deak. *The Last Human: A Guide to Twenty-Two Species of Extinct Humans.* New Haven: Yale University Press, 2007.

Seymour, K. "Size Change in North American Quaternary Jaguars." In *Morphological Change in Quaternary Mammals of North America*, edited by R. A. Martin and A. D. Barnosky. New York: Cambridge University Press, 1993.

Simpson, G. G. "Large Pleistocene Felines of North America." *American Museum Novitates* 1131 (1941): 1–27.

Tseng, Z., X. Wang, G. J. Slater, G. T. Takeuchi, Q. Li, J. Liu, and G. Xie. "Himalayan Fossils of the Oldest Known Pantherine Establish Ancient Origin of the Big Cats." *Proceedings of the Royal Society B* 281, no. 1774 (2013): 20132686. http://dx.doi.org/10.1098/rspb.2913.2686.

Wallace, S. C., and R. C. Hulbert Jr. "A New Machairodont from the Palmetto Fauna (Early Pliocene) of Florida, with Comments on the Origin of the Smilodontini (Mammalia, Carnivora, Felidae)." *PloS ONE* 8, no. 3 (2013): e56173. DOI:10.1371/journal.pone.0056173.

Wei, L., X. Wu, L. Zhu, and Z. Jiang. "Mitogenomic Analysis of the Genus *Panthera*." *Science China Life Sciences* 54, no. 10 (2011): 917–30.

Weissengruber, G. E., G. Forestenpointner, G. Peters, A. Kubber-Heiss, and W. T. Fitch. "Hyoid Apparatus and Pharynx in the Lion (*Panthera leo*), Jaguar (*Panthera onca*), Tiger (*Panthera tigris*), Cheetah (*Acinonyx jubatus*) and Domestic Cat *(Felis Silvestris f. catus)*." *Journal of Anatomy* 201 (2002): 195–209.

Chapter 3: The First People of the Jaguar

Bell, M., and M. J. C. Walker. *Late Quaternary Environmental Change: Physical and Human Perspectives.* New York: Longman Scientific and Technical, J. Wiley & Sons, 1992.

Davis, W. *Shadows in the Sun.* Washington, DC: Island Press, 1998.

Kurten, B., and E. Anderson. *Pleistocene Mammals of North America.* New York: Columbia University Press, 1980.

McKey, D., S. Rostain, J. Iriarte, B. Glaser, J. J. Birk, I. Hoist, and D. Renard. "Pre-Columbian Agricultural Landscapes, Ecosystem Engineers, and Self-Organized Patchiness in Amazonia." *Proceedings of the National Academy of Science* 107, no. 17 (2010): 7823–28.

O'Connell, J. F., K. Hawkes, and N. B. Jones. "Hadza Scavenging: Implications for Plio/Pleistocene Hominid Subsistence." *Current Anthropology* 29, no. 2 (1988): 356–63.

Radding, C. *Landscapes of Power and Identity: Comparative Histories in the Sonoran Desert and the Forests of Amazonia from Colony to Republic.* Durham, NC: Duke University Press, 2005.

Redman, C. L. *Human Impact on Ancient Environments.* Tucson, AZ: University of Arizona Press, 1999.

Saunders, N. *The People of the Jaguar.* London: Souvenir Press, 1989.

Stanford, C. B. *The Hunting Apes: Meat Eating and the Origins of Human Behavior.* Princeton, NJ: Princeton University Press, 1999.

Treves, A., and L. Naughton-Treves. "Risk and Opportunity for Humans Coexisting with Large Carnivores." *Journal of Human Evolution* 36 (1999): 275–82.

Chapter 4: When Jaguars Talked to Man

Ballinger, D. A., and J. Stomper. "The Jaguars of Altar Q, Copán, Honduras: Faunal Analysis, Archaeology, and Ecology." *Journal of Ethnobiology* 20, no. 2 (2000): 223–36.

Hibben, F. *Kiva Art of the Anasazi at Pottery Mount.* Las Vegas, NV: KC Publications, 1975.

Houston, S., and D. Stuart. "The Way Glyph: Evidence for 'Co-essences' among the Classic Maya." In *The Decipherment of Ancient Maya Writing,* edited by S. Houston, O. C. Mazariegos, and D. Stuart, 449–62. Norman, OK: University of Oklahoma Press, 2001.

Milton, G., and R. Gonzalo. "Jaguar Cult—Down's Syndrome—Were-Jaguar." *Expedition* 16, no. 4 (1974): 33–37.

Pavlik, S. "Rohonas and Spotted Lions: The Historical and Cultural Occurrence of the Jaguar, *Panthera onca*, among the Native Tribes of the American Southwest." *Wicazo Sa Review* (U. of Minnesota Press) 18, no. 1 (2003): 157–75.

Perreira, V. *The Last Lords of Palenque.* Boston: Little, Brown and Co., 1982.

Perry, R. *The World of the Jaguar.* New York: Taplinger Press, 1970.

Reichel-Dolmatoff, G. *The Shaman and the Jaguar: A Study of Narcotic Drugs among the Indians of Columbia.* Philadelphia: Temple University Press, 1975.

Saunders, N. J. "The Day of the Jaguar." *Geographical Magazine,* August issue, 1983.

Saunders, N. J. *People of the Jaguar.* London: Souvenir Press, 1989.

Saunders, N. J. *The Cult of the Cat.* London: Thames and Hudson, 1991.

Vitebsky, P. *The Shaman: Voyages of the Soul, Trance, Ecstasy and Healing from Siberia to the Amazon.* London: Watkins Publishing Ltd., 1995.

Wright, R. M. *Mysteries of the Jaguar Shamans of the Northwest Amazon.* Lincoln: University of Nebraska Press, 2013.

Zorich, Z. "Fighting with Jaguars, Bleeding for Rain." *Archaeology* 6, no. 6 (2008): archive.archaeology.org/0811/etc/boxing.html

Chapter 5: The Conquest of Jaguar Land

Coates, A. G., ed. *Central America: A Natural and Cultural History.* New Haven, CT: Yale University Press, 1997.

Kupperman, K. O. *Indians and English: Facing Off in Early America.* Ithaca, NY: Cornell University Press, 2000.

MacLeod, M. J. "Exploitation of Natural Resources in Colonial Central America: Indian and Spanish Approaches." In *Changing Tropical Forests,* edited by H. K. Steen and R. P. Tucker. Durham, NC: Forest History Society, 1992.

Miller, S. W. *An Environmental History of Latin America.* Cambridge, UK: Cambridge University Press, 2007.

Patton, S., A. Rabinowitz, S. Randolph, and S. Strawbridge. "A Coprological Survey of Parasites of Wild Neotropical Felidae." *Journal of Parasitology* 72, no. 4 (1986): 517–20.

Powell, D. "Columbus' Arrival Linked to Carbon Dioxide Drop." *Science News* 180, no. 10 (2011): 12.

Redman, C. *Human Impacts on Ancient Environments.* Tucson, AZ: University of Arizona Press, 1999.

Restall, M. *Seven Myths of the Spanish Conquest.* Oxford: Oxford University Press, 2003.

Scurlock, D. "El Tigre: The Jaguar in the Southwest Borderlands." *Password* 51, no. 4 (2006): 159–75.

Simonian, L. *Defending the Land of the Jaguar: A History of Conservation in Mexico.* Austin, TX: University of Texas Press, 1995.

Chapter 6: The Killing Grounds

Carey, N. *The Epigenetics Revolution: How Modern Biology Is Rewriting Our Understanding of Genetics, Disease, and Inheritance.* New York: Columbia University Press, 2012.

Carmony, N. B., and D. E. Brown, eds. *Mexican Game Trails: Americans Afield in Old Mexico, 1866–1940.* Norman, OK: University of Oklahoma Press, 1991.

Coates, A. G., ed. *Central America: A Natural and Cultural History.* New Haven, CT: Yale University Press, 1997.

Daugherty, H. E. "The Impact of Man on the Zoogeography of El Salvador." *Biological Conservation* 4, no. 4 (1972): 273–78.

De Almeida, T. *Jaguar Hunting in the Mato Grosso and Bolivia.* Long Beach, CA: Safari Press, 1990.

Doughty, R. W., and N. Myers. "Notes on the Amazon Wildlife Trade." *Biological Conservation* 3, no. 4 (1971): 293–97.

Duguid, J. *Tiger Man.* London: Victor Gollancz Ltd., 1932.

Fitzgerald, S. *International Wildlife Trade: Whose Business Is It?* Washington, DC: WWF-US, 1989.

Haig, D. "The (Dual) Origin of Epigenetics." In *Cold Spring Harbor Symposia on Quantitative Biology,* Vol. LXIX, 1–4. New York: Cold Spring Harbor Laboratory Press, 2004.

Kozak, V. "Ritual of a Bororo Funeral." *Natural History* 72, no. 1 (1963): 38–49.

Kroeber, A. L. "A Preliminary Sketch of the Mohave Indians." *American Anthropologist* 4 (1902): 276–85.

Kroeber, A. L. "Two Myths of the Mission Indians of California." *Journal of American Folklore* 19 (1906): 309–21.

Lankford, G. E. "Pleistocene Animals in Folk Memory." *Journal of American Folklore* 93, no. 369 (1980): 293–304.

Leopold, A. "Conservationist in Mexico." *American Forests* 43 (1937): 118–20.

Leopold, A. *A Sand County Almanac.* New York: Oxford University Press, 1949.

Mahler, R. *The Jaguar's Shadow: Searching for a Mythic Cat.* New Haven, CT: Yale University Press, 2009.

Miller, S. W. *An Environmental History of Latin America.* Cambridge, UK: Cambridge University Press, 2007.

Radding, C. *Landscapes of Power and Identity: Comparative Histories in the Sonoran Desert and the Forests of Amazonia from Colony to Republic.* Durham, NC: Duke University Press, 2005.

Schacter, D. L. *The Seven Sins of Memory.* Boston: Houghton Mifflin Co., 2001.

Smith, N. "Spotted Cats and the Amazon Skin Trade." *Oryx* 17, no. 4 (1976): 362–71.

Spector, T. *Identically Different: Why We Can Change Our Genes.* New York: Overlook Press, 2012.

Waddington, C. H. "The Epigenotype." *Endeavour* 1 (1942): 18.

Chapter 7: Into the Jaguar's World

Darwin, C. *Selected Works of Charles Darwin: Journal of Researches into the Natural History and Geology of the Countries Visited during the Voyage of H.M.S. Beagle round the World.* New York: D. Appleton & Co., 1897.

Duguid, J. *Green Hell: A Chronicle of Travel in the Forests of Eastern Bolivia.* Pomona, CA: Pomona Press, 2006. Reprint from original 1931 edition.

Heckadon-Moreno, S. "Spanish Rule, Independence, and the Modern Colonization Frontiers." In *Central America: A Natural and Cultural History,* edited by A. G. Coates. New Haven, CT: Yale University Press, 1997.

Hemley, G. *International Wildlife Trade: A CITES Sourcebook.* Washington, DC: Island Press, 1994.

International Union for the Conservation of Nature (IUCN). *Protected Areas of the World: A Review of National Systems.* Vol. 4, *Nearctic and Neotropical.* Gland, Switzerland: IUCN, 1992.

Miller, S. W. *An Environmental History of Latin America*. Cambridge: Cambridge University Press, 2007.

Miller, C. S., M. Hebblewhite, J. M. Goodrich, and D. Miquelle. "Review of Research Methodologies for Tigers: Telemetry." *Integrative Zoology* 5 (2010): 378–89.

Perry, R. *The World of the Jaguar*. New York: Taplinger Press, 1970.

Redman, C. *Human Impact on Ancient Environments*. Tucson, AZ: University of Arizona Press, 1999.

Shoumatoff, A. *The Rivers Amazon*. San Francisco: Sierra Club Books, 1978.

Simonian, L. *Defending the Land of the Jaguar: A History of Conservation in Mexico*. Austin, TX: University of Texas Press, 1995.

Chapter 8: Meals on the Hoof

Bradley, D. G. "Genetic Hoofprints." *Natural History* 112 (Feb. 2003).

Caras, R. A. *A Perfect Harmony: The Intertwining Lives of Animals and Humans Throughout History*. New York: Simon and Shuster, 1996.

Conforti, V. A., and F. C. C. de Azevedo. "Local Perceptions of Jaguars (*Panthera onca*) and Pumas (*Puma concolor*) in the Iguacu National Park Area, South Brazil." *Biological Conservation* 111, no. 2 (2003): 215–21.

Hoogesteijn, R., and A. Hoogesteijn. "Conflicts between Cattle Ranching and Large Predators in Venezuela: Could Use of Water Buffalo Facilitate Felid Conservation?" *Oryx* 42, no. 1 (2008): 132–38.

Hoogesteijn, R., A. Hoogesteijn, and E. Mondolfi. "Jaguar Predation and Conservation: Cattle Mortality Caused by Felines on Three Ranches in the Venezuelan Llanos." In *Mammals as Predators*, edited by N. Dunstone and M. L. Gorman, 391–407. London: Symposia of the Zoological Society 65, 1993.

Inskip, C., and A. Zimmermann. "Human–Felid Conflict: A Review of Patterns and Priorities Worldwide." *Oryx* 43, no. 1 (2009): 18–34.

Marchini, S., and D. W. Macdonald. "Predicting Ranchers' Intention to Kill Jaguars: Case Studies in Amazonia and Pantanal." *Biological Conservation* 135 (2012): 213–21.

Michalski, R., R. L. P. Boulhosa, A. Faria, and C. A. Peres. "Human-Wildlife Conflicts in a Fragmented Amazonian Forest Landscape: Determinants of Large Felid Depredation on Livestock." *Animal Conservation* 9 (2006): 179–88.

Polisar, J., I. Maxit, D. Scognamillo, L. Farrell, M. Sunquist, and J. F. Eisenberg. "Jaguars, Pumas, Their Prey Base, and Cattle Ranching: Ecological Interpretations of a Management Problem." *Biological Conservation* 109 (2003): 297–310.

Rabinowitz, A. *Jaguar: One Man's Struggle to Establish the World's First Jaguar Preserve.* Washington, DC: Island Press, 1984.

Rabinowitz, A. "Jaguar Predation on Domestic Livestock." *Wildlife Society Bulletin* 14, no. 2 (1984): 170–74.

Rabinowitz, A., and B. Nottingham. "Ecology and Behavior of the Jaguar (*Panthera onca*) in Belize, Central America." *Journal of Zoology, London* (A) 210 (1986): 149–59.

Rosas-Rosas, O. C., L. C. Bender, and R. Valdez. "Jaguar and Puma Predation on Cattle Calves in Northeastern Sonora, Mexico." *Rangeland Ecology and Management* 61 (2008): 554–60.

Zimmermann, A., M. J. Walpole, and N. Leader-Williams. "Cattle Ranchers' Attitudes to Conflicts with Jaguar *Panthera onca* in the Pantanal of Brazil." *Oryx* 39, no. 4 (2005): 406–12.

Chapter 9: Thinking to Scale

Bottrill, M. C., et al. "Is Conservation Triage Just Smart Decision Making?" *Trends in Ecology and Evolution* 23, no. 12 (2008): 649–54.

Eizirik, E., J. Kim, M. Menotti-Raymond, P. G. Crawshaw, S. J. O'Brien, and W. E. Johnson. "Phylogeography, Population History and Conservation Genetics of Jaguars (*Panthera onca*, Mammalia, Felidae)." *Molecular Ecology* 10 (2001): 65–79.

Forman, R. T. T., and M. Gordon. *Landscape Ecology.* New York: Wiley, 1986.

Heckadon-Moreno, S. "Spanish Rule, Independence, and the Modern Colonization Frontiers." In *Central America: A Natural and Cultural History,* edited by A. G. Coates. New Haven, CT: Yale University Press, 1997.

Larson, S. E. "Taxonomic Re-evaluation of the Jaguar." *Zoo Biology* 16 (1997): 107–20.

MacArthur, R. H., and E. O. Wilson. *The Theory of Island Biogeography.* Princeton, NJ: Princeton University Press, 1967.

Medellin, R. A., C. Chetkiewicz, A. Rabinowitz, K. H. Redford, J. G. Robinson, E. W. Sanderson, and A. Taber. *El jaguar en el nuevo milenio: Una evaluación de su estado, detección de prioridades y recomendaciones para la conservación de los jaguares en América*. Mexico City: Universidad Nacional Autónoma de México and Wildlife Conservation Society, 2001.

Meyers, N., R. A. Mittermeier, C. G. Mittermeier, G. A. B. da Fonseca, and J. Kent. "Biodiversity Hotspots for Conservation Priorities." *Nature* 403 (2000): 853–58.

Nelson, E. W., and E. A. Goldman. "Revision of the Jaguars." *Journal of Mammalogy* 14 (1933): 221–40.

Noss, R. F., and L. D. Harris. "Nodes, Networks and MUM's: Preserving Diversity at All Scales." *Environmental Management* 10 (1986): 299–309.

Olson, D. M., and E. Dinerstein. "The Global 200: A Representation Approach to Conserving the Earth's Most Biologically Valuable Regions." *Conservation Biology* 12 (1998): 502–15.

Pocock, R. I. "The Races of Jaguar (*Panthera onca*)." *Novitates Zoologicae* 41 (1939): 406–22.

Quigley, H., and P. Crawshaw. "A Conservation Plan for the Jaguar *Panthera onca* in the Pantanal Region of Brazil." *Biological Conservation* 61 (1992): 149–57.

Rabinowitz, A. *Jaguar: One Man's Battle to Establish the World's First Jaguar Preserve*. Washington, DC: Island Press, 1986.

Read, B. E. *Chinese Materia Medica: Animal Drugs*. Taipei: Southern Materials Center, 1982.

Redford, K. H. "The Empty Forest." *BioScience* 42, no. 6 (1992): 412–22.

Sanderson, E. W., K. H. Redford, C. B. Chetkiewicz, R. A. Medellin, A. Rabinowitz, J. Robinson, and A. Taber. "Planning to Save a Species: The Jaguar as a Model." *Conservation Biology* 16, no. 1 (2002): 58–72.

Soule, M. E. "What Is Conservation Biology?" *Bioscience* 35 (1985): 727–34.

Soule, M. E., and M. Terborgh. "A Global Perspective on Large Carnivore Conservation." *Conservation Biology* 10 (1999): 1045–54.

Swank, W. G., and J. G. Teer. "Status of the Jaguar—1987." *Oryx* 23, no. 1 (1989): 14–21.

Wikramanayake, E. D., E. Dinerstein, J. G. Robinson, U. Karanth, A. Rabinowitz, D. Olson, T. Mathew, P. Hedao, M. Conner, G. Hemley, and D. Bolze. "An Ecology-Based Method for Defining Priorities for Large Mammal Conservation: The Tiger as Case Study." *Conservation Biology* 12 (1998): 865–78.

Wilson, K. A., J. Carwardine, and H. P. Possingham. "Setting Conservation Priorities." *Annals of the New York Academy of Sciences* 1162 (2009): 237–64.

Chapter 10: The Underground Railway of the Jaguar

Adriaensen, F., J. P. Chardon, G. De Blust, E. Swinnen, S. Villalba, H. Gulinck, and E. Matthysen. "The Application of 'Least-Cost' Modeling as a Functional Landscape Model." *Landscape and Urban Planning* 64 (2003): 233–47.

Boecklen, W. J. "Optimal Design of Nature Reserves: Consequences of Genetic Drift." *Biological Conservation* 38 (1986): 323–38.

Chabris, C., and D. Simons. *The Invisible Gorilla: How Our Intuitions Deceive Us.* New York: MJF Books, 2010.

Crawshaw, P., and H. Quigley. "Jaguar Spacing, Activity, and Habitat Use in a Seasonally Flooded Environment in Brazil." *Journal of Zoology London* 223 (1991): 357–70.

Fattebert, J., T. Dickerson, G. Balme, R. Slotow, and L. Hunter. "Long-Distance Natal Dispersal in Leopard Reveals Potential for a Three-Country Metapopulation." *South African Journal of Wildlife Research* 43, no. 1 (2013): 61–67.

Grandia, L. "Between Bolivar and Bureaucracy: The Mesoamerican Biological Corridor." *Conservation and Society* 5, no. 4 (2007): 478–503.

Holland, M. B. "Mesoamerican Biological Corridor." In *Climate and Conservation: Landscape and Seascape Science, Planning, and Action*, edited by J. A. Hilty, C. C. Chester, and M. S. Cross, 56–66. Washington, DC: Island Press, 2012.

Illeuca, J. "The Paso Pantera Agenda for Regional Conservation." In *Central America: A Natural and Cultural History*, edited by A. G. Coates, 241–57. New Haven, CT: Yale University Press, 1997.

Leopold, A. *Wildlife of Mexico.* Berkeley: University of California Press, 1959.

Logan, K. A., and L. L. Sweanor. "Puma." In *Ecology and Management of Large Mammals in North America*, edited by S. Demarias and P. R. Krausman, 347–77. Upper Saddle River, NJ: Prentice Hall, 2000.

Logan, K. A., and L. L. Sweanor. *Desert Puma: Evolutionary Ecology and Conservation of an Enduring Carnivore.* Washington, DC: Island Press, 2001.

Manel, S., M. K. Schwartz, G. Luikart, and P. Taberlet. "Landscape Genetics: Combining Landscape Ecology and Population Genetics." *Trends in Ecology and Evolution* 18, no. 4 (2003): 189–97.

Miller, S. W. *An Environmental History of Latin America.* New York: Cambridge University Press, 2007.

Mills, L. S., and F. W. Allendorf. "The One-Migrant-per-Generation Rule in Conservation and Management." *Conservation Biology* 10 (1996): 1509–18.

Muhly, T. B., C. Sernenluk, A. Massolo, L. Hickman, and M. Musiani. "Human Activity Helps Prey Win the Predator-Prey Space Race." *PLoS ONE* 6, no. 3 (2011): e17050. DOI: 10.1371/journal.pone.0017050.

Steen, H. K., and R. P. Tucker, eds. *Changing Tropical Forests: Historical Perspectives on Today's Challenges in Central and South America*. Durham, NC: Forestry History Society, 1992.

Rabinowitz, A., and K. Zeller. "A Range-Wide Model of Landscape Connectivity and Conservation for the Jaguar, *Panthera onca*." *Biological Conservation* 143 (2010): 939–45.

Ruiz-Garcia, M., E. Payan, A. Murillo, and D. Alvarez. "DNA Microsatellite Characterization of the Jaguar (*Panthera onca*) in Colombia." *Genes and Genetic Systems* 81 (2006): 115–27.

Zeller, K. A., S. Nijhawan, R. Salom-Perez, S. H. Potosme, and J. E. Hines. "Integrating Occupancy Modeling and Interview Data for Corridor Identification: A Case Study for Jaguars in Nicaragua." *Biological Conservation* 144 (2011): 892–901.

Zeller, K. A., A. Rabinowitz, R. Salon-Perez, and H. Quigley. "The Jaguar Corridor Initiative: A Range-Wide Conservation Strategy." In *Molecular Population Genetics*, edited by M. Ruiz-Garcia and J. M. Shostell. Hauppauge, NY: Nova Science Publishers, 2013.

Chapter 11: Borderland Jaguars

Brown, D. F. "On the Status of the Jaguar in the Southwest." *Southwestern Naturalist* 28 (1983): 459–60.

Brown, D. E., and C. A. L. Gonzalez. *Borderland Jaguars*. Salt Lake City, UT: University of Utah Press, 2001.

Childs, J., and A. M. Childs. *Ambushed on the Jaguar Trail: Hidden Cameras on the Mexican Border*. Tucson, AZ: Rio Nuevo Publishers, 2008.

Coues, E. "The Quadrupeds of Arizona." *American Naturalist* 1, no. 6 (1867): 281–92.

Davis, G. P. *Man and Wildlife in Arizona: The American Exploration Period 1824–1865*. Phoenix, AZ: Arizona Fish and Game Department, 2001.

Glenn, W. *Eyes of Fire: Encounter with a Borderlands Jaguar*. El Paso, TX: Printing Corner Press, 1996.

Lopez-Gonzalez, C.A., and D. E. Brown. "Distribución y estado de conservación actuales del jaguar en el Noroeste de México." In *El jaguar en el nuevo milenio: Una evaluación de su estado, detección de prioridades y recomendaciones para la conservación de los jaguares en América*, edited by R.A. Medellin, C. Chetkiewicz, A. Rabinowitz, K. H. Redford, J. G. Robinson, E. W. Sanderson, and A. Taber, 379–91. Mexico City: Universidad Nacional Autónoma de México and Wildlife Conservation Society, 2001.

McCain, E. B., and J. L. Childs. "Evidence of Resident Jaguars (*Panthera onca*) in the Southwestern United States and the Implications for Conservation." *Journal of Mammalogy* 89, no. 1 (2008): 1–10.

Rabinowitz, A. R. "The Present Status of Jaguars (*Panthera onca*) in the Southwestern United States." *Southwestern Naturalist* 44, no. 1 (1999): 96–100.

Salzman, J. "Evolution and Application of Critical Habitat under the Endangered Species Act." *Harvard Environmental Law Review* 14 (1990): 311–42.

Swank, W. G., and J. G. Teer. "Status of the Jaguar—1987." *Oryx* 23, no. 1 (1989): 14–21.

Chapter 12: In Search of Jaguarness

Andrews, T. *Animal-Speak: The Spiritual and Magical Powers of Creatures Great and Small*. St. Paul, MN: Llewellyn Publications, 1998.

Aranda, M. "Importancia de los pecaríes (*Tayassu* spp.) en la alimentación del jaguar (*Panthera onca*)." *Acta Zoológica Mexicana* 62 (1994): 11–22.

Barrett, L. *Beyond the Brain: How Body and Environment Shape Animal and Human Minds.* Princeton, NJ: Princeton University Press, 2011.

Bonner, J. T. *Why Size Matters*. Princeton, NJ: Princeton University Press, 2006.

Christiansen, P. "Canine Morphology in the Larger Felidae: Implications for Feeding Ecology." *Biological Journal of the Linnean Society* 91 (2007): 573–92.

Crandall, L. S. *The Management of Wild Mammals in Captivity*. Chicago: University of Chicago Press, 1964.

Del Moral Sachetti, J. F., F. I. Lameda Camacaro, J. S. Vazquez, and R. Zenteno Cardenas. "Fuerza de mordedura y estrés mandibular en el jaguar: (*Panthera onca*) durante la depredación de pecaríes (Artiodactyla: Tayassuidae) mediante la fractura de sus cráneos." *Acta Zoológica Mexicana* 27, no. 3 (2011): 757–76.

Denis, A. *Cats of the World*. London: Constable & Co., 1964.

Emmons, L. "Feeding Ecology of Felids in a Neotropical Rainforest." *Behavioral Ecology and Sociobiology* 20, no. 4 (1987): 271–83.

Emmons, L. H. "Jaguar Predation on Chelonians." *Journal of Herpetology* 23, no. 3 (1989): 311–14.

Hornaday, W. T. *Hornaday's American Natural History*. New York: Charles Scribner's Sons, 1927.

Meachen-Samuels, J., and B. Van Valkenburgh. "Forelimb Indicators of Prey-Size Preference in the Felidae." *Journal of Mammalogy* 270 (2009): 729–44.

Meachen-Samuels, J., and B. van Valkenburgh. "Carniodental Indicators of Prey-Size Preference in the Felidae." *Biological Journal of the Linnean Society* 96 (2009): 784–99.

Novack, A. J., M. B. Main, M. E. Sunquist, and R. F. Labisky. "Foraging Ecology of Jaguar (*Panthera onca*) and Puma (*Puma concolor*) in Hunted and Non-Hunted Sites within Maya Biosphere Reserve, Guatemala." *Journal of Zoology, London* 267 (2005): 167–78.

Nuñez, R., B. Miller, and F. Lindzey. "Food Habits of Jaguars and Pumas in Jalisco, Mexico." *Journal of Zoology, London* 252 (2000): 373–79.

Rabinowitz, A. R., and B. G. Nottingham. "Ecology and Behavior of the Jaguar (*Panthera onca*) in Belize, Central America." *Journal of Zoology, London* (A) 210 (1986): 149–59.

Sellinger, R. L., and J. C. Ha. "The Effects of Visitor Density and Intensity on the Behavior of Two Captive Jaguars (*Panthera onca*)." *Journal of Applied Animal Welfare Science* 8, no. 4 (2005): 233–44.

Sicuro, F. L. "Evolutionary Trends on Extant Cat Skull Morphology (Carnivora: Felidae): A Three-Dimensional Geometrical Approach." *Biological Journal of the Linnean Society* 103 (2011): 176–90.

Sicuro, F. L., and L. F. B. Oliveira. "Skull Morphology and Functionality of Extant Felidae (Mammalian: Carnivore): A Phylogenetic and Evolutionary Perspective." *Zoological Journal of the Linnean Society* 161 (2011): 414–62.

Taber, A. B., and A. J. Novaro. "The Food Habits of Sympatric Jaguar and Puma in the Paraguayan Chaco." *Biotropica* 29, no. 2 (1997): 204–13.

Van Valkenburgh, B. "Incidence of Tooth Breakage among Large Predatory Mammals." *American Naturalist* 131 (1988): 291–302.

Verissimo, D., D. A. Jones, R. Chaverri, and S. R. Meyer. "Jaguar (*Panthera onca*) Predation of Marine Turtles: Conflict between Flagship Species in Tortuguero, Costa Rica." *Oryx*, 2012: 1–8.

Vogel, S. *Cats' Paws and Catapults.* New York: W. W. Norton and Co., 1988.

Wroe, S., C. McHenry, and J. Thomason. "Bite Club: Comparative Bite Force in Big Biting Mammals and the Prediction of Predatory Behavior in Fossil Taxa. *Proceedings of the Royal Society B* 272 (2004): 619–25.

Yamaguchi, N., A. C. Kitchener, E. Gilissen, and D. W. MacDonald. "Brain Size of the Lion (*Panthera leo*) and the Tiger (*P. tigris*): Implications for Intrageneric Phylogeny, Intraspecific Differences and the Effects of Captivity. *Biological Journal of the Linnean Society* 98 (2009): 85–93.

Chapter 13: The Reluctant Warrior

Estes, J. A., et al. "Trophic Downgrading of Planet Earth." *Science* 333 (2011): 301–6.

Hoogesteijn, R., and E. Mondolfi. *The Jaguar.* Caracas, Venezuela: Armitano Publishers, 1992.

Janzen, D. "The Deflowering of Central America." *Natural History* 83, no. 4 (1974): 48–53.

Nyhus, P. J., C. E. Dufraine, M. C. Ambrogi, S. E. Hart, C. Carroll, and R. Tilson. "Human–Tiger Conflict over Time." In *Tigers of the World: The Science, Politics, and Conservation of* Panthera tigris, edited by R. Tilson and P. J. Nyhus (2nd ed.), 132–35. Waltham, Massachusetts: Academic Press, 2010.

Ripple, W. J., et al. "Status and Ecological Effects of the World's Largest Carnivores." *Science* 343 (2014). DOI: 10.1126/science.1241484.

Terborgh, J., and J. Estes, eds. *Trophic Cascades: Predators, Prey, and the Changing Dynamics of Nature.* Washington, DC: Island Press, 2010.

Wells, W. V. *Explorations and Adventures in Honduras: Comprising Sketches of Travel in the Gold Regions of Olancho (1857).* New York: Harper & Brothers, 1857.

Woodroffe, R., S. Thirgood, and A. Rabinowitz, eds. *People and Wildlife: Conflict or Coexistence?* Conservation Biology Series 9. Cambridge, UK: Cambridge University Press, 2005.

Chapter 14: Survival in a Changing World

Abrams, E. M., and D. J. Rue. "The Causes and Consequences of Deforestation among the Prehistoric Maya." *Human Ecology* 16, no. 4 (1988): 377–95.

Allen, B. *Through Jaguar Eyes: Crossing the Amazon Basin*. London: Harper-Collins, 1994.

Azevedo, F. C. C., R. L. Costa, H. V. B. Concone, A. Pires-da Silva, and L. M. Verdade. "Cannibalism among Jaguars (*Panthera onca*)." *Southwestern Naturalist* 55, no. 4 (2010): 597–99.

Brett, W. H. *The Indian Tribes of Guiana*. London: Bell and Daldy, 1868.

Brown, J. *The Spiritual Legacy of the American Indian*. New York: Crossroad, 1991.

Cavalcanti, S. M. C., and E. M. Gese. "Kill Rates and Predation Patterns of Jaguars (*Panthera onca*) in the Southern Pantanal, Brazil." *Journal of Mammalogy* 91, no. 3 (2010): 722–36.

Chapman, A. *Masters of Animals: Oral Traditions of the Tolupan Indians, Honduras*. London: Gordon and Breach, 1978.

Corlett, R. T. "Impacts of Warming on Tropical Lowland Rainforests." *Trends in Ecology and Evolution* 26, no. 11 (2011): 606–13.

Guterl, F. *The Fate of the Species: Why the Human Race May Cause Its Own Extinction and How We Can Stop It*. New York: Bloomsbury, 2012.

Kohn, E. *How Forests Think: Toward an Anthropology beyond the Human*. Berkeley, CA: University of California Press, 2013.

Saunders, N. J. "The Day of the Jaguar." *Geographical Magazine*, August issue (1983): 400–404.

Silva, J. G. "Religion, Ritual and Agriculture among the Present-Day Nahua of Mesoamerica." In *Indigenous Traditions and Ecology: The Interbeing of Life and Death*, edited by T. Regan, 218–59. Philadelphia: Temple University Press, 2001.

Stanford, C. B. *The Hunting Apes: Meat Eating and the Origins of Human Behavior*. Princeton, NJ: Princeton University Press, 1999.

Wells, W. *Explorations and Adventures in Honduras*. New York: Harper & Brothers, 1857.

Whitehead, N. L. *Dark Shamans: Kanaima and the Poetics of Violent Death*. Durham, NC: Duke University Press, 2003.

Acknowledgments

THE BOOK IS THE RESULT of decades of work and effort by many passionate individuals—students, villagers, government officials, scientists, conservationists, and government leaders—all of whom have been particularly inspired by one of the most magnificent, tenacious species that lives among us: the jaguar. To all those people who have helped me in my struggles to better understand this indomitable beast, or have themselves helped protect the jaguar—I thank you with all my heart. This book is about an animal I love. And about a species that has been a part of my life since early childhood.

First, I would like to thank those who reviewed parts of the book for accuracy: Dr. Eduardo Eizirik, Dr. Helmut Hemmer, Dr. Rafael Hoogesteijn, Dr. Howard Quigley, Dr. Z. Jack Tseng, and Kathy Zeller. Kathy Zeller, both in the field and in the laboratory, provided the knowledge, insight, and passion to help make the jaguar corridor a reality, from the mapping tables to the field. Lisanne Petracca, Panthera's GIS analyst, helped me with maps and tables for the book. Steve Winter, a world-class photographer, spent many months in the field for Panthera photographing jaguars and helping me compile an extraordinary portfolio for my jaguar conservation efforts.

I must give special thanks to two of my oldest friends and jaguar buddies—Rafael Hoogesteijn, who, after almost 30 years of our knowing each other and a decade of working together at Panthera, still provides me with great insight and comfort during countless wonderful nights of sipping Brazilian rum in the Pantanal and discussing jaguars. And Howard Quigley, whom I lived with in a trailer while we tracked bears and raccoons in the mountains of Tennessee, and who has remained one of my best friends and closest confidantes throughout my career. I am thrilled to now have Howard working and traveling by my side as we continue to make the jaguar corridor a reality throughout its range.

My deep gratitude goes to the staff of Panthera, whose passion and drive have helped to ensure the future survival of jaguars, tigers, lions, snow leopards, and other wild cats. Panthera is now the voice for those who have no voice. And to Dr. Luke Hunter and Andrea Hedylauff, president and vice president respectively, who trusted and believed in the vision of Panthera from the onset. Dr. George Schaller, my mentor, my friend, and now vice president of Panthera, helped kick-start my wondrous career and remains the most iconic figure in wildlife conservation today.

A life is measured, at least in part, by friends and family. I have been blessed with some very special people in both those categories. Friends never came easily to me and there were never many adults in my life whom I'd learned to trust. Fortunately, a few individuals saw more in me than perhaps I saw in myself, and they have stuck by me through thick and thin. I have already written about Dr. Tom Kaplan, chairman and founder of Panthera, whom I consider the brother I never had. His vision made Panthera possible, and because of him many more cats are alive today than would be otherwise. Two other friends, Michael Cline and Greg Manocherian, were always there for me when I needed someone to lean on. They too have added vision, creativity, and substance to both my work at Panthera and to my life as a whole.

Then there is my family. My wife Salisa, while working her full-time job as a geneticist at the American Museum of Natural History, has structured her life so that I could run off at a moment's notice to some remote part of the world and save cats. She would rather be splicing DNA than watching animals with me, but she understands every bit of what I am about. I could not be who I am without her. She has also given me the two finest children in the world, Alexander and Alana. As much as the jaguar at the Bronx Zoo helped that little stuttering boy into manhood, my two children have now become the rock to which I am anchored as an adult. They are my greatest pride in life.

Island Press has been a wonderful publisher. They are not only committed to helping save our planet, but their staff rivals that of Panthera in passion, creativity, and drive towards this end. I have had the pleasure of working with wonderful people at Island Press, but none more so than my editor, Barbara Dean. This book truly would not have come about except for her patience, her guidance, and her insight into what I was trying to convey to the world. Thank you, Barbara, for sharing and helping me along this wonderful journey.

About the Author

A LAN RABINOWITZ is CEO of Panthera Foundation. Educated at the University of Tennessee, with degrees in zoology and wildlife ecology, Dr. Rabinowitz has traveled the world on behalf of wildlife conservation and has studied jaguars, clouded leopards, Asiatic leopards, tigers, Sumatran rhinos, bears, leopard cats, raccoons, and civets.

His work in Belize resulted in the world's first jaguar sanctuary; his work in Taiwan resulted in the establishment of that country's largest protected area, its last piece of intact lowland forest; his work in Thailand generated the first field research on Indochinese tigers, Asiatic leopards, and leopard cats, in what was to become the region's first World Heritage Site; and his work in Myanmar has led to the creation of five new protected areas there: the country's first marine national park, the country's first and largest Himalayan national park, the country's largest wildlife sanctuary, and the world's largest tiger reserve.

Dr. Rabinowitz has authored nearly eighty scientific and popular articles and six books, including *Jaguar: One Man's Struggle to Establish the First Jaguar Preserve* (1986/2000), *Chasing the Dragon's Tail: The Struggle to Save Thailand's Wild Cats* (1991/2002), and *Beyond the Last Village: A Journey of Discovery in Asia's Forbidden Wilderness*New York Times, National Geographic Adventure Magazine, Outside Magazine, Scientific American, Men's Fitness, GEO, Natural History, and Audubon. He has been featured in television specials by the National Geographic Society and the BBC, and recently consulted on an IMAX film project about tigers in the Sundarbans of Bangladesh and India.

About Panthera

PANTHERA, founded in 2006, is devoted exclusively to the conservation of wild cats and their ecosystems. Utilizing the expertise of the world's premier cat biologists, Panthera develops and implements global strategies for the largest, most imperiled cats—tigers, lions, jaguars, snow leopards, leopards, cougars, and cheetahs—and the other thirty wild cat species. Representing the most comprehensive effort of its kind, Panthera works in partnership with local and international NGOs, scientific institutions, local communities and governments around the globe. Visit www.panthera.org

Index